In the Court We Trust

The preliminary reference procedure has long been envisaged as a judicial dialogue between the European Court of Justice and national courts. However, in reality the relationship appears to be closer to one of growing separation rather than to a happy marriage between equal partners. This book tries to find out: what is behind this? A study of the existing literature, combined with a case law analysis and interviews with judges, has shown that there are a number of important stumbling blocks hindering the communication between these courts, such as language barriers, time constraints and a failing digital infrastructure. However, on a deeper level there also appears to be a lack of mutual trust that prevents supreme administrative courts from using the possibilities the procedure provides, such as the opportunity to offer provisional answers to the Court of Justice and the use of requests for clarification by the latter.

Rob van Gestel is Professor of Law at Tilburg Law School. He was visiting Professor at the Academy of Legal Theory of the KU Brussels, Professor of methodology of legal research at Leuven University, and Braudel Fellow of the European University Institute in Florence, Chairman of the Dutch Association of Legislation and member of the International Association of Legislation. He has recently edited, with Hans Micklitz and Ed Rubin, *Rethinking Legal Scholarship: A Transatlantic Dialogue* (2017) and articles in the *European Law Journal, Common Market Law Review, European Public Law, Cambridge International Law Journal, Legal Studies* and more.

Jurgen de Poorter is Professor of Administrative Law at Tilburg University and Deputy Judge in the District Court of The Hague. From 2005 until 2018 he was a special advisor to the Dutch Council of State, in particular to the Administrative Jurisdiction Division of the Council of State. His recently published work is about methods of judicial lawmaking, judicial review of evidence-based legislation and judicial dialogues in the European Union.

Cambridge Studies in European Law and Policy

This series aims to produce original works which contain a critical analysis of the state of the law in particular areas of European law and to set out different perspectives and suggestions for its future development. It also aims to encourage a range of work on law, legal institutions and legal phenomena in Europe, including 'law in context' approaches. The titles in the series will be of interest to academics; policymakers, especially those who are interested in European legal, commercial and political affairs; practising lawyers, including the judiciary; and advanced law students and researchers.

Books in the Series

Empire of Law: Nazi Germany, Exile Scholars and the Battle for the Future of Europe
Kaius Tuori

Beyond Minimum Harmonisation: Gold-Plating and Green-Plating of European Environmental Law
Lorenzo Squintani

The Politics of Justice in European Private Law: Social Justice, Access Justice, Societal Justice
Hans Micklitz

The Transformation of EU Treaty Making: The Rise of Parliaments, Referendums and Courts Since 1950
Dermot Hodson and Imelda Maher

Redefining European Economic Integration
Dariusz Adamski

Human Rights in the Council of Europe and the European Union: Achievements, Trends and Challenges
Steven Greer, Janneke Gerards and Rosie Slowe

Core Socio-Economic Rights and the European Court of Human Rights
Ingrid Leijten

Green Trade and Fair Trade in and with the EU: Process-based Measures within the EU Legal Order
Laurens Ankersmit

New Labour Laws in Old Member States: Trade Union Responses to European Enlargement
Rebecca Zahn

The Governance of EU Fundamental Rights
Mark Dawson

The International Responsibility of the European Union: From Competence to Normative Control
Andrés Delgado Casteleiro

Frontex and Non-Refoulement: The International Responsibility of the EU
Roberta Mungianu

Gendering European Working Time Regimes: The Working Time Directive and the Case of Poland
Ania Zbyszewska

EU Renewable Electricity Law and Policy: From National Targets to a Common Market
Tim Maxian Rusche

European Constitutionalism
Kaarlo Tuori

Brokering Europe: Euro-Lawyers and the Making of a Transnational Polity
Antoine Vauchez

Services Liberalization in the EU and the WTO: Concepts, Standards and Regulatory Approaches
Marcus Klamert

Referendums and the European Union: A Comparative Enquiry
Fernando Mendez, Mario Mendez and Vasiliki Triga

The Allocation of Regulatory Competence in the EU Emissions Trading Scheme
Jospehine Van Zeben

The Eurozone Crisis: A Constitutional Analysis
Kaarlo Tuori and Klaus Tuori

International Trade Disputes and EU Liability
Anne Thies

The Limits of Legal Reasoning and the European Court of Justice
Gerard Conway

New Governance and the Transformation of European Law: Coordinating EU Social Law and Policy
Mark Dawson

The Lisbon Treaty: A Legal and Political Analysis
Jean-Claude Piris

The European Union's Fight against Corruption: The Evolving Policy towards Member States and Candidate Countries
Patrycja Szarek-Mason

The Ethos of Europe: Values, Law and Justice in the EU
Andrew Williams

State and Market in European Union Law: The Public and Private Spheres of the Internal Market before the EU Courts
Wolf Sauter and Harm Schepel

The European Civil Code: The Way Forward
Hugh Collins

Ethical Dimensions of the Foreign Policy of the European Union: A Legal Appraisal
Urfan Khaliq

Implementing EU Pollution Control: Law and Integration
Bettina Lange

European Broadcasting Law and Policy
Jackie Harrison and Lorna Woods

The Transformation of Citizenship in the European Union: Electoral Rights and the Restructuring of Political Space
Jo Shaw

The Constitution for Europe: A Legal Analysis
Jean-Claude Piris

The European Convention on Human Rights: Achievements, Problems and Prospects
Steven Greer

Social Rights and Market Freedom in the European Constitution: A Labour Law Perspective
Stefano Giubboni

EU Enlargement and the Constitutions of Central and Eastern Europe
Anneli Albi

In the Court We Trust

Cooperation, Coordination and Collaboration between the ECJ and Supreme Administrative Courts

Rob van Gestel
Tilburg University

Jurgen de Poorter
Tilburg University

CAMBRIDGE
UNIVERSITY PRESS

CAMBRIDGE
UNIVERSITY PRESS

University Printing House, Cambridge CB2 8BS, United Kingdom

One Liberty Plaza, 20th Floor, New York, NY 10006, USA

477 Williamstown Road, Port Melbourne, VIC 3207, Australia

314–321, 3rd Floor, Plot 3, Splendor Forum, Jasola District Centre, New Delhi – 110025, India

79 Anson Road, #06–04/06, Singapore 079906

Cambridge University Press is part of the University of Cambridge.

It furthers the University's mission by disseminating knowledge in the pursuit of education, learning, and research at the highest international levels of excellence.

www.cambridge.org
Information on this title: www.cambridge.org/9781108481274
DOI: 10.1017/9781108686556

First published 2019

Printed in the United Kingdom by TJ International Ltd, Padstow Cornwall

A catalogue record for this publication is available from the British Library.

ISBN 978-1-108-48127-4 Hardback

To Eleanor Sharpston, Advocate General at the European Court of Justice

Contents

Figures

Series Editors' Preface

Judicial co-operation (or the lack of it) is at the centre of judicial activity in EU law; it takes place primarily through the reference procedure for a preliminary ruling on the interpretation and application of EU law, provided for in what is now Article 267 TFEU. Co-operation also takes place in other fora, such as the regular meetings between the Court of Justice and the supreme courts and supreme administrative courts of the Member States of the EU; many informal contacts are also made, renewed, and strengthened in the excellent initiatives of the European Law Institute. The formal judicial dialogue, so praised by the Court of Justice in many judgments, has not always been an easy one, and allegations of overstepping boundaries are not infrequently bandied around.

This work concentrates on the Court of Justice's relationship with national supreme courts and supreme administrative courts; in doing so this work breaks new ground through interviews with members of ten supreme administrative courts about their relationship with the Court of Justice, as most research so far has focused on the relationship between national constitutional courts and the Court of Justice. This work is extremely timely, coming fairly shortly after the Court of Justice found France in breach of its obligations under EU Law because of a failure by the *Conseil d'État* to make a reference for a preliminary ruling when it manifestly should have done.[1]

This work reveals that the proclaimed judicial dialogue is something of an illusion. This conclusion, that there is not really a dialogue, more of a monologue, leads the authors to examine three possible scenarios for improvement: cooperation; coordination, and collaboration. The call

[1] Case C-416/17 *Commission* v. *France* ECLI:EU:C:2018:811, paras. 105–114.

for more involvement of the supreme administrative courts in the decision-making process and shared responsibility is a call that will find an echo in many circles. Whether the response will be more than that remains to be seen.

We are indeed delighted to welcome this latest addition to the *Cambridge Studies in European Law and Policy* series.

Laurence Gormley
Jo Shaw

Preface

European courts are living in challenging times. On the one hand, there appears to be growing discomfort with the ongoing process of European integration in some of the Member States (code word Brexit) and with supranational courts intervening deeper and deeper into the national legal order. On the other hand, one must admit that successive global crises have learned that national and European legislators are all too often incapable of providing solutions for important transnational legal problems, such as tax evasion, drug trafficking and abuse of labour laws, which is why people seek refuge by going to court.

Other than academics, courts do not have the luxury to be able to remain silent or admit to not know the answer. They have to 'rule', at least in case a legal claim or request is admissible. What has made life much more complicated for judges is that we now live in a highly complex multilevel legal order in which supranational and national laws, hard law and soft law, and private law and public law have become intertwined. Moreover, the old days where there was a single highest court in almost every country are lying far behind us. There is no longer a clear-cut hierarchy of courts in the European Union. Even in the field of fundamental rights nobody really knows anymore what the 'highest' court is, let alone which court has the last word. The reason is that judicial law making increasingly takes place in networks, which are not necessarily institutionally, legally or hierarchically embedded in a single system of constitutional checks and balances, but are more often formed ad hoc.

In such a globalizing world, judicial dialogues seem inevitable. How else would one provide legal certainty, protect legal unity and ensure legitimacy of judicial decisions? Little is still known, however, about how inter-court communications operate and to what extent they actually represent something that goes beyond occasionally referring to foreign courts' decisions and attending formal meetings organized by individual courts or professional judicial networks. In order to find out more about this we decided to study the communication between courts in the realm of the preliminary reference procedure. Not only had the European Court of Justice itself on several occasions referred to the relationship with national courts in this procedure as a judicial dialogue, but the fact that the Dutch Council of State served as the presidency of the Association of Councils of State and Supreme Administrative Jurisdictions (ACA Europe) and decided to make the preliminary reference procedure the primary topic of its presidency with a seminar in The Hague on 7 November 2016 proved to be a unique opportunity to study the relationship between the Luxembourg court and national supreme administrative courts up close.

In order to offer input for the survey among ACA members and the debate during the meeting in The Hague, we were asked to do a literature review and interview judges from both the Court of Justice and supreme administrative courts. This project finally grew into the study that we present in this book. We are very grateful of the generous financial, practical, and organizational support from the side of the Dutch Council of State. We especially want to thank Mr Piet Hein Donner, the then–vice president of the Council of State for helping us with getting access to the Court of Justice and to the different supreme administrative courts, which enabled us to do the interviews. Our gratitude further goes out Dr Rob Visser, secretary of the Council of State for his engagement throughout the project and for the inspirational meetings in which we discussed our (first) findings. We certainly could not have done the current book project without his help.

A special token of appreciation also needs to go to Mr Koen Lenaerts, the president of the European Court of Justice, for taking the time to speak to us and for providing us with all the support we needed to conduct our study. Next to this, we of course also want to express our gratitude to all the individual judges and advocates general from the Court of Justice and the supreme administrative courts, who were willing to be interviewed and who often offered us with far more information than we could have hoped for when we started this project. Thankful in a different way are we also for the comments, criticism and suggestions that we received from some (former) colleagues that we asked to read (parts of) the manuscript. In alphabetical order: Dr Peter van Lochem, Prof Jan Vranken and Prof Rob Widdershoven.

Finally, we hope this is not going to be the end of this project in the sense that we believe our study should rather be seen as the beginning than as the end of an endeavour to (further) improve the communication and cooperation between the European Court of Justice and national (supreme) courts. It should not come as a surprise that there is still much room for improvement. The reader of this book will notice that we are critical as academics towards certain established practices, customs, cultures and traditions that influence the relationship between the Court of Justice and national highest courts. We believe this relationship is in transition and will probably need to change significantly over the next decades in order to be able to meet future global and local challenges due to, among other things, legal fragmentation (e.g. growing legal pluralism), digitization (e.g. the rise of social media, artificial intelligence and machine learning), constitutionalisation (e.g. the impact of fundamental rights on contracts and tort law) and emancipation (e.g. less respect for traditional, institutionalized authority).

The central theme of our book is 'trust'. Without trust a meaningful dialogue between national and supranational courts that goes beyond courts on one side asking questions, while the court on the other side provides answers, cannot exist. This implies that where trust is absent or weak it will need to be reinforced, and where it is present it needs to be maintained. We think this book offers at least some useful suggestions to assist trust-building. Since we focus mostly on problems and on room for improvement, it might appear as if we believe the Court of Justice and supreme administrative courts are doing a poor job at the moment. That would be a misconception. It is certainly not how we see things! We sincerely believe that courts on both sides are doing a quite decent job in most of the cases, most of the time. One should not forget, though, that in the end it is the hard cases that really matter. That is where serious judicial law making is required, where judicial leadership is crucial and where legitimacy is put to the test. Luckily, however, this is also where trust and dialogue can make a difference. Unfortunately, this implies that the basis for this must already be there beforehand.

1 Why Don't We Talk?

1.1 Introduction

In its advisory opinion about the draft agreement concerning the creation of a unified patent litigation system and a European patent court the Court of Justice of the European Union (hereafter CJEU) portraits the preliminary reference procedure of article 267 TFEU as a way in which national courts and the CJEU have a shared responsibility for the correct application and uniform interpretation of EU law.[1] This corresponds with previous case law in which the Court repeatedly envisaged the preliminary reference procedure as 'a dialogue between one court and another, the initiation of which depends entirely on the national court's assessment as to whether a reference is appropriate and necessary'.[2] So far, however, the CJEU has never clarified what this mutual responsibility of the courts entails. Moreover, it has been argued that the preliminary reference procedure should rather be seen as a

[1] Opinion 1/09 of the Court (Full Court) of 8 March 2011 on the basis of Article 218(11) TFEU on the Draft agreement – Creation of a unified patent litigation system – European and Community Patents Court – Compatibility of the draft agreement with the Treaties, ECLI: EU:C:2011:123.

[2] Case C-2/06, Willy Kempter KG v. Hauptzollamt Hamburg-Jonas [2008] ECR I-411, par. 42; ECLI:EU:C:2008:78, Case C-210/06, Cartesio Oktató és Szolgáltató bt v. Hungary [2008] ECR I-9641, par. 91; ECLI:EU:C:2008:723 and Case C-104/10, Patrick Kelly v. National University of Ireland [2011] ECR I 0000, par. 63; ECLI:EU:C:2011:506. That the initiation of a dialogue with the CJEU depends entirely on the national court's assessment as to whether a reference is appropriate and necessary is not telling the whole truth of course. Not only do highest national courts, which omit to refer preliminary questions to the CJEU, face the risk of a liability claim due to the Köbler case law of the Court (Case C-224/01, Gerhard Köbler v. Republik Österreich [2003] ECR I-10239; ECLI:EU:C:2003:513), but a refusal to send questions to Luxemburg can also be bypassed by lower courts addressing the CJEU.

series of monologues than as a judicial dialogue. Claes and De Visser formulate it as follows:

> [T]he national court refers a question and is then virtually removed from the procedure before the CJEU; there is no further conversation, much less deliberation. The national courts steps in again only after the CJEU has given its response to the question asked. Furthermore, answers from the CJEU are known to be sometimes volatile and unpredictable: at times restricted to the case at hand and almost doing the work of the national court, at other times general and almost laconic, often open-ended. There are plenty of examples where the answer of the CJEU was not helpful (not only for the case at hand but also for future cases). Very few national courts make the effort of making a new reference in the same case where the answer has not been helpful. In other words, they do not engage in a true dialogue with the CJEU. Finally, the dialogue through the preliminary reference procedure is easy to avoid for the national courts, by simply not making the reference.[3]

We wonder whether these observations about the absence of a judicial dialogue are correct. If so, why does the CJEU nevertheless stress the shared responsibility with national courts for the uniform interpretation of EU law and why would the latter accept this? Is the CJEU, in other words, actually prepared (1) to share power and responsibility with supreme administrative courts regarding decisions about the validity and correct interpretation of EU law; (2) to enable these supreme courts to talk back at the Court to inform it about the consequences of possible preliminary rulings for the national legal order; (3) to show accountability towards national courts regarding the way in which it has taken into account *their* views of how EU law should be interpreted, applied and enforced?

1.2 Focus on Supreme Administrative Courts

In trying to answer these questions, we will concentrate on the relationship between the CJEU and highest administrative courts (hereafter supreme administrative courts or simply supreme courts). The reason for this is that most of the literature on the communication between the CJEU and supreme courts is currently focused on constitutional courts while other highest courts have remained understudied.[4]

[3] M. Claes and M. De Visser, 'Are You Networked Yet? On Dialogues in European Judicial Networks' *Utrecht Law Review*, 6, 2, 104 (2012).

[4] See for a general overview the special issue of the German Law Journal 2015, No. 6 on Constitutional Courts in the European Legal System After the Treaty of Lisbon and the Euro-Crisis: www.germanlawjournal.com/volume-16-no-06/.

That constitutional courts have drawn so much attention is understandable since some of these courts have refused to raise preliminary questions to the CJEU,[5] while others have shown to be reluctant to accept the supremacy of the Court. The German constitutional court is probably the best example here. It has, on the one hand, recognised the primary role of the CJEU in the framework of fundamental rights protection[6] but, on the other hand, reserved the right to declare decisions by the CJEU ultra vires in case they undermine the fundamental rights and democratic values enshrined in the German constitution.[7]

Focusing on supreme administrative courts, however, is not only interesting because their relationship with supreme administrative courts seems less politicized which could enable a more open communication with the CJEU. They are also more familiar with the core business of the CJEU since the bulk of the cases before the Court contain administrative actions in fields, such as, freedom of goods and services, customs, environmental policy, asylum, food safety and so on. Although the importance of the CJEU's case law for private law and criminal law is rapidly growing, it seems fair to say that the communication with supreme administrative courts probably represents the most mature type of judicial dialogue, at least if we can actually speak of a dialogue.

Last but not least, we had the privilege to have access to judges from highest administrative courts and the CJEU because our study coincided with a project issued by the Dutch presidency of ACA-Europe – the association of Councils of State and Supreme Administrative Jurisdictions in Europe. This enabled us to get a look behind the scenes and interview judges about their communication with each other.[8] This led to new insights as to why, for example, some judges coordinate their preliminary questions with other colleagues (e.g the judges from the

[5] Until fairly recently the German and French constitutional courts, for example, did not refer cases to Luxemburg.

[6] The Bundesverfassungsgericht has indicated that it would make a preliminary reference before declaring a measure ultra vires. See: Solange II, BVerfGE 73, 339, Order of 7 June 2000, BVerfGE 102, 147 (*Bananenmarktordnung*) and Order of 6 July 2010, BVerfGE 126, 286 (*Honeywell*).

[7] BVerfGE 14 January 2014, 2 BvR 2728/13, ECLI:DE:BVerfG:2014:rs20140114.2bvr272813 (*Gauweiler*).

[8] We are of course not the only ones or the first ones doing this. See for a recent example: E. Mak, *Judicial Decision-Making in a Globalised World. A Comparative Analysis of the Changing Practices of Western Highest Courts* (Oxford: Hart Publishing, 2013). Nevertheless, as far as we know, there is no previous empirical study in which ten highest administrative courts in the EU have been interviewed about their relationship with the CJEU.

Dutch Council of State are very active in coordinating preliminary references with foreign colleagues and so are the judges of the Conseil d'Etat) within the same court or even with foreign colleagues, while others do not; some judges (e.g. judges in the Bundesverwaltungsgericht) are inclined to provide provisional answers to the questions they raise for the CJEU, while others (e.g. judges from the Belgian Council of State) refuse to do so; and some judges would like to play a much more active role in the proceedings before the CJEU, while others see no point in this.

1.3 Dialogue Before, During and After the CJEU Decides

What sort of communication processes between courts are we going to study? In order to make this more comprehensible, it may be useful to discern between the different moments when a dialogue may occur. As we see it, there are roughly three stages in the preliminary reference procedure where a dialogue could take place: (1) before a preliminary question is submitted to the CJEU, national supreme courts may, for instance, want to communicate with the Court about the necessity of a certain question or perhaps inform themselves about whether similar legal problems exist in other Member States; (2) during the preliminary reference procedure, where national courts can inform the CJEU about the likely consequences of alternative preliminary rulings or where the CJEU may according to article 101 of its rules of procedure request clarification from the referring court about the nature of the questions;[9] (3) after a decision is taken by the CJEU, for example, in case national courts may want to raise new questions when they feel their questions have not really been answered or when the CJEU takes the initiative to inform how its preliminary ruling is applied in national practice.

1.3.1 *Dialogue Before Raising a Question*

With regard to the period before a preliminary question is referred to the CJEU, we are particularly interested in the horizontal dialogue within the national court (e.g. between different chambers of a court) where an issue regarding the interpretation or validity of EU law has come up or between that court and other (international) courts where similar

[9] Article 101, § 1 reads: 'Without prejudice to the measures of organisation of procedure and measures of inquiry provided for in these Rules, the Court may, after hearing the Advocate General, request clarification from the referring court or tribunal within a time-limit prescribed by the Court.'

problems might exist (external dialogue). We believe this horizontal dialogue may also affect the vertical dialogue with the CJEU because the communication between supreme courts could be very informative for the Court with regard to the question whether courts in different Member States share the same views with regard to certain parts of EU law that present problems for national legal actors.

Concerning the dialogue within supreme courts, we discovered that some of them have organized the drafting process of preliminary questions in such a way that EU law specialists from different chambers of the court are involved in the drafting process[10] or that they actively try to pool cases from lower courts and refer them collectively to the CJEU.[11] Other courts, however, see this as an infringement of the principle of judicial independence because it is perceived as limiting the freedom of individual judges via peer pressure. Something similar applies to transnational communications about preliminary references between different supreme courts. Some of these courts (e.g. the Dutch, British and French, appear to be quite active in contacting foreign colleagues on an informal basis or via the ACA-forum on the website,[12] where judges can ask each other questions or provide each other with advice on EU law related questions. Other courts (e.g. the Danish) are less eager to raise preliminary questions,[13] especially when the litigating parties do not ask for it. One possible explanation for this could be that referring questions to the CJEU will usually cause a serious delay of the national proceedings. This could also be why they seek less contact with foreign courts about the formulation of preliminary questions.

[10] This is, for example, the case in the Dutch Council of State where a committee of EU law experts composed of members of different chambers of the court is consulted in case preliminary questions. See Dutch answers to the ACA-questionnaire, which are on file with the authors. There is at least one other highest administrative court where this happens. See the General report ACA Europe Seminar on the preliminary ruling procedure, The Hague, 7 November 2016 § 3.1.

[11] As did the Administrative Jurisdiction Division of the Dutch Council of State in the so-called passport-cases. See CJEU 16 April 2015, C-446/12, C-447/12, C-448/12 and C-449/12, ECLI:EU:C:2015:238.

[12] See: www.aca-europe.eu/forum/. One should realize that the word 'courts' is a generalization here. From the interview we have learned that it is perfectly possible that individual judges within one court show different priorities with regard to contacting foreign colleagues and also have totally different views on the importance of a (transnational) judicial dialogue.

[13] J.E. Rytter and M. Wind, 'In Need of Juristocracy? The Silence of Denmark in the development of European Law' *International Journal of Constitutional Law*, 9, 2, 470–504 (2011).

Nonetheless, it might be useful to inform the supreme courts of other Member States about the intention of raising a preliminary question. This could be an incentive to these courts to raise preliminary questions in similar cases with reference to the first preliminary question in order to set the agenda of the CJEU, as happened in the Dow Benelux-case of the Dutch Council of State.[14] In other cases, one might expect this to encourage foreign courts to provide the referring court with relevant information about the transnational context of the preliminary question. In practice, though, the supreme administrative courts seem to be reluctant to inform each other about the intention of raising preliminary questions.

Regarding the latter, we can refer to a case about 'gay asylum claims' where the CJEU was asked about the kind of evidence that should be taken into consideration to establish the declared homosexual orientation of an applicant for asylum.[15] It was clear in this case that the referring court worried about a possible 'floodgate effect' due to refugees claiming a right to asylum based on a sexual orientation that is hard to verify. The CJEU, however, focused heavily on the fundamental rights aspect in the case (e.g. the right to privacy and human dignity). In its preliminary ruling, the CJEU did not provide any guidelines as to what sort of evidence the referring court was allowed to require from asylum seekers. This might have been different in case national courts would have joined forces in the procedure in order to show the CJEU they had similar issues and were looking for ways to prevent a floodgate of false asylum claims. It could also prevent that courts from different Member States raise similar questions to the CJEU because the previous answers did not provide sufficient guidance for them.

Many other examples could be given of useful horizontal dialogues between supreme courts about whether or not to raise preliminary questions or about the best way to formulate a preliminary question to the CJEU in order to trigger a meaningful answer. More important for the moment, however, is to underline that the horizontal dialogue between national courts and the vertical dialogue with the CJEU might

[14] See CJEU 26 April 2016, C-191/14; ECLI:EU:C:2016:311 (*Borealis* Polyolefine GmbH and Others v. Bundesminister für Land- und Forstwirtschaft, Umwelt und Wasserwirtschaft and Others).

[15] Cases CJEU 2 December 2014, C-148/13, C-149/13 and C-150; ECLI:EU:C:2014:2406 (A, B and C v. Staatssecretaris van Veiligheid and Justitie).

serve as communicating vessels. After all, the more preliminary questions are coordinated across countries, the better the CJEU will be informed about the scope and nature of the legal problems that Member States have with regard to certain provisions in EU law. This information might even be used by the CJEU to draft preliminary rulings that solve a broader range of legal problems in different EU Member States and prevent unnecessary future references from other courts.

1.3.2 Dialogue During the Procedure Before the CJEU

The period between a court's reference and the Court of Justice's ruling is sometimes referred to as the 'black hole'.[16] De Werd has signaled that misunderstandings about a reference often come to light no sooner than after the Advocate General's Opinion. This is because other than the government and the parties involved, national judges cannot communicate directly with the Court after they have referred a case to Luxemburg. They have no other recourse to methods for damage control. The only court that can officially ask for clarification during the period between a reference and a preliminary ruling is the CJEU itself by using article 101 of the Courts rules of proceeding to issue a request for clarification.

Even when preliminary questions are not formulated appropriately, the CJEU may refuse to ask the referring court for clarification. Although the original idea behind the preliminary question was that national courts are responsible for: how the facts of a case are presented, how the question is defined and the decision of the CJEU is applied to the national case at hand, the CJEU has early in the history of the preliminary reference procedure given itself discretionary power to reformulate preliminary questions. It did so, for example, in the famous Costa/Enel case. There the Court decided:

> Nevertheless, the Court has power to extract from a question imperfectly formulated by the national court those questions which alone pertain to the interpretation of the Treaty. Consequently a decision should be given by the Court not upon the validity of an Italian law in relation to the Treaty, but only upon the interpretation of the above-mentioned Articles in the context of the points of law stated by the Giudice Conciliatore.[17]

[16] M. de Werd, 'Dynamics at Play in the EU Preliminary Ruling Procedure' *Maastricht Journal of European and Comparative Law*, 1, 152 (2015).
[17] CJEU 15 July 1964, C-6/64; ECLI:EU:C:1964:66 (Flaminio Costa v. E.N.E.L.).

In the past, the CJEU has gone as far as reframing the question as formulated by a national court into a very different area of EU law,[18] thereby sometimes following its own integration agenda, according to some.[19] In the cases of Van Putten and Martens, the CJEU seems to have done just this. The questions in Van Putten concerned citizenship, but the Court's answer concerned the free movement of capital.[20] In Martens, the questions related to the freedom of establishment and about citizenship, but the Court's only answered the question regarding citizenship.[21] Langer casted serious doubts as to whether the answers by the CJEU were of much use to the referring courts in these cases.[22]

As long as the reformulation of preliminary questions leads to a constructive cooperation with national courts, in which the CJEU ruling manages to solve actual problems regarding a lack of clarity or validity of EU law that referring courts have tried to bring to the fore; there seems little wrong with this. This may be different, though, in case the CJEU would transform a question by a national court into a problem this court did not seek to address. In such a case, about the only thing the national court can do is to ask the same question again and try to influence the CJEU by providing provisional answers. However, for this it fully depends on the cases brought before it by litigating parties. Moreover, it may take a long while before another occasion to refer the same questions presents itself. In practice, this could lead to frustrations and to attempts to informally contact judges or advocates general of the CJEU. Nonetheless, such attempts would suffer from the same lack of transparency as the one-sided reformulation of preliminary questions may have caused. This might be avoided if the referring court would receive an official role in the proceedings before the CJEU, but so far there has been no support for this.

[18] See Case C-279/09, DEB Deutsche Energiehandels- und Beratungsgesellschaft mbH v. Bundesrepublik Deutschland [2010] ECR I-13849; ECLI:EU:C:2010:811 and Case C-368/95, Vereinigte Familiapress Zeitungsverlags- und vertriebs GmbH v. Heinrich Bauer Verlag [1997] ECR. I-3689; ECLI:EU:C:1997:325.

[19] R. Garcia Antón, 'The reformulation of the questions referred to the CJEU for a preliminary ruling in direct taxation: towards a constructive cooperation model', EC Tax Review 2015-5, 258–267.

[20] Case C-578/10, Staatssecretaris van Financiën v. L.A.C. van Putten and Others, ECLI:EU:C:2012:246.

[21] Case C-359/13, B. Martens v. Minister van Onderwijs, Cultuur en Wetenschap, ECLI:EU:C:2015:118.

[22] J. Langer, 'The preliminary ruling procedure: old problems or new challenges?', Inaugural address Groningen University, 31 March 2015, p. 12.

The problems with respect to a reformulation of preliminary questions and the response from the side of the CJEU to provisional answers given by the referring courts – sharing their view on the interpretation of EU law – brings us to another matter directly related to the concept of a judicial dialogue, namely the way courts motivate their decisions. The possibility for national courts to provide provisional answers to the questions they refer to the CJEU offers a great opportunity to inform the CJEU about their interpretation of EU law and the expected consequences of different possible answers to preliminary questions for the national legal order(s). For the national court it may be important, though, not to preclude too much on a particular desirable outcome, because that could give either the litigating parties or the CJEU the idea that the referring court is biased. Hence, the referring court should probably develop other strategies to convince the CJEU. For the CJEU, on the other hand, the justification and motivation of its rulings appears to be crucial for a fruitful dialogue. In case national courts take the effort to provide provisional answers to the preliminary questions they have referred, but the CJEU does not show what is has done with this information, this is likely to discourage national supreme courts to share their views. More in general, one may question whether the rather minimalistic 'French style' of judicial decision making by the CJEU does not stand in the way of an effective dialogue with national courts.[23]

1.3.3 Dialogue After the CJEU Has Ruled

After the CJEU has issued a preliminary ruling, the dialogue with the national court is not necessarily over. Sometimes the ruling of the Court may not be entirely clear to the national court. This may, for example, be the case when the decision contains ambiguities or uses open texture or seems to deviate from an opinion previously expressed by the European Commission. In such a case, it is important to know to what extent it is possible for national courts to directly ask the CJEU to clarify its preliminary ruling without having to start a completely new reference procedure.

From the side of the Court, it may not always be clear what the national court is going to do in order to enforce its ruling in the dispute

[23] See about the minimalist style of the CJEU: D. Sarmiento, 'Half a case at a time: Dealing with judicial minimalism at the European Court of Justice', in M. Claes, M. de Visser, P. Popelier and C. van de Heyning (eds.), *Constitutional Conversations in Europe* (Cambridge: Intersentia, 2012), pp. 13–40.

that led to the preliminary reference. This is why the CJEU usually asks the referring court for a copy of the follow-up decision. It is unclear, though, to what extent national courts actually send their decisions to Luxemburg and, more importantly, whether they always strictly follow the Courts' ruling. Little is known about the enforcement of preliminary rulings via national courts.[24] This implies that it is uncertain whether courts sending references to the CJEU will later evade unwelcome decisions by misinterpreting the CJEU's ruling or reinterpreting the facts of the case to bypass the Court's ruling.

The dialogue between supreme courts and the CJEU after ruling of the latter courts has gained new momentum through the Ajos case. The case involved an employee who at the age of 60 was dismissed by his employer, Ajos. Pursuant to the Danish Salaried Employees Act, the employee had lost his claim for severance allowance. The labour union disagreed with this practice and raised a claim for payment against the employer. The Danish Supreme Court decided to submit two preliminary questions to the CJEU.[25]

The first one concerned the scope of the principle of non-discrimination on grounds of age as developed in the case law of the CJEU. More concretely, the question was whether this principle could override a Danish statute, which deprived an employee of a severance allowance in case he reached the age of 50 and was already entitled to an old-age pension financed by the employer. The second question concerned whether in such situations a national court can weigh the principle of non-discrimination on grounds of age against the principles of legal certainty and the protection of legitimate expectations and conclude that the latter takes precedence.

The CJEU decided that the principle of non-discrimination against age applies with direct effect to private parties and that the principle may thus be used as legal base for ordering a private employer to pay out severance allowance, even if the employer, pursuant to article 2a(3) of the Salaried Employees Act, was exempted from this obligation.

[24] However, see: L. Conant, 'Compliance and what EU Member States make of it' in M. Cremona (ed.), *Compliance and the Enforcement of EU Law* (Oxford: Oxford University Press, 2012), p. 23 and S.A. Nyikos, 'The Preliminary Reference Process: National Court Implementation, Changing Opportunity Structures and Litigant Desistment' *European Union Politics* 4, 397, 399–401 at 410 (2003).

[25] Request for a preliminary ruling from the Højesteret (Denmark) lodged on 24 September 2014 – DI [Dansk Industri], acting on behalf of Ajos A/S v. Estate of Karsten Eigil Rasmussen (Case C-441/14, ECLI:EU:C:2016:278).

Consequently, the ECJ established that the general principle of non-discrimination against age applies unconditionally, also in cases between private parties.[26]

After the decision by the CJEU, the Danish Supreme Court ruled in majority (8–1) that the Danish Accession Act does not confer powers to the EU to allow the unwritten general principle prohibiting discrimination on the grounds of age to overrule a provision in Danish legislation in a dispute between two private parties.[27] In other words, the Danish Court saw no horizontal direct effect of this principle of law and openly refused to comply with the CJEU's judgment.

The Danish Supreme Court concluded that an unwritten principle of law, developed by the CJEU is not binding since it has no basis in a specific Treaty provision. The Supreme Court added that it would act ultra vires – outside the boundaries of its own judiciary powers – if it would set aside Danish legislation in this situation where there is no explicit legal basis for an unwritten principle of EU law to override a decision by the Danish legislature. Consequently, the Danish Supreme Court refused to comply with the preliminary ruling.[28]

1.4 Dialogue: Problem or Solution?

It is unclear who really wants a judicial dialogue. Certainly not all national courts are frequently asking preliminary questions to the CJEU. Few of them systematically provide provisional answers to inform the CJEU about their view on the validity or correct interpretation of EU law or about the consequences of different possible rulings for the national legal order(s). Even when they do, the CJEU usually does not respond to

[26] The judgment implies that all terminated employees who have not received severance allowance due to the fact that they qualified for retirement pension upon termination of the employment may now make a claim against their employer. However, the claims are limited by Danish legislation, pursuant to which the limitation period for claims is five years after the expiry of the employment relationship.

[27] The original Danish text of the decision by the Supreme Court in case 15/2014 can be found at: www.hoejesteret.dk/hoejesteret/nyheder/Afgorelser/Documents/15-2014.pdf. For an English summary see: www.supremecourt.dk/supremecourt/nyheder/pressemeddelelser/Pages/TherelationshipbetweenEUlawandDanishlawinacaseconcerningasalariedemployee.aspx.

[28] This should not come as a total surprise since the Danish Supreme Court already in 1998 declared that it could not be deprived of the competence to review whether EU law had exceeded the limits of the transfer of competence by the Act of Accession. See: Danish Supreme Court, Carlsen et al. v. Rasmussen, April 6, 1998, I-361/1998.

the arguments of the national court, as we will show hereafter, which makes it impossible to determine to what extent the CJEU took the national courts' view into account.

After the CJEU has ruled, we know little about what happens with the implementation of preliminary rulings by national courts. How do national courts, for instance, deal with situations in which the CJEU does not answer all the questions that were referred or reformulates questions in way that is unrecognizable for the referring court? As we will see hereafter, this happens quite frequently. At the same time there appears to be little open protest against this practice. What does this tell us? On the one hand, national courts remain silent with regard to how they transpose preliminary rulings. On the other hand, the CJEU does not seem to keep record with regard to whether national courts interpret preliminary rulings in line with what the Court decided. This raises the question: do courts really want a dialogue or is it enough for them to avoid open conflict?

It is important to stress that we do not believe that a more intensive communication between the CJEU and national courts will automatically solve all problems in the preliminary reference procedure,[29] such as the growing tension between the increasing number of references and the importance of receiving high quality preliminary rulings within a reasonable time. As will be shown throughout the rest of this book, the communication between courts in the preliminary reference procedure is still surrounded by practical problems. Just think of: language barriers, lack of (time for) training, a lack of access to relevant up to date information about references in different Member States, high caseloads and a lack of staff in some of the national courts, which make that preliminary questions not always receive the attention they deserve. These kinds of problems primarily seem to be a matter of resources to invest in human capital and practical supporting systems (e.g. websites, research and documentation, training facilities).

The question of who wants a judicial dialogue is more difficult to answer. This is partly due to the fact that what a judicial dialogue entails, remains rather vague so far. Therefore, we will give a brief overview of the literature on judicial dialogues in the next chapter. Instead of looking for definitions or theoretical clarity, we will focus mainly on the functions attributed to these dialogues. In other words:

[29] See for an overview of these problems: M. Broberg and N. Fenger, *Preliminary References to the European Court of Justice* (Oxford: Oxford University, 2014).

for what sort of problems are judicial dialogues supposed to be the solution? Do different kinds of dialogues attempt to address the same sort of problems or should we not only discern between different types of dialogues, but also between different aims that judicial dialogues are supposed to fulfil?

We will show that major differences can be found in the literature as to what functions judicial dialogues should fulfil, ranging from: a coordination mechanism between courts and legislatures concerning constitutional values within one and same country (e.g. the declaration of incompatibility in the UK Human Rights Act); a strategy for national highest courts to protect sensitive national interests against the power of supranational courts (e.g. the Bundesverfassingsgerichts Solange case law), to a more practical tool for harmonizing decisions of highest courts by referring to each other's case law in order to prevent forum shopping (e.g. 'wedding tourism' in case of same sex marriages) in case courts do not coordinate their decisions.

The answer to the question: who really wants a judicial dialogue, may not only depend on what a certain use of the term 'dialogue' stands for but also whom one asks. So far, we have talked about the position of courts in the dialogue. However, courts are not monolithic institutions in which everybody has automatically the same opinions or expectations about the preliminary reference procedure. This is one of the reasons why we decided to interview judges from supreme administrative courts and from the CJEU. Without going into detail yet, we can already give away that there are different sorts of judges with diverging ambitions and a variety of view on judicial law making. Where some national judges seem to behave as knights of the rule of law, others present themselves more as knaves of the European single market who primarily want to assist the CJEU and solve disputes between litigating parties without undue delay. It is needless to say that with such a diverse range of judges in so many different Member States with distinct legal cultures, there can hardly be consensus about which problems a judicial dialogue is supposed to solve.

1.5 Checks and Balances in the Dialogue?

Meanwhile, the Ajos case raises deeper and more fundamental questions about the dialogue between highest national courts and the CJEU. It shows that, not only influential constitutional courts, but also 'regular' supreme courts may show resistance towards the CJEU in order to control the consequences that preliminary rulings may have for the national legal order. In this respect, the Ajos decision does not seem to stand on its own. It should be seen in light of a broader trend towards a pushback against the CJEU as the motor behind further European integration.[30]

In the famous OMT case, the German Bundesverfassungsgericht decided that the precedence of application of European Union law over national law only extends as far as the Basic Law and the relevant Act of Approval permit or envisage the transfer of sovereign powers.[31] In its ruling on the constitutionality of the Lisbon Treaty,[32] the Danish Supreme Court previously noted that, although the CJEU is charged with settling disputes on the interpretation of EU law: 'this must not result in a widening of the scope of Union powers'.[33] The Court emphasized that since Denmark's implementation of the Lisbon Treaty was based on the government's constitutional assessment that no new powers were transferred to the EU, this promise should be ensured by the Danish authorities, including the judiciary.

Viewed from this perspective, the Ajos case can be seen as an additional attempt to protect the constitutional identity of the national legal order against ongoing competence creep by EU institutions, including the CJEU.[34]

[30] Especially Pollack has shown that and how the CJEU's legitimacy seems to be closely related to the general attitude of the public towards European integration. See: M. Pollack, The Legitimacy of the European Court of Justice, in N. Grossman, H. Cohen, A. Follesdal (eds.), *Legitimacy and International Courts* (Cambridge: Cambridge University Press, 2018), pp. 143–173.

[31] A good overview over the arguments can be found in the English summary of the Judgment of 21 June 2016 – 2 BvR 2728/13, 2 BvR 2729/13, 2 BvR 2730/13, 2 BvR 2731/13, 2 BvE 13/13. See www.bundesverfassungsgericht.de/SharedDocs/Pressemitteilungen/EN/2016/bvg16-034.html;jsessionid=9CE8E53A851F67CC3F7DCA4A655B8CEB.2_cid361.

[32] UfR 2013.1451H.

[33] Court, Case 199/2012 of 20 February 2013 (with a case note by Helle Krunke in European Constitutional Law Review, 10: 542–570, 2014). See for the English translation of the decision: www.hoejesteret.dk/hoejesteret/nyheder/ovrigenyheder/Documents/199-12engelsk.pdf, p. 15.

[34] See about this more in general: A. Prechal, 'Competence Creep and General Principles of Law' *Review of European and Administrative Law*, 3, 1, 5–22, (2010) and S. Weatherill, 'Competence Creep and Competence Control' *Yearbook of European law* 23, 1–55 (2004). See also: T. Wilhelmsson, 'Jack-in-the-Box Theory of European Community Law', in L Krämer, H.W., Micklitz and K. Tonner, (eds.), *Law and Diffuse Interests in the European Legal Order* (Baden-Baden: Nomos, 1997), pp. 177–194 about judicial fiats accomplish that member states did not see coming and for which, upon reflection, they would not have chosen.

Relevant for our study is where the fear of competence creep by the CJEU is coming from. In the past, intergovernmentalists believed that the CJEU acts under serious political constraints from the Member States, which may decide to overrule the CJEU by initiating new EU legislation in case the Court overstretches its competences.[35] Today, however, one may wonder how realistic the possibility of a legislative override of CJEU decisions is. Stone Sweet and Brunell have calculated that 90 percent of all CJEU rulings in which Member States filed observations and demonstrated a real interest in the outcome of the case, would have required unanimity to be revised by subsequent legislation. That would make revision of most CJEU's rulings by the Member States virtually impossible.[36]

At first sight, the highest national courts could prevent further competence creep by the CJEU by referring less questions to the CJEU, especially in delicate matters concerning, for instance, the primacy of the national parliament.[37] Looking closer to how the preliminary reference procedure has developed over the years one cannot ignore that by building upon its doctrines of supremacy, direct effect and state liability, the CJEU has managed to design a system of decentralized enforcement of EU law with the help of (often) lower courts and private litigants, willing to go against national legislation and supreme court rulings with little chance of reprisals.[38]

To override the CJEU on an interpretation of Treaty provisions, for example, Member States must agree unanimously. With the current amount of Member States, this is virtually impossible. Overriding an interpretation by the CJEU of secondary legislation may look easier, but it normally requires the introduction of a proposal for legislation by the European Commission, a qualified majority in the Council, and a

[35] See C.J. Carubba, M. Gabel and C. Hankla, 'Understanding the Role of the European Court of Justice in European Integration' *American Political Science Review*, 106, 214 (2012) and C.J. Carruba, M. Gabel and C. Hankla, 'Juridicial Behavior Under Political Constraints' *American Political Science Review*, 102, 435 (2008).

[36] A. Stone Sweet and T. Brunell, *How the European Union's Legal System Works and Does Not Work: Response to Carrubba, Gabel and Hankla*, Faculty Scholarship Series, Yale Law School, 2010, p. 10.

[37] The H2S case is a good example here. See: R (HS2 Action Alliance Ltd) v. Secretary of State for Transport [2014] UKSC 3 (available at: www.supremecourt.uk/decided-cases/docs/UKSC_2013_0172_Judgment.pdf).

[38] K. Alter, *Establishing the Supremacy of European Law: The Making of an International Rule of Law in Europe* (Oxford: Oxford University Press, 2001).

majority in the European Parliament.[39] As long as one or more crucial players in the EU legislative process support the CJEU's assertions of authority, they can usually shield the Court from being overruled by the EU legislature.[40]

The bottom line here is that where both the EU executive and legislature have found countervailing powers in comitology, indirect member state involvement with delegated acts via the right of opposition and revocation, and influence via the Council of Ministers, the CJEU does not really have any strong intergovernmental opponents.[41] This might explain why supreme courts increasingly seem to feel the need for a dialogue with the CJEU in which they are not only on the receiving end. One cannot rule out that at least some highest courts in the Member States are seeking a possibility to actually influence how preliminary rulings are going to look like.

Several strategies are possible here. Perhaps the most obvious one, in particular for the less powerful national courts, is to find allies for their viewpoints on certain interpretations of EU law.[42] If in the Test-Achats case[43], for example, national courts would have joined forces in claiming that a strict unisex formula for the calculation of insurance premiums is not desirable because there are statistically relevant differences between the risks men and women are facing, while ignoring these can drive up the price for insurance for everybody, the CJEU might have listened. The same goes for the Ajos case,[44] where the Danish court seemed to act in splendid isolation in its quest for discretion, allowing the national

[39] See also Scharpf, who calls this the joint decision trap. See: F. Scharpf, 'The Joint-Decision Trap: Lessons from German Federalism and European Integration' 66 *Public Administration* 239, 239 (1988) and more recently F. Scharpf, 'The Joint-Decision Trap Revisited' *Journal of Common Market Studies*, 44, 845 (2006).

[40] See for a notorious example of lower court successfully bypassing highest national courts and legislatures with regard to the validity of certain terms in a mortgage loan agreement entered into by the parties, and whether they were contrary to the Unfair terms directive: Case C-415/11, *Mohamed Aziz v. Caixa d´Estalvis de Catalunya, Tarragona i Manresa (Catalunyacaixa)*, ECLI:EU:C:2013:164.

[41] See D. Kelemen, 'The Court of Justice of the European Union in the Twenty-First Century' *Law and Contemporary Problems* 79, 117–140 (2016), at 120–121. Available at: https://scholarship.law.duke.edu/lcp/vol79/iss1/5.

[42] This is also argued by M.A. Loth, 'Who has the Last Word? On Judicial Law Making in European Private Law' *European Review of Private Law*, 25, 1, 45–70 (2017).

[43] Case C-236/09, Association Belge des Consommateurs Test-Achats ASBL and Others v. Conseil des ministers [2011] ECR I-00773; ECLI:EU:C:2011:100.

[44] Case C-441/14, Dansk Industri (DI), acting on behalf of Ajos A/S v. Estate of Karsten Eigil Rasmussen, ECLI:EU:C:2016:278.

legislature to balance the principle non-discrimination according to age with the principles of legal certainty and the protection of legitimate expectations. Here again, one may wonder whether the CJEU would have dared to turn against the Danish legislature in case multiple courts had shown serious objections against a precedence of the prohibition against age discrimination over other legal principles without any leeway for the national legislature to balance these principles in the specific national context.

Closely linked to all this, is the respect that national courts can claim from the CJEU with regard to the protection of the national identity as enshrined in article 4(2) TEU. Although the exact scope and meaning of the identity clause is still developing, at least one thing is certain, namely: the CJEU cannot unilaterally decide what the national identity of its Member States entails. That would run against the very idea by the Treaty givers that national identity deserves protection *against* interference by EU institutions. If the CJEU wants to avoid outright rupture or conflict over the interpretation of what sort of things fall within the scope of national identity, it will probably need to engage in some sort of dialogue with national supreme courts.

For some, however, the very idea of a judicial dialogue might run against the principle of supremacy of EU law,[45] which is functional to ensure the equality of the Member States before the law, preventing each country of the EU from cherry picking which provisions of EU law it likes. Nevertheless, others might argue that there is little wrong with legislators and national supreme courts protecting their country's constitutional identity and the unity of their legal system. They will probably take the position that EU institutions, including the CJEU, were never given a blank check to unify national laws in light of an ever-growing European acquis.

1.6 Why the CJEU Might Also Benefit from a Judicial Dialogue

Even if legislative overrides of CJEU rulings are unlikely, this does not mean that the Court has nothing to gain from a judicial dialogue with national highest administrative courts. Apart from avoiding the risk of increased non-compliance, the CJEU may also want to nurture the legitimacy of its judicial decisions. This could explain why an empirical study

[45] F. Fabbrini, 'After the OMT Case: The Supremacy of EU Law as the Guarantee of the Equality of the Member States' *German Law Journal*, 16, 04, 1003–1024 (2015).

by Larsson and Naurin claims that those national courts that make themselves heard stand a better chance of being listened to by the CJEU, even if their preferences are only incomplete representations of the actual objective risk of a legislative override.[46]

From the side of the CJEU, a judicial dialogue could also serve a deeper purpose than receiving clarification from national courts. Provisions, such as article 101 of the Court's rules of procedure, might also serve to create a better understanding about the acceptance of certain interpretations of EU law and foster a better mutual understanding.[47] However, this would require a willingness from the side of the CJEU to use this possibility to engage with the referring national courts and also a preparedness to explain what it has done with the information, arguments and views from national courts.[48] As Davies has formulated it, the CJEU may have the last word, especially in the interpretation of treaty matters, but since treaty provisions often contain abstract reasoning, politically laden choices and policy consequences, the Court should realise that it does not have exclusive expertise over all these matters. The view of legislators – and national supreme courts we would add – should not be replaced by the vision of the CJEU but should contribute to this vision.[49]

What the CJEU has to gain from this is that building trust might prevent national courts from avoidance strategies, such as not raising preliminary questions where this should be done according to the CILFIT criteria or by bending the outcomes of preliminary rulings via selective reading of the Court's decisions when enforcing preliminary rulings in national cases. Although the CJEU may formally have instruments to punish such avoidance strategies, such as punishment via state liability, it is unlikely that this could ever be an effective remedy. This would certainly be the case when multiple supreme courts would abandon following the CJEU's case law in a loyal manner. Hence, mutual trust seems to be a key factor in the success of any judicial dialogue between the CJEU and national highest administrative courts.

[46] O. Larsson and D. Naurin, 'Judicial Independence and Political Uncertainty: How the Risk of Override Affects the Court of Justice of the EU' *International Organization*, 70, 377–408 (2016).

[47] A. Rosas, 'The European Court of Justice in Context: Forms and Patterns of Judicial Dialogue' *European Journal of Legal Studies* (2007), 1–16 at 15.

[48] E. Paunio, Conflict, power, and understanding – judicial dialogue between the ECJ and national courts, *NoFo* 2010, 5–23.

[49] G. Davies, 'Legislative Control of the European Court of Justice' *Common Market Law Review*, 81, 1597–1608 at 1606 (2014).

1.7 Scientific Relevance

What does this book add to the state of the art? The answer to this question is threefold. First, supreme (administrative) courts have remained understudied in the vast amount of literature on judicial dialogues. As we have mentioned above, the bulk of the literature on judicial dialogues concerns constitutional courts and their mutual relations or the relationship with the CJEU or ECtHR. Therefore, we know very little about how the supreme courts actually communicate with the CJEU in the preliminary reference procedure. Moreover, much of the literature on judicial dialogues is rather abstract and theoretical, whereas we intend to combine theory building with the results of a systematic case law analysis, and interviews with judges from Supreme Administrative Courts and from the CJEU.

Second, our research will shed new light on a seemingly paradoxical situation, namely: while the CJEU seems to picture the preliminary reference procedure as the dialogue per excellence with other highest courts, there are very few signs that this dialogue is currently more than a relationship of 'living apart together'. After all, in the preliminary reference procedure, national courts are responsible for raising questions about the interpretation and validity of EU law and especially highest courts have formally little discretion as to decide whether to refer questions according to the CILFIT jurisprudence of the CJEU. Besides this, the highest national administrative courts have no formal rights to access the CJEU to inform the Court about the nature of the questions after these have been submitted or after the CJEU has decided. Only the CJEU may ask for clarification but the Court relatively seldom does. During the procedure before the CJEU, national courts also have no formal role in the proceedings, which makes one wonder about the actual room for these highest administrative courts to engage with the CJEU and express their views on the preferred interpretation of EU law. One of the few possibilities national courts have to influence the CJEU's case law is to provide provisional answers but relatively few courts do and the CJEU rarely seems to respond to these answers in its written motivation of preliminary rulings. How is this possible? Do courts really want a dialogue and share responsibilities or is this merely window dressing?

Third, and building on the previous argument, this book tries to make clear whether a true judicial dialogue between highest administrative courts and the CJEU in which the national courts can leave their mark on the interpretation of EU law, actually fits with the trinity of primacy of EU law, direct effect and state liability. In other words, does a judicial dialogue that goes beyond a 'game' of questions and answers match with the current legal framework in which the CJEU operates? Formulated in more positive terms, how much leeway does the CJEU have, according to the treaties, to share responsibility with national supreme courts for the correct interpretation of EU law while simultaneously protecting the unity of European law? The other way around, what is the margin of interpretation for national highest administrative courts who disagree with the current case law of the CJEU to influence the outcomes of the preliminary reference procedure?

1.8 Outline and Approach

What steps do we need to take to answer the research questions we presented in the introduction, which basically looks to establish the extent there actually is a judicial dialogue between the CJEU and highest administrative and, if not, why would the latter continue to accept that their relationship is presented in terms of a shared responsibility and mutual cooperation?

Our first step needs to be to shed more light on the concept of a 'judicial dialogue' (Chapter 2). We will primarily do this via a systematic literature review. Where did the concept come from, what sort of purposes do different types of dialogues fulfil, and what can be seen as the essential factors for a meaningful conversation between courts in a multi-level legal order as the European Union?[50] Next, we will conduct a case law analysis of preliminary references from ten national highest administrative courts in the Member States between 2010 and 2015 (Chapter 3) and the answers of the CJEU to the preliminary questions raised in these cases. This exercise is meant to check the extent to which the literature about the preliminary reference procedure properly reflects what is actually happening today in the communication between national courts and the CJEU regarding the style in which different supreme administrative courts raise preliminary questions and the way in which the Luxemburg court responds to this.

[50] As we will show in the next chapter, there are various types of 'dialogues' between different actors. Horizontal dialogues between national courts or between supranational courts, vertical dialogues between national highest courts and the CJEU or ECtHR or between lower domestic courts, Supreme Courts and the CJEU et cetera.

In Chapter 4 we present the interviews we conducted with judges from each of the ten supreme administrative courts in the selected Member States and with judges and advocates general from the CJEU in Luxemburg with whom we talked about their formal and informal communications. How do judges from these courts experience the existing information channels, such as the ACA web forum, the regular meetings organised by the CJEU and by ACA-Europe or by more informal study groups? Moreover, how do judges relate to the possibilities the preliminary reference procedure holds to exchange views and share information.

The results from the empirical part will be taken as a point of reference for the more theoretical part of our study (Chapter 5). Without anticipating too much on the conclusions of our empirical study, it may not come as a surprise that quite a number of judges on both sides do not seem to believe they are in a real dialogue with judges from the CJEU that goes beyond one of the partners (the national courts) raising questions which the other partners (the CJEU) then try to answer. Our hypothesis is that this might, at least partly, have to do with a lack of trust from both sides. This is why we will explore the relationship between the communication patterns in the preliminary reference procedure with the literature on trust.

In the final chapter (Chapter 6) we will not only present our conclusion, but will also raise questions for further research and debate concerning the future of the preliminary reference procedure. We will present three scenarios that could give the future relationship between the CJEU and supreme (administrative) courts in the preliminary reference procedure, while simultaneously reviewing where this procedure might need to be changed to improve the conversation between courts on both sides.

2 Dialogue as a Concept

2.1 Introduction

In this chapter, we provide a brief overview of the literature on judicial dialogues, in particular with regard to the relationship between the CJEU and supreme (administrative) courts. We do not intend to be exhaustive with regard to all the different types of dialogues that exist but are more interested in the wide variety of functions they serve and the opportunities and legal challenges that come along with this.

We are first going to study where the idea of a judicial dialogue came from (§ 2.2). This will bring us to the dialogue between courts and legislatures that originated in Canada and spread from there to other jurisdictions. Next, we will look for different purposes that judicial dialogues are supposed to fulfil (§ 2.3). After that, we will turn to a typology of inter-judicial dialogues that was developed by Rosas (§ 2.4) of which we will give an overview and provide current examples. The purpose of this overview is to show that the idea of a judicial dialogue cannot only fulfil different functions but is also a reaction to different types of (constitutional) problems. In the overview, we will mainly concentrate on examples of judicial dialogues outside the realm of the preliminary reference procedure. Now and then, however, we will also show the parallels and differences between this procedure and other inter-judicial dialogues. After we have sketched the different contexts in which dialogues may occur, we will turn back to the question for which problem(s), if any, judicial dialogues could be a solution (§ 2.5).

Finally, we will study the origins of the preliminary reference procedure and the way in which this procedure relates to the dialogue concept (§ 2.6). It is understood that the rise of the number of references, in particular since the turn of the millennium, may also have an impact on the relationship between national courts and the CJEU. What can be said about the opportunities and challenges this poses for the preliminary reference procedure, in general, and the relationship between the CJEU and the supreme administrative courts in the EU, in particular (§ 2.7)? We need this embedding in the literature in order to draw conclusions (§ 2.8) and be able to compare the outcomes of the case law analysis of preliminary references and the interviews we conducted with the judges of the different administrative courts and the CJEU which will be presented in the following chapters of this book.

2.2 The Origins of the Dialogue Concept: Constitutional Conversations between Courts and Legislatures

Judicial dialogues are a specimen of the broader concept within or between branches of government.[1] The literature around "constitutional dialogues" and later on judicial dialogues was sparked by a well-known statement from Alexander Bickel that 'judicial review is a counter-majoritarian force in a legal system' because in particular constitutional courts with the power to review legislation are non-elected institutions.[2] This has led scholars to engage in a debate about how to remedy or circumvent this 'counter-majoritarian difficulty', using the concept of a constitutional dialogue.[3]

Especially in the United States, there has been a lot of criticism over the Supreme Court's style of judicial review starting under the Warren Court, with *Brown* v. *Board of Education* and later on *Roe* v. *Wade* and others. These cases were the start of a whole new chapter of American constitutional law. They were seen as a departure from earlier jurisprudence and legislation that led to much debate about the legitimacy of the Supreme Court and the judicial activism associated with it. Critics argued that the Warren Court departed from the original meaning of the constitutional text and that the Court was wrong to do so.[4] This led

1 A. Meuwese and M. Snel, 'Constitutional Dialogue: An Overview' *Utrecht Law Review*, 9, 2, 123–140 (2013).

2 A. Bickel, *The Least Dangerous Branch: The Supreme Court at the Bar of Politics* (Indianapolis, IN: Bobbs-Merrill 1962), pp. 16–17.

3 G. Dor, 'Constitutional Dialogues in Action: Canadian and Israeli Experiences in Comparative Perspective' *Indiana International & Comparative Law Review*, 11, 1–36 (2000), at 1.

4 R.H. Bork, 'Neutral Principles and Some First Amendment Problems' *Indiana Law Journal*, 47, 1 (1971–72); and R. Berger, *Government by Judiciary: The Transformation of the Fourteenth Amendment* (Cambridge, MA: Harvard University Press, 1977).

constitutionalists to search for new theories of judicial law-making in order to explain and justify the law making by highest courts. A new 'weak-form' of constitutionalism emerged in Canada with the enactment of the Canadian Charter of Rights and Freedoms in 1982.

Section 1 of this Charter is known as the limitation clause, which constitutionally allows legislatures to limit the guaranteed rights under certain justificatory requirements set out by the Supreme Court in *R.* v. *Oakes*.[5] Section 33 of the Charter referred to as the 'notwithstanding' or 'override' provision. This provision grants power to Canadian legislatures, at both the federal and provincial levels, to deviate from or displace judicial rulings that invalidate legislation for violating charter rights in order to avoid the kind of judicial supremacy associated with American-style judicial review, by allowing the legislature to overrule Supreme Court decisions.[6] Where a judicial decision is open to legislative reversal, modification, or avoidance by the legislature, it is meaningful to regard it as a dialogue, according to Hogg and Bushell.[7] Tremblay adds to this that in this theory, the courts and the legislature participate in a dialogue regarding the determination of a proper balance between constitutional principles and public policies in which the judiciary does not necessarily have the last word with respect to constitutional matters and policies.[8] Alternatively, as Roach formulated it, judicial activism may in such cases be answered by legislative activism.[9] Consequently, the counter-majoritarian objection to judicial review would become unsustainable because there are checks and balances build into the law-making process.[10]

This assertion has been heavily criticized, though, because dialogue detractors argue that the interactions that occur in practice between the Canadian legislature and the judiciary are more akin to a monologue

[5] R. v. Oakes, [1986] 1 S.C.R. 103.

[6] C. Bateup, 'Expanding the Conversation: American and Canadian Experiences of Constitutional Dialogue in Comparative Perspective' *Temple International and Comparative Law Journal* 21, 1–58 (2007).

[7] P.W. Hogg and A.A. Bushell, 'The Charter Dialogue Between Courts and Legislatures (Or Perhaps the Charter of Rights Isn't Such a Bad Thing After All)' *Osgoode Hall Law Journal* 35, 75–123 (1997), at 79. See more recently: B. Berger 'Children of Two Logics: A Way into the Canadian Culture' *International Journal of Constitutional Law*, 11, 319 (2013).

[8] L. Tremblay, 'The Legitimacy of Judicial Review: The Limits of Dialogue between Courts and Legislatures' *I-CON*, 3, 4, 617–648 (2005), at 617.

[9] K. Roach, 'Constitutional and Common Law Dialogues between the Supreme Court and Canadian Legislatures' *Canadian Bar Review*, 80, 481–533 (2001), at 532.

[10] Tremblay supra nt. 8 p. 617.

than a dialogue since legislators would normally acquiesce to judicial perspectives rather than express their own views about the Charter.[11] They only rarely use the possibility of a legislative override.[12] Moreover, judges would usually be aware of political attitudes to their decisions and hence think ahead to what kind of political responses are likely, moderating their rulings accordingly. This could lead to a form of judicial self-restraint, which keeps judges from needlessly stepping on political toes.[13] Some have even claimed that courts should stay true to their anti-majoritarian nature, to their precedents, and to their own mode of reasoning in the process of constitutional law-making because their legitimacy flows not from collaboration but from detached and disinterested decision-making in a situation of conflicts of law.[14]

Although dialogue theories have spread from Canada to other countries, such as Australia and the United Kingdom,[15] this should not be mistaken for the explanatory success of dialogue theories. Apart from the fact that legislative overrides of supreme court decisions are rare, Carolan has pointed out that in the majority of the cases, the relationship between courts and legislators does not resemble anything that comes close to a dialogue. This is partly because judicial decision-making is usually fact-specific and backward looking, while legislation entails general rules and forward-looking policy decisions, which normally

[11] F.L. Motyon and R. Knopff, *The Charter Revolution and the Court Party* (Peterborough: Broadview Press, 2000); C.P. Manfredi, *Judicial Power and the Charter* (Oxford: Oxford University Press, 2001).

[12] See C. Manfredi and J.B. Kelly, 'Six Degrees of Dialogue: A Response to Hogg and Bushell' *Osgoode Hall Law Journal*, 37, 513 (1999); T.Kahana, 'The Notwithstanding Mechanism and Public Discussion: Lessons from the Ignored Practice of Section 33 of the Charter' *Canadian Public Administration*, 44, 255 (2001); M. Tushnet, 'Judicial Activism or Restraint in a Section 33 World' *University of Toronto Law Journal*, 53, 89, 91 (2003); T. Kahana, 'Legalism, Anxiety and Legislative Constitutionalism' *Queen's Law Journal* 31, 536 (2006), 555, n.51.

[13] C. Bateup, 'The Dialogic Promise: Assessing the Normative Potential of Theories of Constitutional Dialogue' *Brooklyn Law Review* 71, 16–17 (2006); J. Ferejohn and L. Kramer, 'Independent Judges, Dependent Judiciary: Institutionalizing Judicial Restraint' *New York University Law Review*, 77, 962, 984–986 at 964 (2002).

[14] J. Lecalair, 'Reflexions critiques au sjuet de la métaphore du dialogue en droit constitutionnel canadien' *Revue du Barreau*, 402–412 (2003).

[15] S. Stephenson, 'Constitutional Re-engineering: Dialogue's Migration from Canada to Australia' *International Journal of Constitutional Law*, 11, 4, 870–897 (2013) and A. Young, 'Is dialogue working under the Human Rights Act 1998?' *Public Law*, October, 773–800 (2011). S. Gardbaum, 'Reassessing the New Commonwealth Model of Constitutionalism' *International Journal of Constitutional Law* 8, 167–206 (2010).

makes a dialogue between both branches difficult.[16] There are, however, exceptions to this rule. An interesting example is the declaration of incompatibility in the British Human Rights Act, which functions as a signal from the judiciary to the legislature that action should be undertaken to remedy a violation of fundamental rights. Nevertheless, in practice, this option seems to be a measure of last resort,[17] while the more frequent response of treaty-conform or harmonious interpretation of legislation is far more common but does not provide much room for explicit feedback from the legislature. Moreover, the idea that courts can initiate a dialogue presumes some sort of obligation from the legislature to respond to the courts' reasoning, but this obligation rarely, if ever, exists. Finally, a dialogue between courts and legislatures idealises consensus – usually without any specific practical guideline as to how this consensus should be achieved – but disregards the value of contestation between the different branches of government. According to some, however, healthy democracies need a certain amount of conflict and dissent.[18] They stress that dialogue should not be identified with a relationship of perfect harmony.

2.3 The Purpose(s) of a Judicial Dialogue

Basically, inter-judicial dialogues within the realm of the preliminary reference procedure, which is the subject of our book, fulfil three major purposes, namely: a descriptive, an explanatory and a normative purpose.[19] As a descriptive tool, dialogue is used to define the relationship between the CJEU and national courts in the preliminary reference procedure and to describe the joint characteristics of the role of different participants in the process of judicial law making. Closely related to the purpose of description is explanation. Especially in the political science literature, a lot of attention has been paid to use dialogue as an explanation for the gradual constitutionalization of the EU legal order through landmark cases, such as Van Gend and Loos and Coste Enel, via an

[16] E. Carolan, 'Dialogue Isn't Working: The Case for Collaboration as a Model of Legislative-Judicial Relations' *Legal Studies*, 36, 2, 215 (2016).

[17] R. v. A. (no. 2), [2001] UKHL 25, per Lord Steyn ("A declaration of incompatibility is a measure of last resort. It must be avoided unless it is plainly impossible to do so")

[18] C. Sunstein, *Why Societies Need Dissent* (Cambridge, MA: Harvard University Press 2003). N. Barber, *The Constitutional State* (Oxford: Oxford University Press, 2010), chapter 6.

[19] A. Torres Pérez, *Conflicts of Rights in the European Union: A Theory of Supranational Adjudication* (Oxford: Oxford University Press, 2009), p. 106.

interplay between the CJEU and national courts. As Torres Pérez has rightfully argued, this literature has focused on explaining patterns of resistance to and compliance within the judicial interactions.[20] The development of an interest in fundamental rights by the CJEU has, for instance, been explained by the desire of the Court to protect the supremacy of EU law against the threats posed by different constitutional courts to undermine its authority. Moreover, dialogue has been used to explain differences in the mere number of references made to the CJEU as a sign of acceptance or rejection of supranational court intervention and European integration. Furthermore, judicial dialogue as a concept has been used as a sort of counterfactual to explain interactions between the CJEU and national courts in terms of power games instead of harmonious communicative interactions.[21]

Unfortunately, political science literature has not spend much attention to dialogue as a normative concept. Loth uses judicial dialogue in a normative sense to express a preference for, as he calls it, reciprocal law making over the established alternatives, like the sovereignty of parliament (which gives the parliament the last word), strong forms of judicial review (which gives the judiciary the last word), or a judicial hierarchy (which gives one court authority over another).[22] Closely related to this purpose is the use of dialogue as a legitimacy-seeking exercise. Cartabia, for example, has warned for 'judicial colonialism' in the sphere of the protection of fundamental rights now that the CJEU has its own Charter of fundamental rights and is no longer dependent upon the ECHR and national constitutions with regard to protecting EU citizen's rights. She fears the approval of the Charter of Fundamental rights could produce:

> a centralising effect, gradually drawing the protection of human rights to the European level and at the same time sterilising the protection guaranteed by the national Constitutions and breaking the limits of jurisdiction in which the action of the Community institutions should be carried out. In this centralising movement, the national constitutional traditions risk to be extinguished.[23]

[20] Ibid., p. 107.

[21] See, for example, A. Dyevre, 'Domestic Judicial Defiance and the Authority of International Legal Regimes' *European Journal of Law and Economics*, 44, 3, 453–481 (2017).

[22] M.A. Loth, 'Who Has the Last Word? On Judicial Lawmaking in European Private Law' *European Review of Private Law*, 2017, 45–70 (2017), at 47.

[23] M. Cartabia, 'Europe and Rights: Taking Dialogue Seriously' *European Constitutional Law Review*, 5, 5–31 (2009), at 17.

Entering into a judicial dialogue with national supreme courts is probably the best remedy to guarantee compliance and to warrant acceptance of CJEU decisions. Torres Pérez mentions three critical reasons for doing this. Firstly, dialogue with national supreme courts is important in an attempt to fashion an interpretation of rights that is rationally agreed upon as the *best-reasoned interpretation* that reflects equal respect for the member in the 'interpretative community'. Secondly, dialogue is the best way to *enhance participation* by members of the interpretative community in such a way that the CJEU decision is regarded as a shared outcome instead of as a one-sided dictate. This is, of course, crucial for keeping national courts on board as European courts that are willing to explain and justify the effects that EU law will have within the national legal order. Thirdly, dialogue is probably the best way to build a *common identity* within a pluralist and multi-level legal order.[24]

However, does a judicial dialogue that can fulfil these functions not presuppose – as we will discuss more in detail later in this book – a certain style of law-making that moves away from the technical, apodictic and telegraphic reasoning the CJEU has been known for since the early days of the Court's involvement in EU law making? A style of law-making that requires the CJEU to take into account the constitutional identity of the law in different Member States and, more importantly, to *show* to referring courts that it has taken the national peculiarities into account and that it has listened to the arguments of the national court(s) and is prepared to give feedback on these arguments. Why, otherwise, would supreme courts be prepared to invest time and effort in a European legal order and act as a loyal EU courts when it comes to the implementation and enforcement of preliminary rulings?

2.4 Dialogues Between Courts: A Typology of Different Forms and Functions

Whatever problems dialogues between courts are supposed to solve, these cannot be the same as overcoming the counter-majoritarian difficulty, which is so dominant in the debate about the collaboration between courts and legislatures. This does not imply that inter-court

[24] Torres Pérez supra nt. 19, 110–111.

dialogues do not also serve legitimacy seeking purposes, but the sort of legitimacy that courts are looking for in these dialogues is different and usually more focused on the quality and persuasiveness of judicial decisions in hard cases than on acceptance by the people. Coordination and communication between courts may enhance judicial accountability but it cannot compensate for something that courts do not have, namely: a democratic mandate.

If we want to find out why inter-court dialogues exist, we need to discern between different kinds of judicial dialogues. Rosas mentions five types, namely[25]: (1) vertical dialogues between courts belonging to the same hierarchical judicial system in which lower courts, for example, signal to higher courts that a change of precedent is required and the higher court responds to this; (2) semi-vertical relations, such as between the CJEU and ECtHR, in which the former has committed itself to follow as much as possible, the case law of the latter with regard to fundamental rights enshrined in the convention; (3) coordination between courts with overlapping or 'competing' jurisdictions, like the International Court of Justice (ICJ) and the Law of the Sea Tribunal (LST). Here it is important to make clear who is responsible for what, for instance, in order to avoid forum shopping; (4) dialogues between courts at the same level. Just think of national supreme courts referring to each other's case law as a source of inspiration to solve hard cases or to find general principles of law; (5) dialogues between national courts and supranational courts, such as the ECtHR and CJEU.

2.4.1 *Vertical Dialogues*

It is probably needless to say that the aforementioned 'judicial dialogues' fulfil different functions. Signals from district or appellate courts to the national supreme court to revise existing precedents are usually an attempt to influence the supreme court's case law because it raises unexpected problems for legal practice. Instead of taking a counter initiative and effectively adopt new rules or principles, lower courts often try to avoid contestation because they do not want to run the risk of being overruled higher up in the judicial chain because that could hurt their credibility. Empirical studies show, for example, that there is

[25] A. Rosas, 'The European Court of Justice in Context: Forms and Patterns of Judicial Dialogue' *European Journal of Legal Studies* 1, 2, 1–16 (2007); A. Rosas, 'Methods of Interpretation – Judicial Dialogue', in C. Baudenbacher and E. Busek (eds.), *The Role of International Courts* (Frankfurt: German Law Publishers, 2008), p. 187.

often a strong team spirit within courts trying to prevent it from 'getting it wrong'.[26] For national supreme courts, on the other hand, repeated signals from lower courts that existing precedents raise problems can have an important thermometer function that can help them to keep in touch with how its attempts to guarantee the unity of national law works out in practice. Supreme courts that are receptive to these signals may be able to prevent lower courts by means of a dialogue from deciding their own course.

2.4.2 Semi-Vertical Dialogues

With regard to the semi-vertical relationship, such as the one between the CJEU and ECtHR, courts have an interest in guaranteeing a uniform interpretation and application of fundamental rights law, especially since the introduction of the Charter of Fundamental Rights of the EU, which shows overlap with the rights catalogue of the European Convention on Human Rights. There are also important differences between both courts, though. The Strasbourg court's mission, in accordance with article 53 of the Convention, is to establish a minimum protection of the fundamental rights enshrined in the treaty throughout all forty-seven Member States but does not seek to harmonize the national human rights catalogues. The CJEU, however, is not primarily a human rights court but is first and foremost a supreme court of the European Union protecting the primacy of EU law, concentrating on attaining the socio-economic objectives of the Treaties and guaranteeing a uniform interpretation and application of EU law. The raison d'être of the CJEU is hence not primarily to ensure a minimum protection of fundamental rights in the Member States but to ensure the uniformity of EU law based on the principle of equality of the Member States.[27]

[26] A.F. Daughety and J.F. Reinganum, 'Appealing Judgments' *RAND Journal of Economics*, 31, 502–525 (2000); M.C. Dorf, 'Prediction and the Rule of Law' *UCLA Law Review*, 42, 651–715 (1995); L.A. Kornhauser, 'An Economic "Perspective on Stare Decisis"' *Fordham Law Review*, 65, 63–92 (1989); L.A. Kornhauser, 'Adjudication by a Resource-Constrained Team' *Southern California Law Review* 68, 1605–1629 (1995); J. Rogers, 'Lower Court Application of the 'Overruling Law' of Higher Courts', *Legal Theory* 1, 179–204 (1995); S. Shavell, 'The Appeals Process as a Means of Error Correction' *Journal of Legal Studies* 23, 379–426 (1995).

[27] D. Spielmann, The Judicial Dialogue between the European Court of Justice and the European Court of Human Rights Or how to remain good neighbours after the Opinion 2/13, Brussels 27 March 2017 (www.fp7-frame.eu/wp-content/uploads/2017/03/ECHRCJUEdialog.BRUSSELS.final_.pdf).

Both courts have been referring to each other's case law, already for quite some time before the Lisbon Treaty. Something that resembles a dialogue, however, did not occur until 2005. That was when the Strasbourg Court formulated in the Bosphorus case,[28] the presumption of equivalent protection of ECtHR rights by the EU. Even though the EU is not a party to the European convention, the ECtHR argued that: 'In the Court's view, State action taken in compliance with such legal obligations is justified as long as the relevant organization is considered to protect fundamental rights, as regards both the substantive guarantees offered and the mechanisms controlling their observance, in a manner which can be considered at least equivalent to that for which the Convention provides.'[29] Through the Bosphorus decision, the ECtHR signalled that it was seeking a relationship of comity and cooperation with the CJEU, which could be seen as a judicial dialogue.[30]

Until the Lisbon Treaty, the CJEU seemed to welcome this dialogue with the ECtHR as was shown by numerous references to the ECtHR case law and the promise to apply ECHR standards diligently and conscientiously.[31] After the Lisbon Treaty entered into force, which made the Charter of Fundamental Rights binding, however, the CJEU started to use the Charter more and more as its sole point of reference, thereby sometimes ignoring similar rights enshrined in the Convention, despite the fact that article 52(3) of the Charter initiated in 'interpretative bridge' between Charter rights and Convention rights.

The tendency of the CJEU to interpret the Charter of fundamental rights more autonomously seems to have affected the existing practice of horizontal referencing between both courts. This has become visible in the case *Avotiņš* v. *Latvia*.[32] While the ECtHR mentions that it remains

[28] ECHR Bosphorus Hava Yolları Turizm ve Ticaret Anonim Şirketi v. Ireland, Application No 45036, Merits, 30 June 2006.

[29] Ibid., consideration 155.

[30] S. Douglas-Scott, 'Bosphorus Hava Yollari Turizm Ve Ticaret Anonim Sirketi v. Ireland' *Common Market Law Review*, 43, 1, 243–254 (2006).

[31] Costello, 'The Bosphorus Ruling of the European Court of Human Rights: Fundamental Rights and Blurred Boundaries in Europe' *Human Rights Law Review*, 6, 87, 114 (2006). F. Jacobs, 'Judicial Dialogue and the Cross-Fertilization of Legal Systems: The European Court of Justice' *Texas International Law Journal*, 38, 547 (2003), at 551; L Scheeck, 'The Relationship between the European Courts and Integration through Human Rights' *Heidelberg Journal of International Law*, 65, 837 (2005), at 871; Lock, 'The ECJ and the ECtHR: The Future Relationship between the Two European Courts' *The Law and Practice of International Courts and Tribunals* 375 (2009), at 380.

[32] ECHR Avotiņš v Latvia, Application No 17502/07, 26 May 2016.

mindful of the importance of mutual recognition and trust between the Member States and EU institutions, it warns that these mechanisms must not infringe fundamental rights. In other words, the Bosphorus assumption can be rebutted in case the protection of Convention rights is manifestly deficient. According to Glas and Krommendijk, one may conclude that the ECtHR now applies the Bosphorus doctrine stricter than before Opinion 2/13 in comparison with the handful of judgments in which it dealt with the doctrine previously and wanted to show its dissatisfaction with the way in which the CJEU has one-sidedly altered the tone of the dialogue.[33] Luckily, both courts kept interacting at bilateral meetings, which are organized alternately in Luxembourg and Strasbourg at least every two years and furthermore at conferences and informal meetings.

2.4.3 Dialogues in Overlapping or Competing Jurisdictions

A third category concerns, in fact, the existence of overlapping or competing jurisdictions. Just think of situations where at least two international courts have jurisdiction over the same issue. Recent years have witnessed a sharp increase in the number of international courts and tribunals (e.g., WTO, NAFTA, ITLOS, ICC, etc.) and a greater willingness on the side of states and other international actors to subject themselves to the compulsory jurisdiction of international adjudicative mechanisms. However, as Shany has shown, because of the uncoordinated nature of these developments, overlap between the jurisdictional ambits of the different judicial bodies might occur – i.e., the same dispute could fall under the jurisdiction of more than one forum.[34] An obvious example, mentioned by Rosas, concerns the overlapping jurisdiction of the ICJ and the LST in Hamburg.[35] Since the same dispute could go to either of the two courts, the possibility of 'forum shopping' threatens the unity of international law. Here a judicial dialogue between the ICJ and LST could serve to avoid this kind of forum shopping.

How easily this forum shopping might go wrong can be shown by looking at the preliminary reference procedure of article 214 of the

[33] L. Glas and J. Krommendijk, 'From Opinion 2/13 to Avotiņš: Recent Developments in the Relationship between the Luxembourg and Strasbourg Court' *Human Rights Law Review*, 0, 1–21 (2017). (doi: 10.1093/hrlr/ngw047).

[34] Y. Shany, *The Competing Jurisdictions of International Courts and Tribunals* (Oxford: Oxford University Press, 2003).

[35] A. Rosas, 'The European Court of Justice in Context: Forms and Patterns of Judicial Dialogue' *European Journal of Legal Studies*, 1, 2, 1–16 (2007).

Revised Treaty of Chaguaramas (RTC), which was borrowed from the CJEU.[36] In order to enhance the Caribbean integration, the Caribbean Court of Justice (CCJ) was established in 2001 and inaugurated on 16 April 2005. Thirteen Member States of Caribbean Community (CARICOM) have accepted the CCJ's jurisdiction.[37] CARICOM is an organization established in 1973 of fifteen Caribbean nations and dependencies whose main objective is to promote economic integration and cooperation among its members, to ensure that the benefits of integration are equitably shared, and to coordinate foreign policy. Its major activities involve coordinating economic policies and development planning; devising and instituting special projects for the less-developed countries within its jurisdiction; and most relevant here: operating as a regional single market for many of its members. Just like the CJEU, the CCJ has an important responsibility in deciding regional trade disputes between CARICOM Member States. In its original jurisdiction, the CCJ has the compulsory and exclusive power to interpret and apply the RTC. National courts can refer preliminary questions to the CCJ in a way very similar to the national courts can do this under article 267 TFEU.

It is interesting that while the preliminary references to the CJEU have shown a steady increase over the years, there has not been a single reference from national courts to the CCJ, although the CCJ has repeatedly urged the regional courts to do so, underlining the cooperative relationship with national courts. One possible explanation why national courts have been reluctant to refer cases to the CCJ is that the Court has given special leave on various occasions to private parties under article 222 RTC to address the CCJ directly in order to protect their rights under the treaty from being infringed. After all, providing private parties with the opportunity to address the CCJ directly, makes it possible for them to bypass national courts that are unwilling to enforce the treaty or to refer questions concerning the interpretation or application of the RTC to the CCJ. In other words, why would private citizens or companies take the effort of going through the entire judicial chain in their own country and then wait for an answer of the CCJ to the questions that were referred, if there is also a direct route to address the CCJ? At the same time, one wonders what kind of implications this direct route has for the

[36] The information with regard to the CCJ is derived from the work of Jacintha Asarfi, who is writing her PhD at Tilburg Law School about the dialogue between national courts and the CCJ in the realm of the RTC's preliminary reference procedure.

[37] D. Berry, *Caribbean Integration Law* (Oxford: Oxford University Press, 2014).

preliminary reference procedure and the dialogue between the CCJ and the supreme national courts, and what this could tell us about the preliminary reference procedure of article 267 TFEU, which, according to Pescatore and De Witte, runs the risk of developing into a citizens' infringement procedure.

Pescatore and De Witte have shown for the procedure of article 267 TFEU that, although the CJEU usually claims that this procedure is focused on the validity and interpretation of EU law and not on the compatibility of national law with EU law, which belongs to the competence of national courts, the CJEU does not always restrict itself to a decision about the validity or correct interpretation of EU law.[38] De Witte, for example, refers to the Van Doorne case,[39] where a Belgian appellate court referred a questions to the CJEU about whether Article 58 (1), in conjunction with Article 77(1)(7), of the Belgian Value Added Tax Code, was compatible or incompatible with Article 27 of Sixth Council Directive 77/388/EEC. Here the CJEU starts out with declaring that it is not for the Court to determine whether national provisions are compatible with European Union law. A bit further in its decision, however, the CJEU states that the applicable EU directive 'must be interpreted as not precluding national legislation, such as that at issue in the main proceedings.'[40] Here the CJEU is doing exactly what is says it may not do, namely: deciding whether national law is compatible with EU law. In this case, that probably did not raise tension with the referring court because this is exactly what the appellate court wanted to know. In other cases, however, this could be different.[41]

A risk of backfiring might become apparent as soon as lower courts start to use the possibility of asking for a preliminary ruling to bypass decisions from their own supreme court, as was for example the case in the famous Aziz decision of the CJEU about the legality of the Spanish mortgage system. The CJEU considered the Spanish law to infringe the unfair terms directive, in particular because it precludes the court that

[38] P. Pescatore, 'Van Gend en Loos, 3 February 1963: A view from within', in M. Poiares Maduro and L. Azoulai (eds.), *The Past and the Future of EU Law: The Classics of EU law Revisited* (Oxford: Hart publishing, 2010), pp. 7–8. B. De Witte, 'The Preliminary Ruling Dialogue: Three Types of Questions Posed by National Courts', in B. de Witte, J. Mayoral, U. Jaremba, M. Wind, K. Podstawa (eds.), *National Courts and EU Law/New Issues, Theories and Methods/ Judicial Review and Cooperation* (Cheltenham: Edward Elgar Publishing, 2016), pp. 15–26.

[39] Case C-489/09, Vandoorne NV v. Belgische Staat [2011] ECR I 0000; ECLI:EU:C:2011:33.

[40] Ibid., par. 46.

[41] For another similar example see Case C-614/14, *Ognyanov*; ECLI:EU:C:2016:514.

has jurisdiction to declare unfair a term of a loan agreement relating to immovable property from separately staying the mortgage enforcement proceedings. Some scholars heralded the local court that went against the Spanish legislature and against the case law of the Tribunal Supremo, as was the CJEU's decision.[42] The CJEU ruling was viewed by many as a necessary correction of national mortgage laws that undermined the fundamental rights of consumers (e.g. the right to respect for one's home under article 7 ECHR). Others, however, have warned the CJEU for de facto operating as a court of last instance, which could damage the legitimacy of the Court. Micklitz, for example, pointed out that the Aziz case stood for thousands of similar disputes in other Southern European countries in which the mortgage systems were also heavily affected by the credit crunch. Was the CJEU able to oversee the consequences of its decision in this respect or should the Court have better left this to the (EU or national) legislature?[43]

The question is whether using lower courts as quasi supervisors responsible for the compliance of national laws with EU law might not put the solidarity between lower courts and supreme courts and between the CJEU and supreme courts in jeopardy. A possible consequence of this bypassing could be that supreme courts become unwilling to refer cases to the CJEU, distance themselves from CJEU's decisions that impede national law, and even become more 'flexible' in the implementation of preliminary rulings.

2.4.4 Dialogues Between Courts at the Same Level

Another way in which the concept 'judicial dialogue' is being used is when national judges at the same level refer to each other's case law in (constitutional) interpretation.[44] Here we will limit ourselves to implicit or explicit references of court across national borders. Tzanakopoulos has argued that the use of the term dialogue may be somewhat

[42] I. Ramsay, 'Two Cheers for Europe: Austerity, Mortgage Foreclosures and Personal Insolvency Policy in the EU', in H.W. Micklitz and I. Domurath (eds.), *Consumer Debt and Social Exclusion in Europe* (Aldershot: Ashgate, 2012), pp. 215–216.

[43] H.W. Micklitz, 'Unfair Contract Terms – Public Interest Litigation before European Courts – Case C-415/11 Mohamed Aziz', in E. Terryn, G. Straetmans and V. Colaert (eds.), *Landmark Cases of EU Consumer Law – In Honour of Jules Stuyck* (Cambridge: Intersentia, 2013), pp. 633–653.

[44] G. Halmai, 'The Use of Foreign Law in Constitutional Interpretation', in M. Rosenfeld and A. Sajó (eds.), *The Oxford Handbook of Comparative Constitutional Law* (Oxford: Oxford University Press, 2012), pp. 1328–1349.

misleading in this context given the fact that when a court discusses and/or refers to decisions of foreign courts, the latter will usually not have the opportunity to respond, which means there is not really an exchange of views and opinions. It should be seen more as a matter of influence exercised by the decision of one court on the reasoning or decision of another.[45]

There are grosso modo two types of situations in which this frequently occurs, namely: (1) when courts have difficulties in finding out what is the correct interpretation of international law and (2) in case domestic courts struggle with hard cases with potentially far-reaching consequences that require policy choices. Examples of the first category are: the reference of the High Court of Australia to decisions of Canadian and US courts with regard to the interpretation of the term 'other social group' in article 1A(2) of the 1951 Refugee Convention and the 1967 Protocol relating to the Status of Refugees[46]; the reference from one domestic court to another in order to establish whether certain rules or principles are part of customary international law[47]; references between national courts to establish whether a preliminary reference should be made to the CJEU in light of the CILFIT doctrine (e.g. should the interpretation of a certain EU provision be seen as an Acte Claire?).[48]

Concerning the wicked problems for which domestic courts have sought inspiration from foreign courts, there are many examples to be given, such as: how to deal with questions of liability in cases of 'wrongful birth'; legality of same sex marriages; damages for asbestos victims; and so on. Normally courts do not simply transplant foreign solutions to

[45] A. Tzanakopoulos, 'Judicial Dialogue as a Means of Interpretation', in H. Aust and G. Nolte (eds.), *The Interpretation of International Law by Domestic Courts* (Oxford: Oxford University Press 2016), p. 75.

[46] A. vs Minister for Immigration and Ethic Affairs (1996–1997) 190 CLR 225.

[47] R. O' Keefe, R. van Alebeek, D. Hovell, Y Ronen, S. Olleson, and S. Wittich, in A. Tzanakopoulos and C. Tams (eds.), *Domestic Courts as Agents of Development of International Law*, *LJIL*, 26, 531–665 (2013).

[48] Regarding the latter the case X & Van Dijk (C-72/14 and C-197/14) is interesting because a Dutch court of appeal asked preliminary questions on the application of the social security provisions of Regulation 1408/71 to Rhine boatmen falling under the international Rhine Agreement. The Dutch Supreme Court, in a similar case, however, had reasoned that the answer to those questions was so obvious that it needed no clarification. It then started a preliminary reference to ask whether it had to await the outcome of the pending questions of the lower court, or that it could dismiss the question as an acte clair. Here the CJEU determined that a lower court has referred a question to the ECJ, does not in itself preclude a supreme court from concluding, in line with the Cilfit criteria, that the case is an acte clair.

these kind of problems to the national legal order but try to inform themselves about the ratio and policy choices behind the decisions in different jurisdictions in order to find an interpretation that best matches the national legal order. In some jurisdictions, this practice of referring to foreign law, especially in case fundamental rights are involved, is even recognized by the constitution, as is the case in South Africa.[49]

According to Mak, highest court judges in the United Kingdom, Canada, the United States, France and the Netherlands increasingly take notice of foreign legal sources due to the increased interconnections between legal systems in an increasingly globalizing legal world.[50] Bobek, however, studied the supreme courts in England and Wales, France, Germany, The Czech Republic and Slovakia. He doubts whether voluntary comparative engagement between domestic (supreme) courts is on the rise in Europe.[51] Bobek claims the references to foreign law by the Bundesverfassungsgericht between 1951 and 2007 have, for instance, remained fairly constant and minimalistic,[52] while the French constitutional court never explicitly refers to foreign law, and the Czech and Slovakian courts also seldom speak 'extra-judicially' and stay close to textual interpretation.[53]

It is probably true that the possibilities for a transnational judicial dialogue have increased over the last decades due to factors such as the availability of translated versions of decisions of foreign courts in electronic form, the setting up of judicial networks that enable (physical or electronic) interaction between judges; and the growing intertwinement between national and international law. However, it is questionable whether this has had the biggest impact on the frequency and intensity of references to decisions of foreign courts and to comparative legal reasoning by domestic courts. In particular with regard to constitutional

[49] Article 39(1) of the South African Constitution reads: '[w]hen interpreting the Bill of Rights, a court, tribunal or forum (. . .) may consider foreign law'. See U. Bentele, 'Mining for Gold: The Constitutional Court of South Africa's Experience with Comparative Constitutional Law' *Georgia Journal of International and Comparative Constitutional Law*, 37, 219–265 (2009).

[50] E. Mak, *Judicial Decision-Making in A Globalised World. A Comparative Analysis of the Changing Practices of Western Highest Courts* (Oxford and Portland, Oregon: Hart Publishing, 2013).

[51] M. Bobek, *Comparative Reasoning in European Supreme Courts* (Oxford: Oxford University Press 2013), p. 15.

[52] Ibid., p. 14.

[53] Ibid., chapter 8. Bobek argues that this dates back to the communist era when textualism was the 'survival strategy' of the judiciary against the political regime.

courts, Law and Chang have claimed that institutional factors, such as the composition and staffing of courts, time and case load, and the way legal education is organized and influences the knowledge of foreign law, are probably much more important factors for transnational 'dialogues' in the daily lives of courts.[54]

The reasons for citing foreign courts are manifold. What is interesting, though, is that, on the one hand, citation of a decision from a foreign court seems to reflect the opinion of the citing court that evidence of foreign support or parallel reasoning will strengthen its own decision. In the absence of a defined judicial hierarchy such a calculation is often used by courts in order to enhance the persuasiveness, authority and legitimacy of their individual judicial decisions.[55] On the other hand, critics warn of cherry picking (one can always find arguments for a certain preferred decision somewhere in foreign law) and for institutional isomorphism. The latter implies that especially supreme court decisions will become more homogenous over time due to the emerging of a transnational dialogue between courts which creates a common perspective on an increasing number of border-crossing problems, while at the same time widening the gap between the domestic court and the national audience due to a changing perception of courts of being part of a larger transnational judicial community.[56]

2.4.5 *The Dialogue Between Constitutional Courts and Supranational Courts*

Although this book is about the dialogue between national courts and the CJEU in the course of the preliminary reference procedure, this is certainly not the only form of interchange between national and supranational courts. Popelier, Mazmanyan and VandenBruwaene, discern between four different roles of modern constitutional courts in Europe: guardians of fundamental rights, watchdogs over the institutional balance between different branches of government, regulatory watchdogs, and fora for deliberation and constitutional dialogue.[57]

54 D. Law and W. Chang, 'The Limits of Global Judicial Dialogue' *Washington Law Review*, 86, 523–577 (2011).

55 A.M. Slaughter, 'A Typology of Transjudicial Communication' *University of Richmond Law Review*, 29, 99 (1994) at 119.

56 O. Frishman, 'Should Courts Fear Transnational Engagement?' *Vanderbilt Journal of Transnational Law*, 49, 59–105 (2016).

57 A. Mazmanyan, P. Popelier and W. VandenBruwaene (eds.), *The Role of Constitutional Courts in Multilevel Governance* (Cambridge: Intersentia, 2013), chapter 1.

With regard to the latter, it is important to realize that dialogues between constitutional courts and supranational courts not only occur 'on paper' but also take place via judicial networks in which judges from these courts meet on a regular basis. The ECtHR, for example, organizes meetings with supreme court judges annually and publishes the proceedings under the heading of 'Dialogue between judges', but there are lots of other formal and informal networks in which constitutional courts play a role. Next to this, a practice has developed in which constitutional courts refer in their case law to the jurisprudence of supranational courts, such as the ECtHR and CJEU and vice versa. As mentioned earlier, one may doubt to what extent this kind of referring to foreign or international law constitutes a true dialogue because there is usually no real discussion or interchange between the courts about the actual decision. Nevertheless, the involved constitutional courts probably refer to this supranational case law for expository, empirical and substantive reasons.

Exposition means that the referring constitutional court uses the reference to contrast and explain a certain domestic constitutional rule. Empirically, references show that the court looks to foreign case law in order to find out what the effects of a certain proposed rule have been in other jurisdictions, which is basically a kind of estimation of likely consequences of a ruling. Substantive references indicate that the court has sought guidance in defining the content of the rules it needs to interpret, either via 'reason borrowing' (e.g. what could be the ratio behind a certain rule) or 'moral fact finding' (e.g. does a certain norm actually exist in other jurisdictions or is there a trends towards a certain interpretation of an existing norm).[58] In *Goodwin* v. *United Kingdom*, the ECtHR, for instance, noticed in a case about sexual harassment of a transsexual that there was not only increased social acceptance of transsexuals but also increased legal recognition of the new sexual identity of post-operative transsexuals, which led the Court to conclude there was a violation of Articles 8 and 12 of the Convention.[59] Here, the ECtHR did not resort to deference via the margin of appreciation doctrine but ruled that this practice of sexual abuse runs against the right to private and

[58] See C. Zoethout, 'The European Court of Human Rights and Transnational Judicial Dialogue: References to Foreign Law and the Quest for Justification' *Vienna Journal on International Constitutional Law*, 9, 3, 398–416 (2015) at 406. Zoethout has borrowed her typology from J. Larsen, 'Importing Constitutional Norms from a "Wider Civilization": Lawrence and the Rehnquist Court's use of Foreign and International Law in Domestic Constitutional Interpretation' *Ohio State Law Journal*, 65, 1283 (2004).

[59] ECHR Christine Goodwin v. United Kingdom, Application No 28957/95, 11 July 2002.

family life and the right to marry and found a family. The comparative analysis, which showed increased legal recognition of the rights of transsexuals, legitimized the ECtHR to go further than is would normally be inclined to do.

What is interesting in the relationship between constitutional courts and the ECtHR is that even though the case law of the latter has no erga omnes effect and only obliges the defendant to abide by the judgment, constitutional courts usually spontaneously follow the ECtHR's case law by way of harmonious interpretation when interpreting national constitutional law. They apparently see the ECtHR as a supervising supranational constitutional court, although the court has no power to annul national legislation that is in breach with the Convention. Helfer has argued that since the ECtHR has no coercive powers, the perceived legitimacy of the Court as witnessed by this practice of harmonious interpretation is the result of 'skilful persuasion', which is on its turn due to the recognized expertise of the ECtHR and the high-quality argumentative reasoning of the Court.[60]

The persuasiveness of the ECtHR is also partly fuelled by the fact that the court offers a minimum level of protection of fundamental rights, which leaves states a margin of appreciation to give their own interpretation of convention right. Moreover, the existing system of dissenting and concurring opinions points in the direction of what one might call a 'second order judicial dialogue'. This means that national constitutional courts follow the ECtHR's case law by adopting the Court's method of interpretation in the adjudication of national constitutional provisions because they are convinced by the quality of the arguments of the Court.

However, some constitutional courts have suggested there are limits to the harmonious interpretation of ECtHR case law in the domestic legal order. Both the Italian constitutional court and the German constitutional courts have, for example, argued that application of the Strasbourg case law about the interpretation of the ECHR may not result in a violation of national constitutional rights, which could distort the national legal order and foundations on which the national constitution is build.[61] This indicates that at least these courts feel they cannot just

[60] L.R Helfer, 'Redesigning the European Court of Human Rights: embeddedness as a deep structural principle of the European Court of Human Rights regime' *European Journal of International Law*, 19, 135 (2008).

[61] Italian constitutional court 16 November 2009, no. 311 and German constitutional courts BvR 1481/04, 14 October 2014.

copy the ECtHR's case law when national constitutional rights and principles are at stake. In a certain way, this is a similar argument as the CJEU has made in its advisory opinion about the accession to the ECHR about the autonomy of the EU legal order that needs to be protected primarily by the CJEU.[62] There the CJEU also argues that, although the Court will normally respect the case law of the ECtHR, this cannot be the case when it threatens the autonomy of the EU legal order.

Compared to the overall enthusiasm of constitutional courts to adopt a harmonious interpretation of national constitutional law in light of the ECHR, which of course contains some exceptions, the same courts have so far been far more reluctant to engage with the CJEU. Although members of the CJEU frequently participate in the events of the Conference of European Constitutional Courts and there are regular visits from the CJEU to Constitutional Courts and vice versa, while judges from both courts participate in academic conferences and debates, what has been missing is an active use of the preliminary reference procedure. This procedure applies also in case legislation adopted for complying with primary or secondary EU law is claimed to be in violation with EU constitutional law, such as the Charter of fundamental rights or general principles of EU law.

It took until 1997 for the first constitutional court (of Belgium) to refer a question to the CJEU. Initially this reluctance was mostly due to the fact that constitutional courts believed the preliminary reference procedure applied only to ordinary courts and perhaps also because of the 'judicial ego' of constitutional courts since making a reference implies a voluntary subjection to the authority of an external court, given that it must be presumed that the sender of the question will consider itself

[62] Opinion 2/13 of the Court of Justice of the European Union, ECLI:EU:C:2014:2454. See also: P. Craig, 'EU Accession to the ECHR: Competence, Procedure and Substance' *Fordham International Law Journal*, 36, 5, 1114–1150 (2013); P. Eeckhout, 'Opinion 2/13 on EU Accession to the ECHR and Judicial Dialogue: Autonomy or Autarky' *Fordham International Law Journal*, 38, 4, 955–991 (2015). C. Eckes, 'EU Accession to the ECHR: Between Autonomy and Adaptation' *Modern Law Review*, 76, 254 (2013); J.P. Jacqué, 'The Accession of the European Union to the European Convention on Human Rights and Fundamental Freedoms' *Common Market Law Review*, 48, 99 (2011); T. Lock, 'EU Accession to the ECHR: Implications for Judicial Review in Strasbourg' *European Law review*, 35, 777 (2010); T. Lock, 'Walking on a Tightrope: The Draft ECHR Accession Agreement and the Autonomy of the EU Legal Order' *Common Market Law Review*, 48, 1025 (2011); T. Lock, 'End of an Epic? The Draft Agreement on the EU's Accession to the ECHR' *Yearbook of European Law*, 31, 162 (2012); N. O'Meara, '"A More Secure Europe of Rights?" The European Court of Human Rights, the Court of Justice of the European Union and EU Accession to the ECHR' *German Law Journal*, 12, 1813 (2011).

bound by the answer.[63] For a number of reasons, the hesitance to refer preliminary questions to Luxembourg by constitutional courts has started to change recently.

Firstly, constitutional courts may have realised that lower courts will become their competitors if these courts will choose to refer questions with regard to the constitutionality of national laws in light of EU treaties and the Charter of fundamental rights to the CJEU, even when their constitutional court is unwilling to do so. Doing nothing is therefore no longer an attractive option for constitutional courts because they run the risk of being bypassed by the same domestic courts they are supposed to supervise. After all, in that case the constitutional courts not only lose control over the interpretation of national constitutional law but also risk losing authority towards domestic courts.

Secondly, with the CJEU increasingly entering the realm of fundamental rights law, the CJEU itself became a more visible co-actor and competitor in what constitutional courts consider to be their core business. This does not imply that there was no interchange between constitutional courts and the CJEU before the Lisbon Treaty. On the contrary, the CJEU was probably even encouraged to develop its fundamental rights jurisprudence on instigation of the German and Italian Constitutional Courts, which claimed to be unwilling to accept the primacy of European law unconditionally as long as the EU did not have an adequate system of fundamental rights protection of its own. While this line of 'Solange' and 'contro limiti' cases was not a direct dialogue between the CJEU and constitutional courts,[64] it was again very much a matter of action and reaction spurred by signals in the case law of national constitutional courts that were meant to invoke a response from the side of the CJEU. One might perhaps even call it the 'body language' of the constitutional courts that was picked up by the CJEU.

It is fair to say, though, that because of the advancement of the CJEU's aspirations in the field of fundamental rights law, and constitutional

[63] M. Claes, 'Luxembourg, Here We Come? Constitutional Courts and the Preliminary Reference Procedure' *German Law Journal*, 16, 06, 1332 (2015). She rightfully points out that it is paradoxical that some constitutional courts, such as the German Bundesverfassungsgericht, made it a breach of the constitutional right to a lawful judge for a highest German court not to make a reference without explanation, but have excluded themselves from this obligation.

[64] Bundesverfassungsgericht [BVerfG] [Federal Constitutional Court], 29 May 1974, BVerfGE 37, 271; 22 October 1986, 16 BVerfGE 73, 339; Corte costituzionale, Sentenza of 18 December 1973, n. 183/73, Frontini. Ibid., Claes, p. 1334.

review more in general, constitutional courts have become aware of the fact that there is a new supranational constitutional court to reckon with.[65] This may have spurred counter reactions in which constitutional courts have started to look more critically whether the CJEU respects the limits of EU law. They have done so via their own fundamental rights review, via competence review (ultra vires review) and, more recently, via constitutional identity review.

With respect to fundamental rights review, the Test Achats case in which the Belgium constitutional courts challenged the validity of article 5(2) of Council Directive 2004/113/EC with regard to the equal treatment of men and women by insurance companies is perhaps illustrative. The applicants in that case claimed that the directive infringes upon, among other things, the articles 10, 11 and 11a of the Belgian constitution. Competence review was clearly present in the infamous Landtová case about an alleged discriminatory pension scheme in the Czech Republic that resulted from the dissolvation of Czechoslovakia. In this case, the Czech constitutional court held that the CJEU in its judgment in Case C-399/09 acted ultra vires and subsequently gave Czech national law precedence over EU law. Although this decision raised a lot of criticism, it shows that constitutional courts might in exceptional cases police the boundaries of the CJEU's competence.

Finally, there is identity review. Recently, for example, the Belgium constitutional court rejected several actions for annulment filed against the Act approving the Treaty on Stability, Coordination and Governance in the Economic and Monetary Union but to the surprise of many included in an obiter dictum:

> When approving a treaty which [attributes new competences to EU institutions], the legislature must respect Article 34 of the Constitution. By virtue of that provision, the exercising of specific powers can be assigned by a treaty or by a law to institutions of public international law. While these institutions may subsequently decide autonomously about how they exercise these competences, Article 34 of the Constitution cannot be interpreted as granting an unlimited license to the legislature, when approving that treaty, or to the said institutions, when exercising their attributed powers. Article 34 of the Constitution *does not allow a discriminating derogation to the national identity* inherent in the fundamental structures, political and constitutional, or to the basic values of the protection offered by the Constitution to all legal subjects. [italics RvG/JdP].[66]

[65] See for instance: J. Komarek, 'National Constitutional Courts in the European Constitutional Democracy' *International Journal of Constitutional Law*, 12, 3, 525–544 (2014).

[66] Belgium Constitutional Court, Case no. 62/2016, 28 April 2016, B.8.7.

Here the court refers implicitly to article 4(2) TEU, which requires that the Union respects the national identity of the Member States. As Cloots has rightfully demonstrated this identity clause is closely connected to the notion of democratic legitimacy:

> A common national identity facilitates the attainment of this ideal in at least two ways. First, when citizens are tied by linguistic and national bonds they experience fewer difficulties in communicating with one another, which benefits, in turn, the democratic debate, not only in the decision-making bodies but also in the media. Secondly, democracy can only work if there is sufficient confidence and trust among citizens themselves and among citizens and politicians. Only if people are convinced that their fellow citizens are interested in their opinions too and only if the losers in this election or debate are assured of a chance to win next time is true democracy possible.[67]

In the meanwhile, other constitutional courts have also discovered the identity clause in the TEU as a shield and a sword against judicial activism by the CJEU and as a means to protect national sovereignty and constitutional identity.[68] The latter is not the same as the idea of a national identity. Where the constitutional identity doctrine articulated by certain national courts is based on a claim to sovereignty on behalf of the Member States, Cloots argues that the national identity clause laid down in article 4(2) TEU implements fundamental principles of political morality that call on a multinational polity to pay heed to the identity of its constituent national and local communities.[69] It is to be expected that the identity clause of article 4 TEU will in the future lead to more interaction between the CJEU and constitutional courts with regard to the limits of the competences of EU institutions and the protection of domestic democratic values in the Member States.

2.5 What Have We Learned?

What we have learned from the brief overview of types of dialogues – or perhaps better the various contexts in which the debate about judicial and, somewhat broader, constitutional dialogues, occur – is that the

[67] E. Cloots, 'National Identity, Constitutional Identity, and Sovereignty in the EU' *Netherlands Journal of Legal Philosophy*, 45, 2, 87–88 (2016). See also more in-depth: E. Cloots, *National Identity in EU Law* (Oxford: Oxford University Press, 2015), chapter 3.

[68] T. Konstadinides, 'Constitutional Identity as a Shield and as a Sword: The European Legal Order within the Framework of National Constitutional Settlement' *Cambridge Yearbook of European Legal Studies*, 13, 195–218 (2011).

[69] Cloots supra nt. 67, p. 97.

label is used for different things in different circumstances. The bottom line appears to be that in most of the variants we have discussed above, one cannot really speak of a judicial dialogue in terms of an actual debate or judicial interchange, except perhaps for the informal judicial networks that have been set up over the last decades.[70]

In these networks, the interaction is the most direct and touchable because judges can actually influence each other's views directly by means of an exchange of arguments. The only 'disadvantage' of these meetings is that they will usually have little relevance and informative value for pending cases because the debate is likely to focus on the ex post evaluation of previous cases with which courts have struggled. The word 'disadvantage' is put between quotation marks here because one may wonder to what extent it would be a good idea if foreign judges could directly influence the outcomes of pending cases without being responsible and accountable for those decisions.[71]

This problem of legitimacy brings us back to the roots of the judicial dialogue concept. Especially in the Canadian constitutional model, the idea of a dialogue was presented as a means to overcome the counter-majoritarian difficulty when courts are allowed to review the constitutionality of acts of parliament. Here the 'dialogue' allows legislatures to reverse supreme court decisions and prevents both the judiciary and the legislature to have the last word in a constitutional debate. Idealistically, this creates a world in which legislators and judges stand on each other's shoulders instead of on each other's toes.

Not only in the relationship between courts and legislatures is the concept used to further (democratic) legitimacy and enhance the quality of law-making, but also in inter-judicial dialogues. Even between lower courts and supreme courts there are sometimes informal meetings between judges from both levels in order to create mutual learning

[70] Just think of the Conference of European Constitutional Courts. See: www.confeuconstco.org/en/common/home.html; the Network of Presidents of the Supreme Judicial Courts of the European Union. See: http://network-presidents.eu/page/supreme-courts; or the Association of Councils of State and Supreme Administrative Jurisdictions. See: www.aca-europe.eu/index.php/en/.

[71] It is interesting, though, that while accountability of judges has always been a controversial issue because of the potential conflict with fundamental rights and judicial independence, it is exactly in this area where transnational networks have played an important role in the development of global ethical standards and codes of conduct relating to judicial ethics. See: J. Terhechte, 'Judicial Ethics for a Global Judiciary – How Judicial Networks Create their own Codes of Conduct' *German Law Journal*, 10, 04, 501–514 (2009).

and understanding and in some jurisdictions lower courts are allowed and sometimes encouraged to raise preliminary questions to the Supreme Court. From the side of lower courts both channels of communication may be attractive simply because it can help them to prevent from 'getting it wrong'. For the highest courts, on the other hand, having some sort of open communication channel with lower courts may function as a thermometer that shows the practical consequences of previous decisions and helps to avoid unnecessary tensions and conflicts.

In semi-vertical relationships, such as the one between the ECtHR and CJEU, courts may be referring to each other's case law in order to protect their own jurisdictional territory and avoid legal uncertainty. For the CJEU it made sense to align with the case law of the ECtHR before the entering into force of the Charter of fundamental rights. Once the Charter was in place, though, the CJEU increasingly started to follow its own course, much to the disappointment of the ECtHR. It showed that the CJEU is no longer prepared to submit itself automatically to the interpretation of fundamental rights by the ECtHR. Meetings between judges from both courts will now probably be necessary to create an actual dialogue about how to avoid future competence conflicts.

Closely related are the conflicts between courts with competing jurisdictions in the Caribbean context we described. Here the CCJ seems to be competing with supreme courts in the region by providing private litigants direct access instead of requiring that domestic courts use the preliminary reference procedure that was borrowed from the EU to solve problems regarding the uniform interpretation of the treaties that established a single market between CARICOM countries. So far, domestic courts have not referred cases to the CCJ, which may perhaps be seen as a silent protest against the CCJ's case law that allows private parties to bypass the national judicial chain. The example shows what might happen if the preliminary reference procedure of article 267 TFEU changes colour and turns into an actual citizen's infringement procedure. It would probably change the nature of the dialogue between courts and may ruin the faith that supreme courts have in the preliminary ruling procedure. This shows how important it is for courts with competing competences to communicate with each other in order to avoid conflict by showing respect for the other court's constitutional role.

As far as mutual referencing to each other's case law by courts at the same level is concerned, there is again no real dialogue but rather a series of judicial monologues. The fact that a court is citing another foreign court may, however, reveal where the referring courts is deriving it arguments from, which can make its own decisions more transparent, persuasive and legitimate. It is hard to measure to what extent this is actually the case though. Moreover, there is a risk that the citations are cherry-picked and hence arbitrary simply due to familiarity with certain other jurisdictions. Perhaps even more important is that referring to the case law of foreign courts may create a transnational common judicial identity, which over time could drive national courts away from national democratic actors. In other words, the horizontal dialogue between courts in a transnational context might go to the detriment of the vertical dialogue between national courts and national democratic institutions.

Finally, we have studied the dialogues between constitutional courts and supranational courts. In particular in relation to the ECtHR, constitutional courts have often adopted a harmonious method of interpretation, even though the case law of the ECtHR has no erga omnes working. The other way around, the ECtHR has sometimes 'borrowed reasons' from national courts and looked for 'moral facts' in the case law of constitutional courts to strengthen its own decisions in hard cases. As far as the CJEU is concerned, constitutional courts have, for a long time, refused to refer questions, but this appears to have changed. Since the CJEU has entered the realm of fundamental right review, constitutional courts have become more aware of the risk of being displaced by the CJEU. The fact that the CJEU does not have similar mechanisms as the ECtHR, such as the margin of appreciation doctrine, may explain why constitutional courts have become more assertive towards the CJEU, developing their own competence review and using the identity clause of article 4(2) TEU as a shield.

In almost all the inter-judicial forms of communication that Rosas discerns, we cannot really detect a 'judicial dialogue' in the sense of an actual exchange of arguments to decide a specific case. What is interesting, though, is that one way or the other all these inter-judicial communications can be seen as a quest for legitimacy. This can be legitimacy in terms of strengthening one's own decision in a hard case for which there is no simple answer in legislation or precedent, legitimacy in the sense of defining and defending ones judicial territory towards other courts or legitimacy as in acceptance of one's decisions by other courts and/or litigating parties. In particular in a globalizing legal world where hierarchies between courts are fading and law-making increasingly takes place in transnational networks, which are not necessarily constitutionally embedded in a solid system of checks and balances, courts are looking for ways to strengthen the legitimacy of their decisions.

2.6 Where Does the Preliminary Reference Procedure Fit In?

Now that we have listed different types of judicial interchange that are sometimes presented as a judicial dialogue, we have to ask ourselves where the preliminary ruling procedure fits in.

One first has to realise that the preliminary ruling procedure has undergone dramatic changes in the past. Under the regime of article 41 of the Paris Treaty (ECSC), the Court of Justice only had the power to give preliminary rulings to determine the validity of Community acts. Accordingly, national courts were entitled to give their own authoritative interpretation of the Treaty in all other matters. Fear of conflicting national interpretations, however, made changes necessary. Since the Treaty givers did not want to turn the Court of Justice into a constitutional court with the exclusive power to interpret the Treaty,[72] a revised preliminary ruling procedure was introduced inspired by the preliminary references of the Italian and German constitutional courts and by the French system, where general courts could refer certain issues to specialized administrative courts, such as the Conseil d'État.

In this new procedure, national courts applied Community law and, when confronted with a question of interpretation, would refer to the European court of justice. The result was a unique system with the contours of a quasi-federal system of judicial review,[73] but one that would 'depend completely on the co-operation of national courts in order to function'.[74] In this procedure, domestic courts are exclusively responsible for fact-finding, deciding questions of national law, estimating whether it is appropriate to make a reference according to the CILFIT criteria, and applying the preliminary rulings of the CJEU, while the

[72] A. Boerger-De Smedt, 'Negotiating the Foundations of European Law, 1950–57: The Legal History of the Treaties of Paris and Rome' *Contemporary European History*, 21, 3, 339–356 (2012), at 352.

[73] A.M. Slaughter, 'A Typology of Transjudicial Communication' *University of Richmond Law Review*, 29, 99, 101 (1994).

[74] M. Rasmussen, 'Constructing and Deconstructing "Constitutional" European Law: Some Reflections on How to Study the History of European Law', in H. Koch, K. HagelSørensen, U. Haltern and J. Weiler, (eds.), *Europe: The New Legal Realism* (Århus: DJØF Publishing, 2010), 642–643.

CJEU is entitled to give an authoritative and final interpretation of the relevant EU provisions.

The fact that the reference is drawn up by national courts, which have the possibility to offer provisional answers according to the Court's rules of procedure,[75] whereas the CJEU may ask the national court for clarification after having heard the Advocate General, makes it possible to have an actual exchange of views on the interpretation of EU law.[76] Hence, from a procedural point of view, the preliminary rulings procedure has the potential to facilitate an actual dialogue between the referring national court and the CJEU about the interpretation of EU law in the case at hand. Discourse-wise, however, the communication between the CJEU and national courts is far from ideal. Although the design of the preliminary rulings procedure of article 267 TFEU does not necessarily imply a hierarchical relationship between the CJEU and national courts, the case law of the CJEU seem to leave little room to view the communication with the national courts as horizontal and reciprocal. The CJEU's communication is always bound by the triangle of supremacy,[77] direct effect,[78] and State liability.[79] Under the CILFIT doctrine, domestic courts are no longer free to raise preliminary questions in all situations. Moreover, the introduction of state liability for neglecting to refer certain questions to the CJEU (e.g. about the validity of EU law) has put a potentially very serious penalty on disregarding the rules of procedure.

Nonetheless, the shared jurisdiction between the national courts and the fact that the treaties still require that domestic courts raise questions in order for the CJEU to be able to provide binding interpretations, while the enforcement of these binding interpretations rests with the national courts, makes close cooperation inevitable.[80] As a consequence, the CJEU is put in a position where it must justify its decisions towards domestic courts because the latter are the 'foot soldiers' of the CJEU, who need to

[75] See article 107(2) of the CJEU's rules of procedure.

[76] See F.G. Jacobs, 'Judicial Dialogue and the Cross-Fertilization of Legal Systems: The European Court of Justice' *Texas International Law Journal*, 38, 3, 548–549 (2003).

[77] See CJEU 15 July 1964, C-6/64; ECLI:EU:C:1964:66 (Flaminio Costa v. E.N.E.L.).

[78] See CJEU 5 February 1963, C-26/62; ECLI:EU:C:1963:1 (NV Algemene Transport- en Expeditie Onderneming van Gend & Loos v. Netherlands Inland Revenue Administration).

[79] See CJEU 19 November 1991, joined cases C-6/90 and C-9/90; ECLI:EU:C:1991:428 (*Francovich* and *Daniela Bonifaci*); CJEU 5 March 1996, joined cases C-46/93 and C-48/93; ECLI:EU:C:1996:79 (Brasserie du Pêcheur and Factortame Ltd.) and CJEU 30 September 2003, C-224/01; ECLI:EU:C:2003:513 (Gerhard Köbler v. Republik Österreich).

[80] See J.H.H. Weiler, 'The Transformation of Europe' *Yale Law Journal*, 100, 2403 (1991).

be prepared to even go against executive and legislative resistance towards complying with EU law from their own government.[81] In other words, the effectiveness of the CJEU's rulings relies on active cooperation from the side of especially the highest national courts because these are the central supervisors in the different Member States. Without their help, the CJEU can never actually warrant compliance. It follows that in order for CJEU interpretations of EU law to gain acceptance, they should be based on a shared understanding of the underlying values of the legal order.[82] Therefore, it seems crucial that the CJEU shows itself receptive for the signals that are send by the referring courts about the consequences of its case law for the national legal orders. So far, however, as we have argued before, one may doubt whether the CJEU has used the full potential of the preliminary ruling procedure to set-up an actual dialogue with national courts and give them an actual voice in the procedure that goes beyond the role of a provider of questions and an enforcement agent.

2.7 Future Challenges: The CJEU's Caseload

One cannot ignore that the preliminary ruling procedure is very successful if one looks at the increasing number of references from different types of national courts (lower courts, supreme courts, constitutional courts) over the years. The procedure of article 267 TFEU is today, by far, the most popular route to the CJEU from the side of national courts, which is reflected in the Court's growing caseload. Not only is there a wider spread of preliminary references over the different Member States and have constitutional courts recently started to find their way to the CJEU, but we have also seen that a growing number of private parties started to use the preliminary reference procedure in article 267 TFEU to try to attain judicial coherence across courts in different jurisdictions.[83]

The increasing number of actors that have discovered the preliminary reference procedure has also brought some challenges. The most serious one is, undoubtedly, the growing caseload of the Court. Although the CJEU has managed to keep the length of the procedure under control by

[81] I. Maher, 'National Courts as European Community Courts' *Legal Studies*, 14, 226 (2000).

[82] E. Paunio, 'Conflict, power, and understanding – judicial dialogue between the ECJ and national courts' *NoFo* 7 (April 2010) 9, 14–15.

[83] M. Broberg, 'Judicial Coherence and the Preliminary Reference Procedure' *Review of European Administrative Law*, 8, 2, 9–37 (2015).

taking procedural measures, it has been predicted that eventually the Court will face another crisis due to its workload.[84] This is why a number of remedies have been presented in the literature, ranging from: the introduction of a green light procedure and a docket control system to limiting the right to refer preliminary questions to courts of last instance and setting up decentralized EU courts, for example, by appointing a number of national courts to become auxiliary branches of the CJEU.[85] What is interesting, though, is that none of these proposals received approval from the side of the CJEU. The question we will address later in this book is: what could be the reason for this?

The often mentioned 'green light' procedure, whereby national judges could include their proposed answers to the questions they refer to the Court of Justice, which could then decide within a given period whether to accept the proposed judgment and give it a green or red light, has been rejected. This, even though organisations, such as ACA-Europe, and Advocates General have openly shown to be in favour of such a procedure and there have been ample opportunities to experiment with it. In the Melloni case,[86] for instance, the Spanish Constitutional Court offered the CJEU different possible interpretations of the Framework Decision on the European Arrest Warrant. It even presented a preferred solution: the interpretation of the Framework decision in conformity with article 24 of the Spanish Constitution and the right to defence, which could prevail over the protection offered by Articles 47 and 48 of the EU Charter. The provisional answers were, however, all disregarded by the CJEU in the name of the primacy and unity of EU law, without really engaging with the arguments of the national court.[87] It is probably needless to say that this will not encourage national courts to try to dialogue with the CJEU by providing provisional answers or otherwise informing the Court. Cases like Melloni, but also the negative opinion of

[84] House of Lords, European Union Committee, 14th report of Session 2010–2011, The Workload of the Court of Justice of the European Union at p. 8 and 17–18. See: www.publications.parliament.uk/pa/ld201011/ldselect/ldeucom/128/128.pdf.

[85] See for an overview: M. Broberg and N. Fenger, *Preliminary References to the European Court of Justice* (Oxford: Oxford University Press 2014), pp. 23–33. See also: A. Arnull, 'Judicial Architecture or Judicial Folly? The Challenge Facing the European Union' *European Law Review*, 24, 5, 516–524 (1999).

[86] Case C-399/11 Melloni Judgment of 26 February 2013; Judgment of 26 February 2013 ECLI:EU:C:2013:107.

[87] M. Dicosola, C. Fasone and I. Spigno, 'Foreword: Constitutional Courts in the European Legal System After the Treaty of Lisbon and the Euro-Crisis' *German Law Journal*, 16, 6, 1327 (2015).

the CJEU on the accession to the ECHR might suggest that the Luxembourg court is not truly seeking a dialogue with other courts but wants to have the final word.[88]

A second way to reduce the CJEU's workload could be the introduction of a docket control system as is known by the certiorari decisions of the US Supreme Court. Such a system is supposed to filter out, already at a preliminary stage, cases of lesser importance for the uniformity and development of EU law. It has the advantage that it would prompt national courts and tribunals to exercise selectivity in choosing which questions to refer and would thus encourage them to exercise yet more fully their responsibility as EU courts. The CJEU could then focus on the most notable issues and thereby steering the development of EU law more effectively. In a discussion paper on the future of the judicial system of the European Union, the Court itself argued that such a system, in which it can decide which questions to answer, is unattractive. The reason is that where a question is relevant and the background to the case has been properly set out by the referring court, a refusal by the CJEU to answer would risk serious damage to the spirit of cooperation on which the procedure depends.[89] At first sight, this seems to be a sign that the Court attaches value to a dialogue with the national courts. The discussion paper presented to the Council of Ministers even refers to the Schwartze case in which the Court declared that the preliminary reference procedure: 'requires the national court and the Court of Justice, both keeping within their respective jurisdiction, and with the aim of ensuring that Community law is applied in a unified manner, to make direct and complementary contributions to the working out of a decision'.[90]

Although 'complementary contributions working out a decision' sounds like an open invitation to a dialogue with national courts, the CJEU appears to be most concerned about the inflow of preliminary questions. It does not explain at all, why a reduced caseload and a stricter selection of cases would necessarily have a negative effect on the willingness to cooperate from the side of referring courts. As long as

[88] M. Poli, 'The Judicial Dialogue in Europe' *ICL Journal*, 11, 3, 351–364 (2017).

[89] See Court of Justice and Court of First Instance, The Future of the Judicial System of the European Union: Proposals and Reflections, Luxembourg 1999, p. 24 See: www.alanuzelac.from.hr/Pdf/eu-postdip/Buducnost%20suda%20Europskih%20zajednica%20-%20ave.pdf.

[90] Case 16/65, Firma G. Schwarze v. Einfuhr- und Vorratsstelle für Getreide und Futtermittel [1965] ECR 877; ECLI:EU:C:1965:117.

it is clear for national courts how the filtering works and which cases will no longer be taken on board by the CJEU, we do not see a problem here, certainly if the Court would be more prepared to engage with the arguments of national courts in the remaining cases. Put slightly different, if the only thing that national courts are good for is bringing cases to Luxembourg; what does that tell us about the willingness to take the idea of a dialogue, cooperation or partnership seriously?

Similar objections have been raised against proposals to reduce the workload of the CJEU by limiting the right to raise preliminary questions to highest national courts and to introduce decentralized EU courts by setting up a decentralized system of regional courts, which could then deal with certain (simpler) preliminary questions. With regard to the first proposal, the Court has objected because of reasons of 'procedural economy'. It believes that it would result in proceedings being brought before supreme courts in the Member States solely in order to enable the parties to seek a referral to the Court of Justice. Rasmussen, however, has argued that this line of thought does not carry much weight.

First of all, he states correctly that it is certainly not uncommon to require from litigating parties to exhaust the national procedural remedies before turning to a supranational court (e.g. see the access to the ECtHR) and circumventing the national judicial hierarchy. Secondly, he believes that since references by lower courts concern a substantial part of the cases it would really be an efficient reduction of the workload. A lot of these references would in practice not be mature enough to be decided by the Court anyway. Instead, Rasmussen argues that the Court wants to keep the gateway to the lower domestic courts open because it enables the Court to follow its own political agenda and police the highest national courts.[91] The question we are going to address later in this book, though, is whether it is still necessary for the Court to control the lack of willingness of highest national courts to refer questions to the CJEU since the Köbler case law of the court which enables the Court to hold courts accountable for neglecting the CILFIT standards for referring cases.[92]

Similar objections from the side of the CJEU have been raised against the proposal to set up a system of specialized satellite courts in the

[91] H. Rasmussen, 'Remedying the Crumbling EC Judicial System' *Common Market Law Review* w 37, 1071–1112 (2000), at 1104–1106.

[92] See the opinion of the Advocate General in Case C-173/09, Georgi Ivanov Elchinov v. Natsionalna zdravnoosiguritelna kasa [2010] ECR I-08889; ECLI:EU:C:2010:581.

Member States to filter out preliminary questions that could be decided at a lower level by regional courts close to the litigants and in the language of the jurisdiction in which the question was brought up. Such a system could be completed with the right to appeal to the CJEU under certain conditions in order to guarantee uniformity. The Luxembourg court, however, saw noting in such a system because of the alleged risk of diverging decisions between the regional courts and the risk of delaying the procedure in case of appeals to the CJEU.[93]

Overall, the resistance from the side of the CJEU towards more fundamental reforms of the preliminary reference procedure questions the willingness to involve these courts more actively in the interpretation of EU law. While the Treaty givers have deliberately chosen not to design the preliminary reference procedure as an appeal system with a European constitutional court at the top of the hierarchy, the CJEU appears to see itself increasingly as such when looking at how the Court behaves both towards other supranational courts like the ECtHR and national supreme courts. Some have argued in favour of the withdrawal of power to decide conflicts of competences between the EU and Member States from the CJEU in order to transfer it to a specialized court. This court should then be composed of judges from the CJEU and national constitutional courts and sit ad hoc to decide competence conflicts and prevent the competence creep, which the CJEU has often been accused of.[94] Others have suggested some sort of override clause permitting, for example, the Council to override CJEU decisions under certain circumstances.[95] However, both options have not gained substantial political support so far.

2.8 Conclusion

In this chapter, we have given an overview of the debate on the idea of a judicial dialogue, in particular with regard to what this concept could mean for the preliminary reference procedure. We have discovered that 'dialogue' means different things in different contexts but almost never

[93] See the report, The Future of the Judicial System of the European Union, supra nt. 79, p. 26–27.

[94] D. Grimm, 'Europe's Legitimacy Problem and the Courts', in D. Chalmers, M. Jachtenfuchs and C. Joerges (eds.), *The End of the Eurocrats' Dream* (Cambridge: Cambridge University Press, 2016), p. 260.

[95] F. Scharf, 'Legitimacy in the Multi-Level European Polity' *European Political Science Review*, 1, 2, 173–204 at 199 (2009).

does there seem to be an actual exchange of ideas and opinions between courts about what is supposed to be a correct interpretation of the law. Sometimes courts are referring to each other's case law to borrow arguments or study the impact of a certain choice of law in another jurisdiction, but closer forms of cooperation are rare. What most inter-judicial communications have in common, though, is a quest for legitimacy and better quality of law-making by deriving information from other (foreign) courts. However, we have also mentioned that a judicial dialogue within the realm of the preliminary reference procedure may serve a legitimacy-seeking purpose: (1) by offering input from national courts to the CJEU in order to come up with the best-reasoned interpretation of EU law; (2) by providing a platform for participation in the process of judicial law-making by all the member of the interpretative community; and (3) thereby building a common identity between the EU and national legal orders which is necessary in a multilevel and pluralist legal order.

Furthermore, we have noticed that the preliminary ruling procedure has more potential for dialogue due to the fact that national courts in the procedure could be enabled to do more than 'just' refer questions to the CJEU and implement the rulings that come out of this procedure. The procedure offers possibilities, such as the instrument of provisional answers to involve national courts more. The other way around, the CJEU could also enhance dialogue by making more use of instruments like the request for clarification before reformulation preliminary questions and, more in general, by a more open and responsive style of argumentation and decision making.

Although the preliminary ruling procedure is often considered the jewel in the crown of the EU's judicial system,[96] we have sketched why this jewel might lose its shine in the future due to the steady growth in the number of references.[97] According to some, there is a serious risk

[96] P. Craig, 'The Jurisdiction of the Community Courts Reconsidered', in G. de Búrca and J. Weiler (eds.), *The European Court of Justice* (Oxford: Oxford University Press, 2001), p. 559.

[97] T. de la Mare and C. Donnelly, 'Preliminary Rulings and EU Legal Integration: Evolution and Stasis', in P. Craig and G. de Búrca (eds.), *The Evolution of EU Law* (Oxford: Oxford University Press, 2011), p. 363–407; G. Davies, 'Abstractness and Concreteness in the Preliminary Reference Procedure: Implications for the Division of Powers and Effective Market Regulation', in N.N. Shuibne (ed.), *Regulating the Internal Market* (Cheltenham: Edward Elgar, 2006), p. 210–244.

that the procedure will collapse if serious reforms stays out.[98] After all, the pressure on national courts to refer questions to Luxembourg seems mounting.[99]

Firstly, the CJEU itself keeps hanging on to the CILFIT criteria as can be witnessed in the Ferreira da Silva case,[100] in which the Court stated for the first time that a supreme court had breached its duty to make a preliminary reference under article 267(3) TFEU, finding that the acte clair doctrine could not be applied in this case even though there has been severe criticism against this doctrine. AG Colomer, for example,[101] has claimed that the 1982 CILFIT test, which requires among other things that national courts may not invoke the acte clair exception without first comparing all the (by now 24!) language versions of a disputed EU rule against the backdrop of all the different national legal systems, was already unviable at the time it was formulated but is today 'preposterous'.[102] Nevertheless, in Ferreira da Silva the CJEU in fact determined that the Portuguese Supreme Court could be held liable according to the Köbler case law for not referring a question in this case.

Secondly, the ECtHR has also contributed to the increasing pressure on national courts to refer questions to Luxembourg in case of uncertainty. In the cases of Dhahbi and Schipani, the Court found a violation of article 6 ECHR because the highest Italian court had not sufficiently motivated its decision that a preliminary reference would not be necessary in the case at hand. In the AFNE case, the CJEU seems to have aligned with the ECtHR by arguing that a national court against whose decisions there is no longer any judicial remedy under law is in principle required to make a reference to the Court for a preliminary ruling:

[98] M. Vink, M. Claes and C. Arnold, 'Explaining the Use of Preliminary References by Domestic Courts in EU Member States: A Mixed-Method Comparative Analysis' (Paper presented at the 11th Biennial Conference of the European Studies Association), 2009, p. 23 (see: http://aei.pitt.edu/33155/1/vink._maarten.pdf).

[99] See more in-depth J. Krommendijk, 'It Takes Two to Tango: De Prejudiciële Verwijzingsdans Tussen Het Europees Hof Van Justitie En Nationale Rechters' *Trema* 2017(1) : pp. 10–16.

[100] Case C-160/14, João Filipe Ferreira da Silva e Brito and Others. v. Estado português [2015]; ECLI:EU:C:2015:565.

[101] Opinion of AG Colomer in case C-461/03, Gaston Schul Douane-expediteur BV v. Minister van Landbouw, Natuur en Voedselkwaliteit [2005] ECR I-10513; ECLI:EU:C:2005:415 (par. 52).

[102] See also AG Wahl in case C-72/14 and C-197/14 of September 9th 2015, ECLI:EU:C:2015:564 (*X* en *Van Dijk*), paragraphs 53, 62 and 67, who argues that if the CJEU would apply the CILFIT criteria strictly the chances that an actual acte clair would occur are about as realistic as encountering a unicorn!

In particular, given that the exercise of that exceptional power could adversely affect observance of the principle of the primacy of EU law, that national court could be relieved of the obligation to make a reference to the Court for a preliminary ruling only if it is convinced that the exercise of that exceptional power does not give rise to any reasonable doubt. In addition, it must be established in detail that there is no such doubt.[103]

Thirdly, this line of reasoning by both the CJEU and ECtHR is likely to encourage private parties whose request to refer of questions to the CJEU by the national courts is denied to take appeal against such as decision. They may, for example, file a complaint by the Commission against the national court for misinterpreting the CILFIT criteria on the basis of article 258 TFEU.[104] Another possibility could be to turn to the ECtHR and ask this court whether the refusal to refer results in an infringement of article 6 ECHR.[105]

Taken together, it is not unlikely that the CJEU will eventually suffer the consequences of this in terms of an unmanageable increase in its workload. In case the CJEU does not want to delegate a significant portion of the less important and pressing cases to the General Court or to satellite courts in the Member States, there may not be too many other possibilities than to share more responsibility with national supreme courts. After all, there are limits to the current route to make the preliminary ruling procedure less time-consuming and more efficient by invoking the urgent preliminary ruling procedure or dismiss more cases by reasoned order under article 181 under the Court's Rules of Procedure and by shifting the burden of processing these cases more to the Advocates General.[106]

Looking for possibilities to involve national supreme courts more actively as co-interpreters of EU law would, however, imply that these courts are: (1) willing and able to engage in a more meaningful dialogue with the CJEU and that the possibilities the preliminary reference procedure offers them to become more active are investigated more

[103] Case C-379/15, Association France Nature Environnement v. Premier ministre and Ministre de l'Écologie, du Développement durable et de l'Énergie [2016]; ECLI:EU:C:2016:603, par. 52.

[104] See for a Dutch example: www.jahae.nl/wp-content/uploads/2015/08/150730-Brief-EC-EAB-vragen-HvJ-EU-ex.-bijlagen.pdf.

[105] See for an example: ECHR Baydar v. The Netherlands, Application No 55385/14, 24 April 2018.

[106] E. Sharpston, 'Making the Court of Justice of the European Union More Productive', *Maastricht Journal of European and Comparative Law*, 763–770 (2014).

thoroughly; (2) that the CJEU is ready to entrust national courts with a greater responsibility to interpret EU law on their own without referring; (3) also reduce the burden of evidence and motivation that currently rests on the shoulders of the CJEU by, for example, relying more on the provisional answers and other types of information that domestic courts can provide in order to determine what should be the interpretation of EU law.

In the coming chapters, we are going to study these kind of options for a more intensive dialogue by looking at the different ways in which national highest administrative courts refer cases, by exploring the results from the interviews we held with members of the national supreme administrative courts and the CJEU in which we asked both parties how they envisage the dialogue, and by looking into the literature in order to look for explanations why certain possibilities to enrich the communication, coordination and cooperation between courts on both sides have been neglected so far.

3 Case Law Analysis

3.1 Purpose of the Case Law Analysis

Since the 1978 Simmenthal case, the reference for a preliminary ruling is repeatedly seen as a dialogue,[1] which has been of vital importance in the development of some of the most important principles of the EU's constitutional legal order, such as the principles of direct effect (Van Gend en Loos) and supremacy of community law (*Costa* v. *Enel*).[2] Little is known, however, about the sort of interactions and the style of communication that is actually taking place between the referring courts and the CJEU.

Here we can roughly discern between three different stages in the communication, namely: (1) the preparatory phase in which the reference is drawn up lasting until the submission of a preliminary question to the CJEU. During this phase, national courts can inform each other and the CJEU about whether similar legal problems with the explanation of EU law exist in other Member States and about what sort of consequences alternative preliminary rulings could have for the national legal orders. This information can be used, not only for the formulation of the questions for the CJEU, but also for the offering of provisional answers to those questions; (2) during the preliminary reference procedure there is little room for the referring courts to bring in new information, unless the CJEU files a request for clarification from the referring court about

[1] D. Galetta, 'European Court of Justice and Preliminary Reference Procedure Today: National Judges, Please Behave!', in U. Becker, A. Hatje, M. Potacs, N. Wunderlich (Eds.), *Verfassung und Verwaltung in Europa* (Festschrift für Jürgen Schwarze zum 70. Geburtstag, Nomos Verlag, Baden-Baden, 2014), pp. 674–691.

[2] F. Jacobs, 'Judicial Dialogue and the Cross-Fertilization of Legal Systems, The European Court of Justice' *Texas International Law Journal*, 38, 548 (2003).

the nature of the questions that have been brought to its attention by the referring court, according to article 101 of its rules of procedure; (3) after a decision is taken by the CJEU, the referring court gets a chance to translate the preliminary ruling into its own decision of the case that led to a reference and inform the CJEU about the outcome. Moreover, it may happen that the referring court raises new questions in case it feels its original questions have not actually been answered properly. In case the referring court does not inform the CJEU about the final decision by itself, the CJEU could take the initiative to inform whether and how its preliminary ruling has been applied in the national procedure.

The case law analysis presented hereafter is meant to find out to what extent the literature about the preliminary reference procedure reflects the sort of communication that takes place between supreme administrative courts and the CJEU. The analysis is mainly focused on the second stage of the communication as described above: the actual process of submitting and answering questions in the preliminary reference procedure. The outcome of the case law review is meant to support our literature review about judicial dialogues and, more importantly, to fuel the questions for the interviews with judges from both the national courts and the CJEU. Is there, for example, any light between how the communication on paper and in practice is perceived on both sides of the spectrum?

3.2 Research Design

3.2.1 The Sample

In our case law analysis, we studied the references of ten supreme administrative courts (Germany, France, the UK, Spain, Austria, Czech Republic, Poland, Denmark, the Netherlands and Belgium) over the years 2013, 2014 and 2015. We have chosen for this period because it not only provides us with a recent picture of the state-of-the-art, while at the same time it may be assumed that the CJEU has already decided on the references during this period. Moreover, the database of the Dutch Ministry of Foreign Affairs offers full translated versions of all preliminary references from highest administrative courts from 2013 onwards,[3] which enabled us to study the references in-depth which is a huge practical advantage.

[3] See: www.minbuza.nl/ecer/hof-van-justitie/nieuwe-hofzaken-inclusief-verwijzing suitspraak, accessed on 19 January 2019.

The primary reason for choosing a sample of the above-mentioned ten courts is to offer a broader picture of the practice of preliminary questions and provisional answers. Because studying the references of all the supreme administrative courts would be too time consuming, we selected a sample of courts. This sample is not intended to offer a representative picture of the dialogue between the CJEU and all the national supreme administrative courts but to show the diversity in the style of preliminary references and reveal possible differences between courts in the use of provisional answers. Therefore, we first selected the 'big three': France, Germany and the UK, because these courts have been very influential for the case law of the CJEU and they represent the most important legal traditions. Secondly, we have chosen a Scandinavian court (Denmark) because the Nordic courts have a strong tradition of respecting the primacy of the legislature and were reluctant in the past to raise preliminary references.[4] Thirdly, we wanted to include two supreme administrative courts from founding Member States with a longstanding EU tradition (Belgium and the Netherlands), which are known to be supportive toward the CJEU and two courts from relatively new Member States with a completely different legal and political background (Poland and the Czech Republic), which have had more difficulties to adjust to EU law in general (e.g. think about the controversy with the EU over the recent court reforms in Poland) and the case law of the CJEU more in particular (think about the dispute between the Czech supreme administrative court and constitutional court vs the CJEU over the Czech pension system resulting in the Landtova case law). Fourth and finally, we have chosen two courts with about a similar amount of references and known tensions between the supreme administrative court and lower administrative courts: the Austrian Verwaltungsgerichtshof (e.g. the court reform act of 2012, eliminates a system of more than one hundred independent quasi-judicial bodies within administrative agencies) and the Spanish Tribunal Supremo (where as a result of the Aziz case law a discussion is started about 'leap frogging' the Supreme Court by lower courts).

Despite the modest total number of references (98) and the limited period, the case law analysis helped us getting an idea of what is going on in the communication between the supreme administrative courts

[4] See, for instance, the research by Marlene Wind, 'The Nordics, the EU and the Reluctance Towards Supranational Judicial Review' *JCMS*, 48, 1039–1063 (2010).

and the CJEU. This helped us to raise relevant questions for the interviews we conducted with two judges of each of the ten supreme administrative courts covered by the case law analysis and afterwards with five judges and two Advocates General of the CJEU (see Chapter 4). In order to get an idea about what is going on in the communication between the CJEU and the supreme administrative courts of the ten aforementioned Member States, we have built an analytical framework in order to see whether the communication between these courts goes beyond a simple sender-receiver model in which national courts and the CJEU might still be 'living apart together.' Therefore, we have developed a number of indicators to detect possible signs of dialogue, which we will explain first before moving to the outcomes of the analysis.

3.2.2 Does the Preliminary Question Invite a Response?

In order for a true dialogue to take place in ordinary life, but probably also in the communication between courts, requires that the initial question raised in the conversation needs a certain openness for response. If someone is asked, 'Would you like to be shot to death?', the one raising the question is probably not interested in the answer, because such a rhetorical question should probably be seen more as a warning sign than as an inquiry. There are, of course, also less drastic questions that limit the variety of answers. If we, for instance, ask for someone's age, there is usually only one correct answer possible and that is, 'I am X years old'. This may of course lead to follow-up questions, such as 'Are you not too old/young to. . .?', but there is little to debate about the initial question. On the other end of the spectrum, one may raise a question that is an open invitation to share one's broadest thoughts, such as, 'How are you feeling today?' or 'What do you think about this weather?'

Something similar applies to preliminary questions by national courts to the CJEU. In extreme situations, referring courts sometimes also raise questions that are clearly intended to be answered in a certain way. The questions may even be rhetorical as we have, for example, seen in the notorious Gauweiler case, where the German constitutional court tried its best to persuade the CJEU to put a stop to the European Central Bank's 'Outright Monetary Transactions' (OMT) programme, a new scheme conferring power to purchase government bonds in secondary markets in order to protect the value of the Euro.

3.2.3 *Gauweiler: Example of an Attempt to Dictate the Outcome of a Preliminary Ruling*

In Gauweiler, the Bundesverfassungsgericht for the first time raised a preliminary question about the legality of the ECB's OMT programme. The announcement of this programme by the ECB was supposed to protect the single currency and thereby rendering its actual application unnecessary, but the decision triggered a clear warning sign from the side of the German constitutional court that took the view that, unless interpreted in a certain way, the OMT decision was an obvious and structurally significant ultra vires act which had adverse consequences for core provisions of the Basic Law and would hence be considered unconstitutional. In those circumstances, the Bundesverfassungsgericht made a preliminary reference to the CJEU, but as Tridimas and Xanthoulis have argued,[5] the way the question was formulated suggests that it was, 'less an invitation to provide a binding ruling and more an opportunity to repent'. In other words, this preliminary question was more of an attempt to dictate a certain outcome than an open invitation to the CJEU to interpret the basic EU treaties as to whether the OMT programme was in accordance with primary EU law. This is why some Member States argued the CJEU should have declared the preliminary questions inadmissible. Raising questions, while at the same time threatening not to follow the answers in case of disagreement, would run against the very nature of the preliminary reference procedure and turn it into an advisory opinion. Advocate General Cruz Villalón also hinted in this direction by bringing the functionality of the preliminary reference procedure to the fore.[6]

> This 'cooperative relationship' is far from being precisely defined but it is clear that it purports to be something more than the imprecise 'dialogue' between courts. It is said to derive ultimately from the notion that the obligation of the BVerfG to safeguard the basic order under the national constitution must always be guided by an open and receptive attitude to EU law ('europarechtsfreundlich'), a notion which it might also have been possible to derive from the principle of sincere cooperation (Article 4(3) TEU). Therein lies all the ambiguity with which the Court of Justice is faced in this reference for a preliminary ruling: there is a

[5] T. Tridimas and N. Xanthoulis, 'A Legal Analysis of the Gauweiler Case: Between Monetary Policy and Constitutional Conflict' *Maastricht journal of European and Comparative Law*, 23, 1, 17–39 (2015), at 17–18.

[6] Opinion AG Cruz Villalón 14 January 2015, Case C-62/14, Peter Gauweiler e.a. v. Deutscher Bundestag ECLI:EU:C:2015:7, consideration 46

national constitutional court which, on the one hand, ultimately accepts its position as a court of last instance for the purposes of Article 267 TFEU, and does so as the expression of a special 'cooperative relationship' and a general principle of openness to the so-called 'integration programme' but which, on the other hand, wishes, as it makes clear, to bring a matter before the Court of Justice without relinquishing its own ultimate responsibility to state what the law is with regard to the constitutional conditions and limits of European integration so far as its own State is concerned. That ambivalence runs all through the request for a preliminary ruling, so that it is extremely difficult to disregard it entirely when analysing the case.[7]

The CJEU, however, does not bend for the ultra vires threat from the Bundesverfassungsgericht and decides that the ECB's OMT programme is in accordance with the Treaties, as long as it implemented in the way that the ECB assured the Court it would be. Hence, certain safeguards have to be built into the system, but these safeguards are not new or especially onerous, and they do not go as far as the ones put forward by the German Federal Constitutional Court as conditions of legality. Ultimately, the Bundesverfassungsgericht goes along with this line of reasoning by the Court. If the conditions formulated by the Court of Justice of the European Union in its judgment, intended to limit the scope of the OMT programme are met, the complainants' rights under article 38 in conjunction with article 79 of the Basic Law are not violated by the fact that the federal government and the Bundestag have not taken suitable steps to revoke or limit the effect of the policy decision of the European Central Bank of 6 September 2012 concerning the OMT programme. Furthermore, if these conditions are met, the OMT programme does not currently impair the Bundestag's overall budgetary responsibility. Such was the final decision of the Second Senate of the Federal Constitutional Court. In other words, as long as the OMT programme is carried out in the restrictive way as formulated by the CJEU after the preliminary reference by the German constitutional court, the Bundesverfassungsgericht is prepared to go along with it. Should we see this as giving in to the CJEU, as a successful negotiation to restrict the conditions under which the OMT programme may be carried out or as only a conditional yes that could in the future turn into a no, in case the ECB does not respect the conditions put forward by the CJEU?

Admittedly, the Gauweiler case is exceptional, but what is learns is that courts that refer questions to the CJEU can give the Luxembourg

[7] Ibid., consideration 48–49.

court more or less leeway to decide in a certain direction and add signals about what it expects from the latter court in terms of the outcome of a preliminary reference.

3.2.4 *Open or Closed Questions: A Matter of Trust?*

On the one hand, preliminary questions can be formulated in a binary way, which means that only two answers are possible: yes or no (e.g. yes, something falls within the scope of a directive or regulation, or no, it does not). Open formulated questions, on the other hand, give the CJEU the opportunity to come up with a much broader range of answers. In terms of potential for law making it gives the CJEU more leeway to give its own interpretation of what is needed in response to the preliminary reference. At the same time, it may have the disadvantage that the CJEU reads more and other things into a preliminary question than was intended by the referring court, although the rules of procedure offer the CJEU a possible way out of this dilemma by formulating a request for clarification by the Court (see hereafter), which might intensify the dialogue between both courts.

We expect national courts that anticipate on a preferred outcome of the preliminary rulings procedure to sooner submit closed (binary) questions instead of open ones in order to leave the Court less leeway to give its own interpretation to the question of the referring court, although there is of course also the possibility for the CJEU to reformulate the question that was referred one-sidedly, but this is a more blunt tool that is unlikely to improve the dialogue with the national highest administrative courts. The type of questions being raised may also have an influence on the sort of outcome one expects from the CJEU as we have already witnessed in the Gauweiler case. We distinguish between: (1) ready-made answers, (2) guideline decisions and (3) (quasi) compliance judgments.[8] Open questions will probably invite the Court more often to provide guidance or show deference towards national courts. Apart from requests for clarification, open questions provide the CJEU with more opportunity for judicial law-making and will probably lead more often to follow-up questions because the CJEU interprets the questions in a different way than expected by the referring court. Moreover, formulating open questions can also be seen as a sign of trust in the CJEU from the

[8] These categories are based on T. Tridimas, 'Constitutional Review of Member State Action: The Virtues and Vices of an Incomplete Jurisdiction', *I-CON*, 9, 3–4, 737–756 (2011).

side of national courts because this type of question makes it by definition more complicated to steer the answers or at least prevent certain types of answers.

Closed questions, on their turn, do not necessarily have to be seen as a sign of distrust. In the most innocent form, closed questions may be an attempt to pinpoint the CJEU to shed light on a matter that could genuinely have two different outcomes while the referring court simply does not know the answer to the question it has raised. Whether a certain (provision of a) European act is valid or invalid could be such a binary question.

3.2.5 *Compatibility Questions*

Sometimes, however, referring courts simply want the CJEU to say whether, for example, a national legal provision is compatible with EU law. Although, the answer to such a question belongs to the prerogative of the national courts, while the CJEU is responsible for a uniform interpretation of EU law, we will see hereafter that the CJEU is quite regularly prepared to step in and answer such a question. Sometimes both the preliminary question and the ruling by the CJEU are formulated in a rather subtle way. An interesting case in point is the Petersen case. Here the German Finanzgericht asked:

> Is a legal provision compatible with Article 49 of the Treaty establishing the European Community (in the version of the Nice Treaty signed on 26 February 2001; now Article 56 of the Treaty on the Functioning of the European Union) if it makes a tax exemption for income of an employee who is taxable in Germany dependent on the employer being established in Germany, but does not provide for such exemption if the employer is established in another EU Member State?

Instead of saying that the CJEU does not rule on hypothetical questions and declaring the request for a preliminary ruling inadmissible, as the Court regularly does,[9] it first reformulates the question as a matter of free movement of workers (article 45 TFEU) and then answers the question by arguing that:

[9] See for instance: Case C-83/91 Wienand Meilicke v. ADV/ORGA F. A. Meyer AG [1992] ECR I-4871, ECLI:EU:C:1992:332; Case C-197/10, Unió de Pagesos de Catalunya v. Administración del Estado [2011] ECR I-08495, ECLI:EU:C:2011:590; Case C-101/08 Audiolux SA and Others v. Groupe Bruxelles Lambert SA (GBL) and Other and Bertelsmann AG and Others [2009] ECR I-9823, ECLI:EU:C:2009:626, paragraph 31 and the case-law cited there and Case C-392/16, Marcu Dumitru v. Agenția Națională de Administrare Fiscală (ANAF) and Direcția Generală Regională a Finanțelor Publice București [2017], ECLI:EU:C:2017:519.

Article 45 TFEU must be interpreted as precluding national legislation of a Member State pursuant to which income received for employment activities by a taxpayer who is resident in that Member State and has unlimited tax liability is exempt from income tax if the employer is established in that Member State, but is not so exempt if that employer is established in another Member State.[10]

Although presented as a matter of interpretation of article 45 TFEU, the CJEU is in fact answering the referring court whether the provision of national law is compatible with EU law. De Witte has shown that this happens more often. He also refers to the Van Doorne case,[11] where a Belgian court had asked the CJEU whether a certain Belgian law was compatible with an EU directive. Even though the CJEU started out by declaring that the preliminary reference procedure is not meant to answer questions regarding the compatibility of national law with EU law but can only provide the national court with the criteria for the interpretation of the necessary provision of EU law, in the operational part of the judgment the CJEU went beyond that. It argued literally that the relevant EU directive 'must be interpreted as not precluding national legislation, such as that at issue in the main proceedings.' Here De Witte rightfully argues, '[I]s this not simply another way of doing precisely what the Court declared that it could not do at the start of the judgment?'[12] The CJEU is sometimes prepared to declare that certain norms of EU law must be interpreted as (not) precluding national rules of the sort applicable in the case at hand, although this is in fact for national courts to decide. This begs the question: why do national courts accept this and sometimes even ask for it?

3.2.6 Linking Preliminary Questions to Provisional Answers from the Referring Court

Did we notice above that courts referring questions to the CJEU sometimes simultaneously try to dictate the answer; there is also another less threatening possibility for national courts to start a dialogue with the Luxembourg court.

Article 107(2) of the Rules of Procedure of the Court states that: 'The referring court or tribunal shall set out the matters of fact and law which

[10] Case C-544/11, Helga Petersen and Peter Petersen v. Finanzamt Ludwigshafen [2013], ECLI:EU:C:2013:124, consideration 62.

[11] Case C 489/09 Vandoorne NV v. Belgische Staat [2011] ECR I-00225, ECLI:EU:C:2011:33.

[12] B. De Witte, 'The Preliminary Ruling Dialogue: Three Types of Questions Posed by National Courts', in B. De Witte et al. (ed.), *National Courts And EU Law: New Issues, Theories and Methods* (Cheltenham: Edward Elgar, 2016), p. 19.

establish the urgency and justify the application of that exceptional procedure and shall, *in so far as possible, indicate the answer that it proposes* to the questions referred' [italics RvG/JdP]. In other words, the CJEU invites referring courts to think with the Court about what the best answer to the referred question might be in light of a uniform interpretation of EU law.

One of the first authoritative sources we found about the use of provisional answers is the 'Report on the Future of the European Communities Courts System' form a working group led by former president of the CJEU, Ole Due. This group proposed to the European Commission to change the Court's rules of procedure in order to: 'include in the preliminary questions reasoned grounds for the answers that the national court considers most appropriate.'[13] In a 2008 resolution of the European Parliament, this idea was picked-up. The European Parliament urges consideration of a 'green light' system whereby national judges could include their proposed answers to the questions they refer to the Court of Justice, which could then decide within a given period whether to accept the proposed judgment or whether to rule itself in the manner of an appellate court.[14]

This idea not only gained some support in the literature.[15] It was also embraced by a working group of ACA-Europe in collaboration with the Network of Supreme Courts of the European Union, which was established in 2007 to formulate practical suggestions on ways of reducing the delays involved in the preliminary rulings procedure.[16] According to this

[13] Report by the Working party on the future of the European Communities Court system, January 2008, p. 18. See: http://ec.europa.eu/dgs/legal_service/pdf/due_en.pdf, accessed on 19 January 2019.

[14] European Parliament Resolution of 9 July 2008 on the role of the national judge in the European judicial system (2007/2027(INI)), sec. 31

[15] Francis Jacobs, 'Possibilities for further reforming the preliminary reference procedure. Papers for the Colloquium on the Judicial Architecture of the European Union' (Papers from the Colloquium on the Judicial Architecture of the European Union, May 2004) 62. See: www.ccbe.eu/document/events/colloquium.pdf, accessed on 19 January 2019; Alan Dashwood and Angus Johnston, 'Synthesis of the Debate', in Alan Dashwood and Angus Johnston (eds), *The Future of the Judicial System of the European Union* (Hart publishing 2001) 68–69; Arjen Meij, 'Effective preliminary cooperation: some eclectic notes', in *The Uncertain Future of the Preliminary Rulings Procedure*, Symposium Council of State, the Netherlands (30 January 2004), pp. 11–17 (available at: www.raadvanstate.nl/publicaties/publicaties.html, accessed on 19 January 2019).

[16] Association of the Councils of State and Supreme Administrative Jurisdictions of the European union and Network of the Presidents of the Supreme Judicial Courts of the European Union, 'Report of the working group on the preliminary rulings procedure', The Hague (2007). See: www.aca-europe.eu/seminars/2007_DenHaag/Final_report.pdf, accessed on 19 January 2019.

group, the Court of Justice could easily dispose of a considerable number of preliminary questions by introducing such a green light procedure. This would also fit well with the design of the preliminary rulings procedure as a dialogue between courts.[17] It was seen as an additional advantage that the national courts 'would be inspired to play a greater role' in the procedure.[18] Exactly the same argument was given by former Advocate General Jacobs, who believed that working with provisional answers would enable national courts to contribute more directly and substantially to the development of European law. According to Jacobs, this would be a particular advantage in the case of the highest national courts, which might be able to contribute substantially to the development of Community law but would currently see themselves as little more than a 'judicial post-box' for the CJEU.[19]

Making use of the possibility to provide provisional answers undoubtedly offers opportunities for dialogue with the CJEU. When national courts simply hand over questions to the CJEU raised by the litigating parties without taking position, it is clear that the referring court probably sees itself more as an intermediary than as a partner of the CJEU in the preliminary reference procedure. However, even if provisional answers can still take different shapes. Referring courts might provide: (1) one 'right' answer, (2) different possible answers from which the CJEU can choose and (3) several potential answers alongside with an assessment of their likely impact on the national legal order(s).

Providing one 'right' answer may be seen primarily as a communication style that is aiming for persuasion (e.g. we really want the CJEU to follow us on this). In a way this is also a dangerous communication strategy because if the CJEU does not follow the answer, the outside world will see that the CJEU ignored the referring court, which will give the impression that the latter 'got it wrong'. The other two options will probably be perceived more as an invitation to communicate with the CJEU. Especially when national courts express the legal and practical (socioeconomic, cultural, political, ethical, etc.) consequences of different possible answers to a preliminary question in their communication with the CJEU, however, this could be seen as a more subtle way to steer

[17] Here the working group also pointed to Article 104b, para.1, of the Rules of Procedure of the Court of Justice, which prescribed in this respect that: 'the national court or tribunal indicates in so far as possible the answer it proposes to the questions referred.' This rule can now be found in Article 107(2) under the heading of the urgent preliminary ruling procedure.

[18] Jacobs, supra nt. 15, p. 8. [19] Jacobs ibid., p. 68.

the Court's decision in a certain direction and invite it to take certain sensitive national interests into account.

Interesting is to what extent the CJEU shows responsiveness to the argumentation of referring courts. We realize that great caution is in order here because of the danger of reading things into the case law, which only exist in our own minds (Hineininterpretieren). After all, one can never establish with absolute certainty what the intentions of the judges of the CJEU have been while they answer the question that was raised. What can be observed with a certain amount of objectivity is to what extent the CJEU actually responds to the questions and to the concerns that were raised by the referring court. How discursive is the reasoning of the CJEU? Does it make any difference whether the referring court has (not) provided a provisional answer? Does the CJEU somehow take position towards the referring national courts' signals concerning the preferred outcome of the preliminary ruling? Of course, there may be different reasons why the CJEU does not explicitly respond to provisional answers provided by the referring court. Perhaps the answer was found not convincing, perhaps the CJEU was internally divided about whether to respond or it did not want to go against the referring court too openly in case it felt the answer was wrong.

One cannot conclude from the case law analysis why the CJEU shows (a lack of) responsiveness towards the argumentation by the referring court. Nevertheless, what can be derived from it is whether the arguments that the referring court has provided in its provisional answer were picked up, either by the advocate-general or by the parties to the proceedings before the CJEU. Moreover, what can be observed is whether the CJEU has explicitly taken the arguments into consideration in its ruling. If this is not visible in the judgment, it does not necessarily mean that the CJEU has ignored the provisional answers during the (secret) decision-making process, but one may also safely conclude that provisional answers have not led to a dialogue between courts.

3.3 What Does the Case Law Show Regarding Open, Binary and Compatibility Questions?

3.3.1 Binary or Open Questions?

Taking a closer look at the way in which preliminary questions are formulated by the domestic courts, we indeed find a distinction between at least two types of questions. On the one hand, we see many questions that have been formulated in a binary way, which means that only two answers are possible: yes or no (e.g. yes something falls within the scope of a directive or regulation or no it does not). Binary questions provide no leeway for the CJEU to engage in any dialogue, whereas this is different for more open formulated questions.

The case law analysis shows that the supreme administrative jurisdictions in the majority of the cases (in 89 per cent of the cases that have been subject of our case law analysis) formulate the preliminary questions in a binary way. Only in a few cases have we seen a preliminary question formulated in a very open way. Good examples are the Client Earth case of the Supreme Court of the United Kingdom ('to what extent . . . and under which conditions . . .'),[20] the third sub question in the Bund Naturschutz case of the German Federal Administrative Court ('under what circumstances . . .'),[21] and the cases on the assessment of the homosexual orientation of the Dutch Council of State ('what limits do (. . .) impose on the methods of assessing the credibility of a declared sexual orientation . . .').[22] An interesting variant can be found in the Ajos-case of the Danish cases where the Højesteret statet: 'Guidance is also sought as to whether the fact that the employee, depending on the circumstances, may claim compensation from the State as a result of the Danish legislation's incompatibility with EU law [. . .]'.[23] This also seems to leave the CJEU more answers than a simple yes or no. We have also found an interesting combination of asking for guidance on the one hand while framing the question in a binary way on the other hand: the UK Supreme Court asked the CJEU what the circumstances are an affirmative answer to the first question depends on, while at the same time asking the CJEU in a binary way if these circumstances could possibly be A, B and C.[24] Here we see that although the question is in

[20] Case C-404/13, ClientEarth v. The Secretary of State for the Environment, Food and Rural Affairs [2014], ECLI:EU:C:2014:2382.

[21] Case C-461/13, Bund für Umwelt und Naturschutz Deutschland e.V. v. Bundesrepublik Deutschland [2015], ECLI:EU:C:2015:433.

[22] Joint Cases C-148/13, C-149/13 and C-150/13 A and Others v. Staatssecretaris van Veiligheid en Justitie [2014], ECLI:EU:C:2014:2406.

[23] Case C-441/14, Dansk Industri (DI), acting on behalf of Ajos A/S v. Estate of Karsten Eigil Rasmussen [2016], ECLI:EU:C:2016:278.

[24] Case C-316/15, Timothy Martin Hemming and Others v. Westminster City Council [2016], ECLI:EU:C:2016:879.

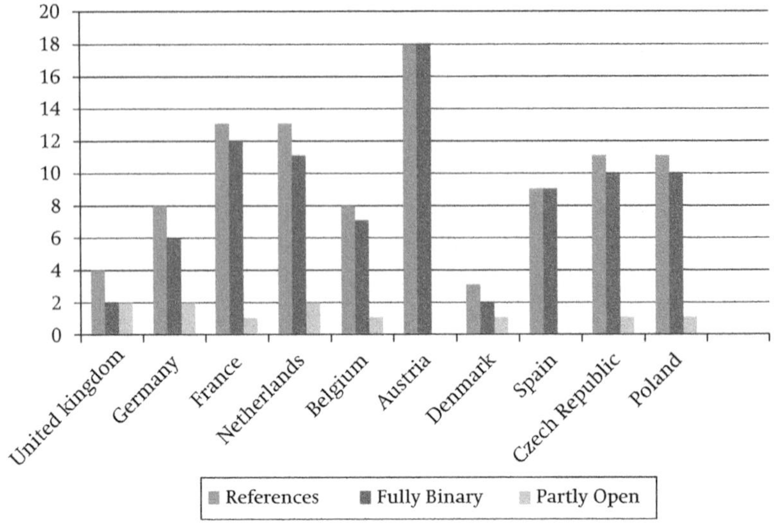

Figure 3.1 Fully binary and partly open questions.

nature framed as an open question, it leaves the CJEU little leeway but to say yes or no (see Figure 3.1).

Although the case law analysis shows a preference for binary questions, it does not provide an answer to the question as to what the explanation is for this preference. However, our hypothesis that this preference for binary questions may have to do with the fact that it prevents the CJEU from avoiding the question or coming up with unexpected or unuseful answers. For the phase of the interviews, it is interesting, not only to find out what exactly is behind this preference, but also to find out to what extent the CJEU would perhaps prefer more room to manoeuvre in certain cases. In this respect, it is conceivable that differences exist in the perception between the referring courts and the CJEU regarding the purpose of the preliminary reference procedure. This will probably have an effect on how they envisage the advantages and disadvantages of binary versus open questions. For the referring courts it seems primarily of interest to make sure that the question is framed in such a way that the answer from the CJEU is sufficiently tailored to the decision the referring court has to take in the case at hand. The perspective of the CJEU, though, might be different as it has not only a role to play in providing the referring court with a useful answer, but also in developing EU-law by constituting a precedent that affects 27 other Member States as well. A question for the interviews is therefore whether the CJEU perhaps needs more leeway in certain cases in order to fuel a dialogue or perhaps needs to take more freedom to deviate from the exact formulation of preliminary question if it feels that is necessary.

3.3.2 *Questions that Should Not Be Asked: Compatibility of National Law with EU Law*

A special category of binary questions that we have found in the case law of the supreme administrative courts are those references in which the referring court basically asks the CJEU if a provision of national law is in accordance with EU-law. In terms of dialogue this appears to be a strange practice, because the CJEU has stressed time and again that the preliminary reference procedure is not meant for answering questions regarding the compatibility of national provisions with EU law, because that is the duty of the national courts. That is also why the CJEU normally provides a general ruling concerning an issue of uniform interpretation of validity of EU law and does not decide the dispute in the case from which the referral comes itself but leaves that to the national judge.

One straightforward example of this kind of preliminary question is the reference of the Austrian Supreme Administrative Court in the Stadt Wiener Neustadt case in which it submits a question that reads as follows[25]:

> Does EU law, in particular Directive 2011/92 and in particular Article 1(4) thereof, or Directive 85/337 and in particular Article 1(5) thereof, preclude a provision of national law whereby projects subject to an obligation to carry out an environmental impact assessment, which have not been granted a consent under the UVP-G 2000 but only consents under various sectoral laws (such as the Abfallwirtschaftsgesetz (Law on Waste Management)) which, since 9 August 2009 . . ., can no longer be annulled as a result of the expiry of the three-year time limit laid down in national law (Paragraph 3(6) of the UVP-G 2000), are regarded as approved under the UVP-G 2000, or is such a provision consistent with the principles of legal certainty and the protection of legitimate expectations established in EU law?

In the case law study we have found no less than 36 cases in which the reference for a preliminary ruling has been framed like: 'Is EU-law

[25] Case C-348/15, Stadt Wiener Neustadt v. Niederösterreichische Landesregierung, ECLI: EU:C:2016:882.

to be interpreted as precluding a provision of national law that . . .'. We have found this kind of references in thirteen Austrian,[26] five Polish,[27] six Spanish,[28] four Czech,[29] four Dutch cases,[30] and two

[26] Case C-529/15, Gert Folk [2017], ECLI:EU:C:2017:419; Case C-348/15, Stadt Wiener Neustadt v. Niederösterreichische Landesregierung [2016], ECLI:EU:C:2016:882; Case C-159/15, Franz Lesar v. Beim Vorstand der Telekom Austria AG eingerichtetes Personalamt [2016], ECLI:EU:C:2016:451; Case C-2/15, DHL Express (Austria) GmbH v. Post-Control-Kommission and Bundesminister für Verkehr, Innovation und Technologie [2016], ECLI:EU:C:2016:880; Case C-175/14, Ralph Prankl [2015], ECLI:EU:C:2015:142; Case C-166/14, MedEval - Qualitäts-, Leistungs- und Struktur-Evaluierung im Gesundheitswesen, GmbH [2015], ECLI:EU:C:2015:779; Case C-66/14, Finanzamt Linz v. Bundesfinanzgericht, Außenstelle Linz [2015], ECLI:EU:C:2015:661; Case C-589/13, F.E. Familienprivatstiftung Eisenstadt v. Unabhängiger Finanzsenat, Außenstelle Wien [2015], ECLI:EU:C:2015:612; Case C-570/13, Karoline Gruber v. Unabhängiger Verwaltungssenat für Kärnten and Others [2015], ECLI:EU:C:2015:231; Case C-531/13, Marktgemeinde Straßwalchen and Others v. Bundesminister für Wirtschaft, Familie und Jugend [2015], ECLI:EU:C:2015:79; Case C-530/13, Leopold Schmitzer v. Bundesministerin für Inneres [2014], ECLI:EU:C:2014:2359; Case C-529/13, Georg Felber v. Bundesministerin für Unterricht, Kunst und Kultur [2015], ECLI:EU:C:2015:20 and Case C-338/13, Marjan Noorzia v. Bundesministerin für Inneres [2014], ECLI:EU:C:2014:2092.

[27] Case C-277/14, PPUH Stehcemp sp. j Florian Stefanek, Janina Stefanek, Jaroslaw Stefanek v. Dyrektor Izby Skarbowej w Łodzi [2015], ECLI:EU:C:2015:719; Case C-500/13, Gmina Międzyzdroje v. Minister Finansów [2014], ECLI:EU:C:2014:1750; C-499/13, Marian Macikowski v. Dyrektor Izby Skarbowej w Gdańsku [2015], ECLI:EU:C:2015:201; Case C-370/13, Henryk Teisseyre and Jan Teisseyre v. Minister Skarbu Państwa [2014], ECLI:EU:C:2014:2033 and Case C-349/13, Minister Finansów v. Oil Trading Poland sp. z.o.o. [2015], ECLI:EU:C:2015:84.

[28] Case C-424/15, Xabier Ormaetxea Garai and Bernardo Lorenzo Almendros v. Administración del Estado [2016], ECLI:EU:C:2016:780; Case C-333/15/C-334/15, María Pilar Planes Bresco v. Comunidad Autónoma de Aragón [2016], ECLI:EU:C:2016:426; Case C-470/14, Entidad de Gestión de Derechos de los Productores Audiovisuales (EGEDA) and Others v. Administración del Estado and Asociación Multisectorial de Empresas de la Electrónica, las Tecnologías de la Información y la Comunicación, de las Telecomunicaciones y de los contenidos Digitales (AMETIC) [2016], ECLI:EU:C:2016:418; Case C-177/14, María José Regojo Dans v. Consejo de Estado [2015], ECLI:EU:C:2015:450; Case C-168/14, Grupo Itevelesa SL and Others v. Oca Inspección Técnica de Vehículos SA and Generalidad de Cataluña [2015], ECLI:EU:C:2015:685 and Case C-165/14, Alfredo Rendón Marín v. Administración del Estado [2016], ECLI:EU:C:2016:675.

[29] Case C-638/15, Eko-Tabak s.r.o. v. Generální ředitelství cel [2017], ECLI:EU:C:2017:277; Case C-318/14, Slovenská autobusová doprava Trnava a.s. v. Krajský úřad Olomouckého kraje [2015], ECLI:EU:C:2015:352; Case C-43/14, ŠKO–Energo s. r. o. v. Odvolací finanční ředitelství [2015], ECLI:EU:C:2015:120 and Case C-80/13, Strojírny Prostějov, a.s. and ACO Industries Tábor s.r.o. v. Odvolací finanční ředitelství [2014], ECLI:EU:C:2014:2011.

[30] Case C-158/14, A and Others v. Minister van Buitenlandse Zaken [2017], ECLI:EU:C:2017:202; Case C-153/14, Minister van Buitenlandse Zaken v. K and A [2015], ECLI:EU:C:2015:453; Case C-133/13, Staatssecretaris van Economische Zaken and Staatssecretaris van Financiën v. Q [2014], ECLI:EU:C:2014:2460 and Case C-91/13, Essent Energie Productie BV v. Minister van Sociale Zaken en Werkgelegenheid [2014], ECLI:EU:C:2014:2206.

French,[31] as well as in one Belgium,[32] one German[33] and one Danish case.[34] This is much more than we expected. Even though one could argue that there is a thin line between interpretation and adjudicating, it is striking that in 37 per cent of the cases the referring court asks the CJEU to settle an issue that is supposed to be for the national courts to decide. What should we make of this?

Different answers could be given. Perhaps one should bear in mind that for the referring court it might come in handy to leave things to the CJEU, especially if the questions that needs to be decided are controversial and could fire back at the referring court in case there is a good chance that the answer is not welcomed by the national legislature or executive. In other words, it might sometimes be attractive to make the CJEU say that a certain national legal practice is in breach with EU law because this can take the (political) heat away from the national court.[35] More down-to-earth reasons could be that the referring court wants to facilitate the litigating parties as much as possible by asking the CJEU what it thinks about how national law relates to EU law, in particular in case the referring court is afraid the CJEU may only come up with a catalogue of criteria to answer a compatibility question that would then still be very difficult to answer for the national court without risking faults. In line with this could be that the referring court wants to prevent the necessity to raise follow-up questions in case it does not understand how to translate the preliminary ruling to the case that was the reason for referral. If the national court feels the CJEU is better equipped to answer a compatibility question it becomes very tempting to formulate the question as such. Perhaps this explains the relatively high number of compatibility questions, we found in the case law (see Figure 3.2).

[31] Case C-530/15, Leopold Schmitzer v. Bundesministerin für Inneres [2014], ECLI:EU:C:2014:2359 and Case C-301/15, Marc Soulier and Sara Doke v. Premier ministre and Ministre de la Culture et de la Communication [2016], ECLI:EU:C:2016:878.

[32] Case C-225/13, Ville d'Ottignies-Louvain-la-Neuve and Others v. Région wallonne [2014], ECLI:EU:C:2014:245.

[33] Case C-443/14, Kreis Warendorf v. Ibrahim Alo en Amira Osso v. Region Hannover [2016], ECLI:EU:C:2016:127.

[34] Case C-441/14, Dansk Industri (DI), acting on behalf of Ajos A/S v. Estate of Karsten Eigil Rasmussen [2016], ECLI:EU:C:2016:278.

[35] See for instance the Polish Case C-370/13, Henryk Teisseyre and Jan Teisseyre v. Minister Skarbu Państwa, ECLI:EU:C:2014:2033.

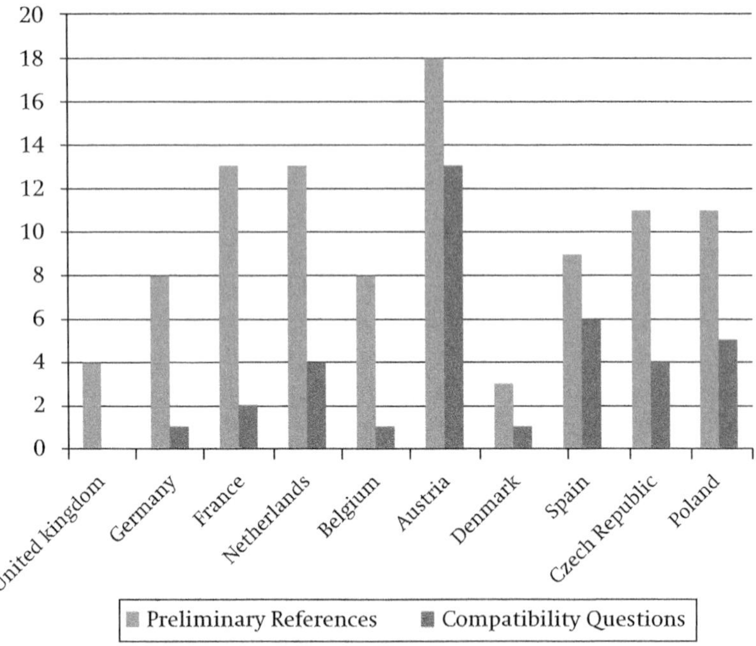

Figure 3.2 Compatibility questions.

3.3.3 *Provisional Answers*

3.3.3.1 How Frequently Are Provisional Answers Being Offered?

What does the case law analysis tell us about referring courts taking position towards the CJEU by providing provisional answers to the question they refer? For the purpose of this case law study the term 'provisional answers' has to be understood as offering one 'right answer', offering a number of alternative answers and offering several answers with an additional assessment of their potential consequences for the national legal order (see Figure 3.3).[36]

Looking at Figure 3.3, one can see that there are not only significant differences between the number of references between supreme administrative courts during our period of investigation, but also with regard to the degree to which these courts provide the CJEU with provisional answers. On the one hand, the German Federal Administrative Court

[36] The basis for the use of provisional answers can be found in rule 17 of the Recommendations to national courts and tribunals, in relation to the initiation of preliminary ruling proceedings (2016/C 439/01).

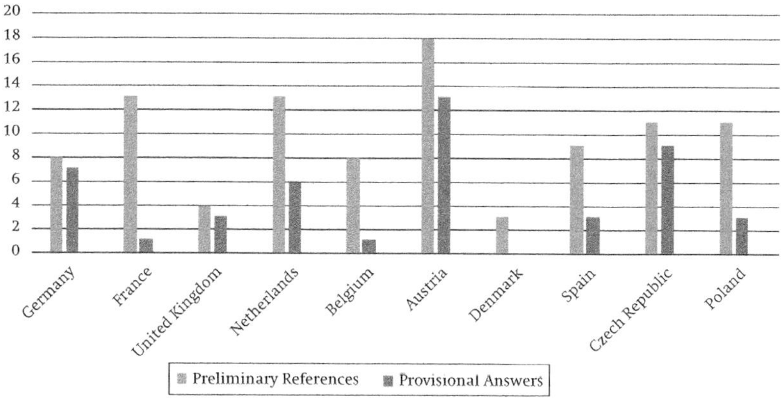

Figure 3.3 Preliminary references and provided provisional answers.

seems to almost systematically offer provisional answers to the questions it raises.[37] A court that appears to follow the German court in the large majority of the cases is the Supreme Administrative Court of the Czech Republic.[38] On the other hand, the French Conseil d'Etat, the Danish Supreme Court and the Belgium Council of State seem to be very reluctant to take position with regard to the preferred outcome to the preliminary questions during the period 2013–2015.[39] The other courts can be positioned somewhere in the middle. These supreme administrative courts (from the UK,[40] the Netherlands,[41]

[37] The only case of the German Federal Administrative Court in which we have not found a provisional answer is Case C-301/14 Pfotenhilfe-Ungarn eV v. Ministerium für Energiewende, Landwirtschaft, Umwelt und ländliche Räume des Landes Schleswig-Holstein [2015], ECLI:EU:C:2015:793.

[38] The only two cases of the Supreme Administrative Court of the Czech Republic in which we have not found a provisional answer are Case C-394/13, Ministerstvo práce a sociálních věcí v. B. ECLI:EU:C:2014:2199 and Case C-638/15, Eko-Tabak [2017], ECLI:EU:C:2017:277.

[39] The French Conseil d'Etat did warn the CJEU for the consequences of a possible decision in Case C-379/15, Association Nature Environnement [2016], ECLI:EU:C:2016:603 and the Belgium Council of State did the same in Case C-290/15, d'Oultremont [2016], ECLI:EU:C:2016:816.

[40] The UK Supreme Court provided a provisional answer in Case C-360/13, Public Relations Consultants Association Ltd v. Newspaper Licensing Agency Ltd and Others [2014], ECLI:EU:C:2014:1195; Case C-430/15, Tolley [2017], ECLI:EU:C:2017:74 and Case C-316/15, Hemming [2017], ECLI:EU:C:2017:74.

[41] The Council of State of The Netherlands took position towards the outcome of the preliminary ruling at least on certain aspects in Joined Cases C-340/14 and C-341-14, R.L.

Austria,[42] Spain[43] and Poland[44]) sometimes explicitly take position towards the CJEU and towards the preferred outcome of the preliminary ruling, while on other occasions they refuse to do so for no apparent reason.[45] At least, the reason itself is not explained in the order for reference.

Why do some courts systematically refuse to provide the CJEU with a provisional answer? One reason could be that this has to do with practicalities, such as a high caseload and worries about delaying the procedure. However, avoiding taking a position could also be a matter of

Trijber v. College van Burgemeester en Wethouders van Amsterdam and J. Harmsen v. Burgemeester van Amsterdam [2015], ECLI:EU:C:2015:641; Case C-295/14 in Joined Cases C-191/14, C-192/14, C-295/14, C-389/14 and C-391/14 to C-393/14, Dow Benelux [2016], ECLI:EU:C:2016:311; Case C-158/14, A, B, C,D v. Minister van Buitenlandse Zaken [2017], ECLI:EU:C:2017:202; Case C-153/14, Minister van Buitenlandse Zaken v. K and A [2015], ECLI:EU:C:2015:453; Case C-81/14, Nannoka Vulcanus Industries BV v. College van gedeputeerde staten van Gelderland [2015], ECLI:EU:C:2015:575 and Case C-158/15, Elektriciteits Productiemaatschappij Zuid-Holland [2016], ECLI:EU:C:2016:422.

42 The Austrian Supreme Administrative Court took position towards the outcome of the preliminary ruling sometimes by providing a provisional right answer (in Case C-589/13, F. E. Familienprivatstiftung Eisenstadt [2015], ECLI:EU:C:2015:612; Case C-282/13, T-Mobile Austria GmbH v. Telekom-Control-Kommission [2015], ECLI:EU:C:2015:24; Case C-453/14, Vorarlberger Gebietskrankenkasse and Alfred Knauer v. Landeshauptmann von Vorarlberg and Rudolf Mathis [2016], ECLI:EU:C:2016:37; Case C-347/14, New Media Online GmbH v. Bundeskommunikationssenat and Der Bundeskanzlerand [2015], ECLI:EU:C:2015:709 and C-175/14, Ralph Prankl [2015], ECLI:EU:C:2015:142) or by providing arguments for multiple alternative answers (Case C-531/13, Marktgemeinde Straßwalchen and Others v. Bundesminister für Wirtschaft, Familie und Jugend [2015], ECLI:EU:C:2015:79; Case C-530/13, Leopold Schmitzer v. Bundesministerin für Inneres [2014], ECLI:EU:C:2014:2359; Case C-529/13, Georg Felber v. Bundesministerin für Unterricht, Kunst und Kultur [2015], ECLI:EU:C:2015:20; Case C-338/13, Marjan Noorzia v. Bundesministerin für Inneres [2014], ECLI:EU:C:2014:2092; Case C-355/15, Beitergemeinschap Technische Gebäudebetreuung GesmbH [2016], ECLI:EU:C:2016:988; Case C-348/15, Stadt Wiener Neustadt [2016], ECLI:EU:C:2016:882; Case C-159/15, Lesar [2016], ECLI:EU:C:2016:451 and Case C-2/15, DHL Express Austria [2016], ECLI:EU:C:2016:451).

43 In the case law of the Supreme Court of Spain we found three cases in which it took position toward the outcome of the preliminary ruling: Case C-165/14, Alfredo Rendón Marín v. Administración del Estado [2016], ECLI:EU:C:2016:675; Case C-424/15, Ormaetxea Garai [2016], ECLI:EU:C:2016:780 and Case C-333/15, Planes Bresco [2016], ECLI:EU:C:2016:426.

44 The Polish Supreme Administrative Court did provide a provisional answer in the cases: Case C-277/14, PPUH Stehcemp sp. j Florian Stefanek, Janina Stefanek, Jaroslaw Stefanek v. Dyrektor Izby Skarbowej w Łodzi [2015], ECLI:EU:C:2015:719; Case C-276/14, Gmina Wrocław v. Minister Finansów [2015], ECLI:EU:C:2015:635 and Case C-42/14, Minister Finansów v. Wojskowa Agencja Mieszkaniowa w Warszawie [2015], ECLI:EU:C:2015:229.

45 At least the reasons for not providing provisional answers in these cases are not being articulated in the order for reference.

risk-aversion: courts not wanting 'to get it wrong'. Finally, some judges might want to avoid being seen as biased. By taking position with regard to the outcome of the preliminary ruling, courts could damage their appearance of impartiality, which might be harmful once the case returns from the Luxembourg court. Based on the case law analysis, it is impossible to explain why national courts refrain from giving provisional answers. This sort of information can only be obtained via interviews (see Chapter 4).

3.3.3.2 Different Styles of Provisional Answers

It is important to realise that provisional answers can be found in different shapes and sizes. Some courts seem to take a neutral standpoint with regard to the outcome of the preliminary reference procedure, while others suggest different possible answers and sometimes even provide an overview of the most likely consequences of these answers. Other courts, such as the German and Czech federal administrative courts, appear to prefer offering 'one right answer' to the CJEU, which is explicitly substantiated in the reference. An example of the 'one right answer' modus operandi can be found in the request the Bundesverwaltungsgericht has made in the Nordzucker AG-case.[46]

This case concerns a decision imposing a penalty of EUR 106 920, on Nordzucker AG for infringement of its obligation to surrender sufficient greenhouse gas emission allowances to cover its emissions during the preceding year. By its question, the referring court asks, in essence, whether Article 16(3) of Directive 2003/87 must be interpreted as meaning that the sanction for excessive emissions should also be applied with retrospective force in case both the company and the verification body have misinterpreted the amount of emission trading rights that should be bought and have corrected their mistake as soon as it became clear that a certain part of the installation should also be brought under the realm of the directive whereas the company initially thought these emissions should not be included. The German court discusses the advantages and disadvantages of the possible answers at length and goes in-depth into what it considers to be the correct interpretation of EU law. The referring court clearly takes position with regard to what should be the outcome of the case: no penalty because the penalty would not have a preventative effect and would probably violate the proportionality principle because the company was not aware that it was not complying with the Emission trading directive. The German court does not shirk away from clear warning signs. It suggests in

[46] Case C-148/14, Bundesrepublik Deutschland v. Nordzucker AG [2015], ECLI:EU:C:2015:287.

consideration 20 that retroactive penalties for violations of reporting requirements are unconstitutional. A more direct message to the CJEU as to the consequences of the preliminary ruling is hard to imagine.

Although this style of referring appears to have the advantage of sending a very clear message about the point of view of the national court, it is exactly this message that could cause controversy. This can be seen in the decision from the CJEU in the Ognyanov case.[47] This case concerns a Bulgarian rule providing that the national court should be disqualified because it stated a provisional answer in the request for a preliminary ruling when setting out the factual and legal context of the case. In its preliminary ruling, the CJEU has taken a final decision on whether domestic criminal procedural rules concerned with safeguards against judicial bias need to be set aside if their application is such as to jeopardize the functioning of the system of referrals for a preliminary ruling in the interpretation of EU law established by Article 267 TFEU. In short, the CJEU followed the Opinion of AG Bot and decided that such a rule is incompatible with EU law:

> [I]t must be observed at the outset that the assumption that underlies that question, that the national rule at issue in the main proceedings provides an individual with enhanced protection of his right to a fair trial, within the meaning of the second paragraph of Article 47 of the Charter, cannot be accepted. As was stated in paragraph 23 of this judgment, the fact that a national court sets out, in the request for a preliminary ruling, in accordance with what is required by Article 267 TFEU and Article 94 of the Rules of Procedure, the factual and legal context of the main proceedings is not, in itself, a breach of that fundamental right. Consequently, the obligation to disqualify itself, imposed by that rule on a referring court which has, in a reference for a preliminary ruling, acted in that way cannot be considered as serving to enhance the protection of that right.

The CJEU decided that the domestic courts not only cannot be obliged to refrain from taking any further decisions in a given criminal case on the basis that they referred a preliminary question to the CJEU where they laid out the facts of the case and the law applicable to them, but they are also prevented from voluntarily stepping down of the case on the basis that they consider themselves biased after having referred the question to the CJEU. Although this decision is fully understandable, it does not answer the question whether provisional answers provided by the

[47] Case C-614/14, Atanas Ognyanov [2016], ECLI:EU:C:2016:514.

referring court could never be seen as a sign of bias that runs against Article 6 ECHR and Article 47 of the Charter of Fundamental Rights. In particular when the referring court strongly defends one right answer and leaves little room for the CJEU to deviate from this answer, as we have seen with the ultra vires claim of the Bundesverfassungsgericht in the OMT-case,[48] it is possible that the ECtHR would decide differently. One must bear in mind, though, that whatever provisional answers national courts might give, the CJEU does not have to follow these, whereas national courts are obliged to follow the ruling of the Luxembourg courts in its final decision in order to guarantee the effet utile of EU law.

3.4 How Does the CJEU Respond: What Sort of Answers Does It Provide?

3.4.1 Reformulating Preliminary Questions

One of the first things the CJEU will probably do when receiving a preliminary reference is to try to make sense of what the referring court wants to know or learn from it. In case the Court has great difficulties in understanding what the referring court meant to ask, it is not unusual that it reformulates the initial question. The CJEU may then rule something like: the referring court is 'asking in essence (. . .)'. By reformulating the question, the CJEU might want to help the referring court in order to provide the latter with a decision that is tailored to the case pending before it. There might also be another reason for the CJEU to rephrase a preliminary question. This has to do with the fact that the CJEU realizes that when it answers a question submitted by a court from one Member State, it at the same takes a guiding decision for 27 other Member States. In order for the CJEU to achieve and safeguard the unity of EU-law it might be necessary to sometimes reformulate a preliminary question in such a way that the answer serves this purpose.

Although reformulating the preliminary question might happen with the best intentions, it bears an inherent risk of answering a question that does not meet the needs of the referring court. Therefore, there are good reasons for the CJEU to operate cautiously in interpreting what the referring court might want to learn. The Court is not always successful in doing as we can derive from the case law.

[48] BVerfGE 134, 366; 2 BvR 2728/13.

3.4.2 *The Case of Trijber and Harmsen: An Example of an Unsuccessful Interpretation of the Preliminary Question*

In the joined cases of Trijber and Harmsen, the Dutch Council of State referred a question concerning the interpretation of Directive 2006/123/EC on the services in the internal market.[49] The requests were made in proceedings between Mr. Trijber and the mayor and municipal council of Amsterdam to grant him a license for the operation of open boat tours to take tourists through the canals of Amsterdam. The Harmsen case concerned the refusal by the same municipal council to grant him a license for his 'window prostitution' business in Amsterdam. The Council of State of the Netherlands stayed the proceedings and referred questions to the CJEU for a preliminary ruling, asking inter alia: 'Does Chapter III of Directive 2006/123 … apply to purely internal situations, or is the assessment of the question as to whether that chapter applies subject to the case-law of the Court of Justice concerning the Treaty provisions on freedom of establishment and the free movement of services in purely internal situations?'

The CJEU, however, concludes there is no need to examine the question whether the provisions of Chapter III regarding freedom of establishment are applicable to purely internal situations nor to establish what the relevant criteria are for determining whether such a situation exists, since the situations which are the subject of the questions referred for a preliminary ruling would not be purely internal. The CJEU draws this conclusion based on an interpretation of what the referring court has noted in its order for reference:

> In that regard, it should be noted that in Case C-340/14, while it is true that, according to the wording of the third question, the service provided by Mr Trijber which is the subject of the application for authorisation at issue in the main proceedings is in essence intended for residents of the Netherlands, the fact remains that the referring court itself notes, in the order for reference, that that service may also be enjoyed by nationals of other Member States and that the scheme at issue could impede access to the market for all service providers, including those from other Member States who wish to establish themselves in the Netherlands in order to provide such a service. Moreover, with respect to Case C-341/14, that court clearly states that the recipients of the services provided by Mr Harmsen which are the subject of the applications for authorisation at issue in the main proceedings are nationals of Member States other than the Kingdom of the Netherlands.

[49] Joint Cases C-340/14 and C-341/14, *Trijber and Harmsen* [2015], ECLI:EU:C:2015:641.

The CJEU declares this part of the preliminary questions inadmissible, although Advocate-General Szpunar strongly warned the CJEU for doing so:[50]

> Rather, the Court should reply to the questions as they are asked, namely whether Chapter III of Directive 2006/123 applies in situations which constitute purely internal situations. I would submit to the Court that the questions deserve to be answered, and this for two reasons. First, according to settled case-law, preliminary questions enjoy a presumption of relevance, that is to say, unless it can be demonstrated that, for example, they are hypothetical they should be answered. Secondly, Directive 2006/123 still being fairly young and this question being hotly debated, I would consider that there is an interest in the Court shedding light on this issue.

The Advocate-General stresses the importance to give the referring court the benefit of the doubt: preliminary questions enjoy a presumption of relevance. Only if the CJEU is absolutely certain that the question is of a purely hypothetical nature it does not need to be answered. To what extent should the CJEU by itself go into the facts of the case in order to answer this question? Establishing the relevant facts is, after all, primarily up to the national courts. One of the problems here is that the referring court does not participate in the proceedings before the CJEU and therefore cannot be consulted about the factual background of the preliminary question unless the CJEU makes use of the possibility to issue a request for clarification. According to article 101(1) the Rules of procedure of the Court:

> Without prejudice to the measures of organisation of procedure and measures of inquiry provided for in these Rules, the Court may, after hearing the Advocate General, request clarification from the referring court or tribunal within a time-limit prescribed by the Court.

The CJEU did not make use of this instrument and if one looks at the aftermath of the Trijber and Harmsen case, it becomes clear that the answer of the CJEU disappointed the Dutch Council of State to a large extent. After all, within three months after the CJEU had given its ruling in the Trijber and Harmsen case, the Council of State submitted the same question for a preliminary ruling in the Visser-case, stating that it still has doubts as to the applicability of Chapter III of Directive 2006/123 to

[50] Opinion of Advocate-General Szpunar in joined cases C-340/14 and C-341/14, *Trijber and Harmsen* [2015], ECLI:EU:C:2015:505.

purely internal situations.[51] This could have been prevented if the CJEU would have taken the opportunity to engage in a dialogue with the referring court, for example via a request for clarification.

3.4.3 *Request for Clarification*

What happens in preliminary reference procedures – the Trijber and Harmsen case is a perfect example – is that the submitted questions may raise doubts as to the admissibility or that the CJEU in the preparatory process to the oral hearing asks the parties for information about the facts of the case or about the applicable national law. The referring court, however, is absent in the proceedings before the CJEU. The shared responsibility for the interpretation of EU law advocated by the Luxembourg court is often not recognizable after the referring court has submitted its request for a preliminary ruling. The time between submitting a question and the decision of the CJEU is therefore also known as 'the black box'. A possibility for a more effective dialogue in these situations for the CJEU to issue a request for clarification but the Court rarely seems to use this possibility.

In the case law analysis, we have not found a single case in which the CJEU has in its decision explicitly mentioned to have applied article 101 (1) of the Rules of procedure of the Court. That does not necessarily mean that the CJEU has not used this instrument, but one would think that in case the CJEU does issue such a request it would somehow mention it in its ruling. In case the CJEU would truly see the interpretation and application of EU-law as a shared responsibility with national courts, one would expect the Court to engage in a conversation with the referring court in case it is not perfectly clear what the national court meant to ask. The reasons why the CJEU frequently chooses to reformulate questions without seeking a request for clarification first cannot be derived from a case law analysis and hence needs to be answered via the questionnaire or interviews with CJEU judges.

Some scholars have claimed that a request for clarification causes procedural complications for the referring court since it might need to reopen the case and perhaps even consult the parties in order to provide the CJEU with the necessary clarification.[52] Others have claimed that

[51] See the request of the Council of State of 13 January 2016 in case C-31/16, ECLI:NL:RVS:2016:75.

[52] J. Langer, The preliminary ruling procedure: old problems or new challenges? Inaugural lecture held on 31 March 2015 on acceptance of the Professorship of European law and

asking for clarification might even make things worse since some of the referring courts simply lack sufficient knowledge of EU-law. However, if the latter would be true, it also tells us something about the possibilities for a judicial dialogue within the confines of the preliminary reference procedure.

3.4.4 *Different Types of Answers From the CJEU*

The type of questions submitted by national courts is likely to influence the sort of response from the CJEU. We distinguish between three types of answers: (a) ready-made answers, (b) guideline decisions and (c) quasi compliance judgments.[53] In case of ready-made answers, the CJEU in fact provides an answer to the referring court that offers a ready-made solution for the decision in the case the national court needs to decide. More complex are the guideline cases. This category can be split up in decision by the CJEU, in which the Court offers concrete guidelines for the national court(s) to decide not only the case that was referred but also similar future cases and cases in which the CJEU may have wanted to show deference towards the referring court by offering more freedom to take responsibility for an interpretation of national law that is in line with EU law or chose for 'deliberate ambiguity' simply because that was the only way for the judges deciding the case to reach an agreement. Compliance decisions are the CJEU's equivalent of the aforementioned category of (quasi) citizens' infringement cases in which the Court de facto decides whether a certain provision of national law or a domestic court ruling is in breach with EU law.

Especially the second category is a more fluid one. Sometimes it is hard to determine to what extent the CJEU wanted to offer (vague) guidelines for further decision-making, show deference towards the referring national court or was simply unable to provide a preliminary ruling that points the way because consensus between CJEU judges could only be reached by taking an ambiguous decision. In the second and third case, the amount of guidance offered by preliminary rulings is rather minimal. A good example is another Dutch case *A, B, C*

the national legal order, p. 13. Available at SSRN: https://ssrn.com/abstract=2885256 or http://dx.doi.org/10.2139/ssrn.2885256 accessed on 19 January 2019. See also R. Barents, Procedures en procesvoering voor het Hof van Justitie en het Gerecht van eerste aanleg van de EG (Kluwer, 2005), p. 334.

53 This distinction draws on the varying degrees of specificity as described by T. Tridimas, 'Constitutional Review of Member State Action: The Virtues and Vices of an Incomplete Jurisdiction' *I-CON*, 9, 3–4, 737–756 (2011).

v. *Staatssecretaris van Veiligheid en Justitie*.[54] Here the Dutch Council of State asked the CJEU what proof may be taken into account to 'establish' the declared homosexual orientation of an applicant for asylum. However, the question was formulated in a negative way, asking about what the legal limits were:

What limits do Article 4 of [Directive 2004/83] and [the Charter], in particular Articles 3 and 7 thereof, impose on the method of assessing the credibility of a declared sexual orientation, and are those limits different from the limits which apply to assessment of the credibility of the other grounds of persecution and, if so, in what respect?

It was clear from the case referred that the Dutch court worried about a possible 'floodgate' effect due to refugees claiming a right to asylum on the basis of a sexual orientation, which can be difficult to verify in case of doubts. Hence, it was clear that the Council of State was seeking guidance from the CJEU. The Dutch court even substantiated its position by referring to a report that describes the practice in different EU member states with respect to the complexity of this problem. The question, however, is how one should qualify the preliminary ruling from the CJEU. The Court responded by declaring that Article 4(3)(c) of Directive 2004/83/EC precludes an assessment that is based on:

Stereotyped notions concerning homosexuals instead of on the individual and personal circumstances [paras 60–63];

Detailed Questioning of Sexual Practices, which should not be asked as this would violate the right to respect private and family life of article 7 of the Charter of fundamental rights [paras 64–65];

Tests of the applicant in order to demonstrate sexual identity (such as production of video evidence of sexual acts, which would infringe the right to human dignity of article 1 of the Charter) [paras 65–66];

Adverse findings with respect to delay in not declaring sexual identity at the outset cannot be found to be a point against the applicant's credibility, as sexuality is an intimate aspect of sexual identity [paras 67–71]. To rely on delay would violate both Article 4 of the Qualification Directive and Article 13 of the Procedure Directive, due to the vulnerability of gay applicants.

This case is a good example of what may happen if the CJEU is given a rather open preliminary question. In its decision, the CJEU concentrates almost completely on the fundamental rights aspects of the case, such as the right to privacy and human dignity, which do not allow requesting

[54] Joined Cases C-148/13 to 150/13, A e.a. v. Staatssecretaris van Veiligheid en Justitie [2014], ECLI:EU:C:2014:2406.

empirical evidence concerning one's sexual orientation. However, this seemed to be but one aspect of what concerned the Dutch Council of State and the immigration authorities in different Member States. The referring court was probably also seeking guidance as to the rules of evidence that could (still) be applied without infringing upon fundamental rights in order to filter out as many false claims as possible. On this aspect: the Council of State was left almost completely in the dark. Accordingly, it is difficult how one should label such a decision: is it a guidance case, a deference case, or simply a matter of taking the easy way out by the CJEU by agreeing on which screening methods are precluded instead of signaling what sort of methods would be allowed according to EU law. We have labeled cases, such as this one, as guidance decisions because whether CJEU judges want to defer to the national court or cannot agree among themselves is something that cannot be proven by simply studying case law since it has to do with the intentions of judges.

3.4.5 *A Case Law Analysis into the Different Types of Responses by the CJEU*

Studying the rulings of the CJEU shows that in many cases the Court provides the referring court with a ready-made answer to the preliminary question that the national court can simply take over. We found these decisions in 46 cases, which corresponds with 47 per cent of the cases that were subject to our case-law study. In 36 cases, the CJEU was responding to a question about the compatibility of national legislation in the light of EU law. In 16 cases, the CJEU provided more or less specific guidelines for the national court or showing deference towards the referring court

Sometimes we found a combination of approaches. If the CJEU takes a decision about the compatibility of national legislation with EU-law, the judgment of the Court sometimes also shows characteristics of a ready-made answer. For the purpose of our analysis, though, we have qualified the decision as a compliance judgment. Preliminary questions may also consist of different sub questions each with their own characteristics: binary and/or (partly) open. In answering this kind of questions, it may very well be that the answers by CJEU also differ per sub question. In case we found a combination of ready-made answers and providing guidelines we have chosen to call the case a guidance decision because overall, the CJEU answers could not be copy pasted by the referring court (see Figure 3.4).

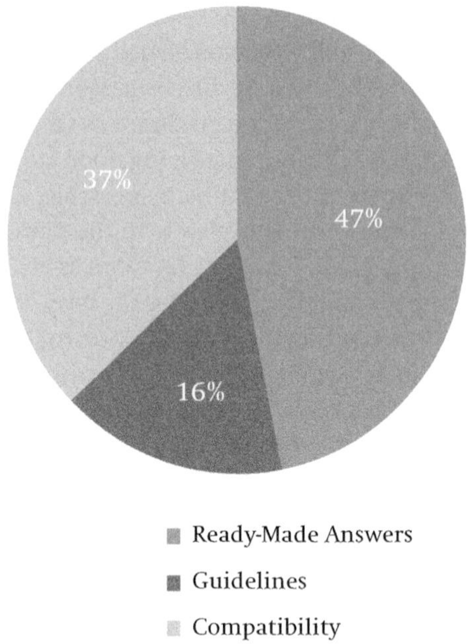

Figure 3.4 Ready-made answers, guidelines and compliance decisions.

3.4.5.1 The CJEU's Response to Binary Questions

Taking a closer look at these 46 decisions in which the CJEU provided a ready-made answer to the referring national court, it is striking that the vast majority of them have been preceded by a binary question. Hence, there seems to exist a correlation between the both. However, there are two categories of binary questions: the purely binary questions and the binary compatibility questions. In the case law analysis, we have found binary questions in 87 cases. In 50 cases, the referred question is of a purely binary nature. Here the CJEU has responded 40 times with a ready-made solution to the dispute. Take for example the case of Mateusiak. The Polish Supreme Administrative Court submitted a question for a preliminary ruling that reads as follows:

Must Article 18(c) of the [VAT Directive] be interpreted as meaning that, on expiry of the adjustment period referred to in Article 187 of the directive, a taxable person's fixed assets upon the acquisition of which he deducted VAT, should not be subject to tax and included in the winding-up inventory at the time he ceases his activity, if the period laid down in law for adjusting the input tax on the acquisition thereof, which arises from the estimated period for using those assets in the taxable person's economic activity, has passed, or as meaning that the fixed assets are subject to tax at the time the taxable person ceases his economic activity, regardless of the adjustment period?[55]

The CJEU responded by providing a ready-made answer to the referred question:

The answer to the question asked is that Article 18(c) of the VAT Directive must be interpreted as meaning that, when a taxable person ceases to carry out a taxable economic activity, the retention of goods by that taxable person, where VAT on such goods became deductible upon their acquisition, can be treated as a supply of goods for consideration and be subject to VAT if the adjustment period laid down in Article 187 of the VAT Directive has passed.

In the remaining 10 cases, the national court referred a purely binary question without the CJEU responding to it with a clear yes or no answer. In these cases, the CJEU provided the national court with more or less specific guidelines. An example can be found in the Austrian case of GD European Land Systems – Steyr GmbH.[56] The request has been made in proceedings between GD European Land Systems – Steyr and the Customs Office, Eisenstadt, Vienna Airport concerning the customs classification of a turret system (Multi Gun Turret System weapon station). The Austrian Vewaltungsgerichtshof submitted a reference for a preliminary ruling raising two pure binary questions:

(1) Does the exception specified in point (c) of note 1 to Chapter 93 of the CN, in the version applicable to the facts in the present case, which is worded 'armoured fighting vehicles (heading 8710)', apply also to 'parts thereof'?
(2) Must note 3 to Section XVII of the CN be interpreted as meaning that a 'weapons station (armoured turret)' which may be used on armoured fighting vehicles or on 'mobile maritime transport systems' or in stationary installations must be classified under heading 8710 of the CN as a part of an armoured fighting vehicle because that weapons station was imported by the manufacturer of armoured fighting vehicles for the production or assembly of armoured fighting vehicles and is used in fact for that purpose?

[55] Case C-229/15, Minister Finansów v. Jan Mateusiak [2016], ECLI:EU:C:2016:454.
[56] Case C-262/15, GD European Land Systems – Steyr GmbH v. Zollamt Eisenstadt Flughafen Wien [2016], ECLI:EU:C:2016:365.

The CJEU does not provide the referring national court with a yes or no and explicitly points out why it does so: 'When the Court is requested to give a preliminary ruling on a matter of tariff classification, its task is to provide the national court with guidance on the criteria which will enable the latter to classify the products at issue correctly in the CN, rather than to effect that classification itself, *a fortiori* since the Court does not necessarily have available to it all the information which is essential in that regard (judgments of 7 November 2002 in *Lohmann and Medi Bayreuth*, C-260/00 to C-263/00, EU:C:2002:637, paragraph 26, and 22 November 2012 in *Digitalnet and Others*, C-320/11, C-330/11, C-382/11 and C-383/11, EU:C:2012:745, paragraph 61).' Therefore the CJEU offers the referring court some guidelines by stating that if the turret system: 'is "principally" intended for use on an armoured fighting vehicle, this being a matter for the referring court to determine on the basis of the objective characteristics and properties of the turret system, without the end use to which it is put in the case at hand being determinant for the purpose of its classification. If that is not the case, that turret system must be classified, as a part or accessory of a "military weapon", under subheading 9305 91 00 of the CN.' In other words, the CJEU in this case offers guidelines to the national court but does not step into the tariff classification, simply because the court lacks information to do so, but perhaps also because it does not want to engage in the politically sensitive compliance issue of how to classify military weapons for the purpose of customs tariffs.

3.4.5.2 The CJEU's Response to Compliance Questions

A special category of binary questions the CJEU is invited to assess concerns the legality of provisions of national law, although this is in fact for the national court to decide. Nevertheless, as we have argued above, national courts often do not take the trouble to formulate their preliminary questions in such a way that they focus on the correct interpretation or validity of EU law only, but often simply want to know whether a certain national legal rule is in breach of EU law. In such a case the referring court often disguises the compliance issue by formulating the question in such a way that it is abstracting out the exact national provision. Take for example the Gruber-case in which the Austrian Verwaltungsgerichtshof asked[57]:

[57] Case C-570/13, Karoline Gruber v. Unabhängiger Verwaltungssenat für Kärnten e.a. [2015], ECLI:EU:C:2015:231.

Does European Union law, in particular Directive 2011/92/EU of the European Parliament and of the Council of 13 December 2011 on the assessment of the effects of certain public and private projects on the environment (Directive 2011/92), in particular Article 11 thereof, preclude a provision of national law under which a decision finding that a particular project does not require an environmental impact assessment is also binding on neighbours who did not have the status of parties in the previous proceedings for a declaratory decision and can be relied on as against them in subsequent development consent proceedings even though they have the opportunity to raise their objections to the project in those consent proceedings (the objection in the main proceedings being that the effects of the project will pose a risk to the appellant's life, health or property or represent an unreasonable nuisance to her in the form of smell, noise, smoke, dust, vibration or otherwise)?

In fact, this question was raised because the applicant in the referring case disputed the lawfulness of the decision of the Province of Carinthia's government, by which that government declared, on the basis of Paragraph 3(7) of the Umweltverträglichkeitsprüfungsgeset 2000, that no environmental impact assessment needed to be carried out in relation to the project at issue. How does the CJEU respond to these compatibility questions? In theory, the Court should probably rule either that it is not able to deliver advisory opinions or rule on general or hypothetical questions, according to its established case law,[58] or that the preliminary reference procedure does not give the CJEU the power to decide whether a national provision is compatible with EU law.[59] It is exclusively for the national court to decide whether a given national legal provision or administrative decision complies with EU law or not.[60]

The CJEU is competent to provide the national court with all criteria for the interpretation of EU-law which may enable it to determine the issue of compatibility for the purposes of the decision in the case before it.[61] Nevertheless, how should the CJEU do this in case the direct occasion is, as in the Gruber case, the unlawfulness of the decision of the government by which it declared, on the basis of Paragraph 3(7) of the UVP-G 2000, that no EIA needed to be carried out in relation to the project at issue? In the Gruber case the CJEU responded like this:

[58] See Case C-197/10, Unió de Pagesos de Catalunya v. Administración del Estado [2011], ECLI:EU:C:2011:590, para 17-18 and the references to other cases there.

[59] See Case C-172/82, Inter-Huiles [1983] ECR 555, ECLI:EU:C:1983:69, para 8.

[60] Case C-55/94, Reinhard Gebhard v. Consiglio dell'Ordine degli Avvocati e Procuratori di Milano [1995], ECLI:EU:C:1995:411, para. 19.

[61] Ibid., para. 19.

> Article 11 of Directive 2011/92/EU of the European Parliament and of the Council of 13 December 2011 on the assessment of the effects of certain public and private projects on the environment must be interpreted as precluding national legislation, *such as that at issue in the main proceedings pursuant to which an administrative decision declaring that a particular project does not require an environmental impact assessment* [Italics added RvG/JdP], which is binding on neighbors who were precluded from bringing an action against that administrative decision, where those neighbors, who are part of the 'public concerned' within the meaning of Article 1(2) of that directive, satisfy the criteria laid down by national law concerning 'sufficient interest' or 'impairment of a right'. It is for the referring court to verify whether that condition is fulfilled in the case before it. Where it is so fulfilled, that court must hold that the administrative decision not to carry out such an assessment is not binding on those neighbors.

Is this not just another way of saying that Paragraph 3(7) of the UVP-G 2000 is incompatible with the EU directive? As we mentioned before, De Witte has asserted that the CJEU never answers compatibility questions in a straightforward way.[62] What this means is that the CJEU does not use 'compatibility' language, which is reserved for the infringement procedure, but maintains in its interpretive role although in many cases there can be no doubt about the compatibility between national law and EU law.

We found evidence for this claim in our case law study. In answering the preliminary question, the CJEU consequently starts by stating that 'EU law has to be interpreted as (...)'. This echoes the sound of an interpretive judgment rather than of a declaratory decision. Also, the CJEU has in some cases mitigated the declaratory effect by not referring directly to the legislation at stake, but more abstractly referring to 'legislation pursuant to which (...)'. Despite all this, the actual answer given by the CJEU in response to a compatibility question is – in essence – nothing less than a decision about the compatibility of national law with EU law. Using standard language like 'EU law must be interpreted as (not) precluding national legislation such as that at issue in the main proceedings pursuant to which (...)' the CJEU is in fact acting like a supreme court that is deciding the case at hand.

Similar remarks could be made when the CJEU does not give a direct answer to the compatibility question, but the Court provides the national court with criteria to assess whether the provisions of national law are

[62] B. de Witte, 'The preliminary ruling dialogue: three types of questions posed by national courts', in B. de Witte, J. Mayoral, U Jaremba, M. Wind, K Podstawa (eds.) *National Courts and EU Law* (Cheltenham: Edward Elgar, 2016), p 18.

compatible with EU law. In a minority of the compatibility cases we have found an answer of the CJEU leaving the referring court a margin of appreciation. Take for example the Spanish case of Grupo Itevelesa.[63] The Spanish Supreme Court referred a question consisting of four sub questions. The fourth sub question reads as follows:

> Is it compatible with Articles 10 and 14 of [the Services Directive] or, if that directive is not applicable, Article 43 EC (now Article 49 TFEU), for national legislation to make the number of licences for roadworthiness testing centres subject to a local plan which justifies the quantitative restriction on the grounds of ensuring adequate local coverage, ensuring the quality of the service and encouraging competition between operators and, to that end, includes factors relating to economic planning?

What the Supremo Tribunal is de facto asking here is whether the national law subjecting roadworthiness testing subject to a local plan justifying quantitative restriction of the kind mentioned is compatible with the Services Directive. Again, the CJEU answered in a way avoiding compatibility or compliance language:

> In the light of the foregoing considerations, the answer to the third and fourth questions is that Article 49 TFEU must be interpreted as precluding national legislation, such as that at issue in the main proceedings, which makes the authorisation for an undertaking or group of undertakings to open a vehicle roadworthiness testing centre subject to the condition, first, that there is a minimum distance between that centre and centres belonging to that undertaking or group of undertakings which are already authorised and, secondly, that that undertaking or group of undertakings will, if such an authorisation is granted, not hold a market share in excess of 50%, unless it is established that that condition is genuinely appropriate in order to achieve the objectives of consumer protection and road safety and does not go beyond what is necessary for that purpose, these being matters for the referring court to determine.

Although the CJEU leaves room for the national court to have the final say, it is clear from the outset that the Court is doing more than just interpreting EU-law.

In our case law analysis we found a compatibility question in 36 references for a preliminary ruling. In all of these cases, the CJEU basically adjudicates on the compatibility of national provisions with EU law. The CJEU sometimes leaves a margin of appreciation to the national courts and has in earlier judgments replied by saying that '(. . .) it is necessary to

[63] Case C-168/14, Grupo Itevelesa SL e.a. v. Oca Inspección Técnica de Vehículos SA en Generalidad de Cataluña [2015], ECLI:EU:C:2015:685.

point out that it is not for the Court, in the context of the procedure provided for in Article 267 TFEU, to determine whether national provisions are compatible with European Union law', this circumlocutory language, however, cannot hide the fact that what the CJEU is doing, is actually acting like a supreme court, otherwise the CJEU should have ruled that it is not competent to answer hypothetical questions regarding the compatibility of certain national provisions with EU law nor to answer compatibility questions. One can only speculate why the Luxembourg court does not do this. Perhaps the courts wants to be seen as a citizens' court that offers protection to individuals who are entitled to protection according to EU law against governments or other influential 'repeat players' or perhaps the Court is arguing that whenever national courts frame their preliminary questions as such, they apparently want the CJEU do decide whether national law is compatible with EU law which makes the answer legitimate.

3.4.5.3 The CJEU's Response to (Partly) Open Questions

In the minority of the cases the referring courts have submitted a preliminary question that is at least partly open. How does the CJEU respond to this type of questions? We found 11 cases in which the preliminary question was of a partly open nature, leaving the CJEU some discretion with regard to the way in which to answer the questions. In most of the cases in which the referring court launched such a question we have seen the CJEU responded by providing the referring court with guidelines to decide the case at hand.

ClientEarth, an environmental NGO, brought proceedings for an order that, with respect to sixteen zones and agglomerations, including London, the UK government had failed to meet the limit values laid down in Directive 2008/50 on ambient air quality and cleaner air for Europe. The defendant conceded that these limit values had not been met. Where a deadline cannot be met with regard to a particular zone or agglomeration, Article 22 of the Air Quality Directive allows Member States to postpone that deadline by five years, provided that they notify the Commission thereof. If the Commission does not object within nine months, the conditions laid down in the Directive for postponing the deadline are deemed to be satisfied. However, the UK had not notified the postponement to the Commission.

In these circumstances, the Supreme Court granted the order sought but also referred four preliminary questions to the European Court of Justice. The Supreme Court asked the CJEU whether (1) where the limit values were not met by 1 January 2010, a Member State was obliged to apply for a postponement of the deadline and (2) whether the establishment of an air quality plan is relevant to decide if a Member State has complied with the directive, and, if it has not complied, what measures the national court is required to take.

The CJEU notes that, as regards nitrogen dioxide, the directive provides that the limit values 'may not be exceeded', which amounts to an obligation to achieve a certain result. Postponement of the original deadline is possible only where acute compliance problems exist.

In those circumstances, in order to postpone for a maximum of five years, a Member State is required to make an application for postponement when it is objectively apparent, having regard to existing data, and notwithstanding the implementation by that Member State of appropriate pollution abatement measures, that conformity with those values cannot be achieved in a given zone or agglomeration by the specified deadline. The directive does not contain any exception to that obligation.

Next, the CJEU recalls that, where the limit values for nitrogen dioxide are exceeded after the deadline and no application for postponement had been submitted, Member States are equally required to establish an air quality plan that sets out appropriate measures so that the period during which the limit values are exceeded can be kept as short as possible. However, the mere fact that such a plan has been established does not mean that the Member State concerned has entirely satisfied its obligations under the directive. Where a Member State has not complied with the limit values and has not applied for a postponement of the deadline in accordance with the prescribed conditions, it is for the competent national court, should a case be brought before it, to take, with regard to the national authority, any necessary measure, such as an order in the appropriate terms, so that the authority establishes the plan required by the directive to ensure, in particular, that the period during which the limit values are exceeded is as short as possible.

On the one hand, the CJEU provides guidelines as to how article 22(1) of Directive 2008/50 must be interpreted. In order to be able to postpone by a maximum of five years the deadline specified by the directive for achieving conformity with the limit values for nitrogen dioxide, a Member State is required to make an application for postponement *when it is objectively apparent, having regard to existing data, and notwithstanding the implementation by that Member State of appropriate pollution abatement measures*, that conformity with those values cannot be achieved in a given zone or agglomeration by the specified deadline. On the other hand, the

CJEU seems to shows deference towards the national court: *it is for the national court having jurisdiction, should a case be brought before it, to take, with regard to the national authority, any necessary measure*, such as an order in the appropriate terms, so that the authority establishes the plan required by the directive in accordance with the conditions laid down by the latter.

If we look at these 11 cases in which the referring courts have submitted a (partly) open question we might assume a certain correlation between the open nature of the question and the CJEU acting as a signpost offering guidelines to national courts. In six cases the CJEU clearly answered by giving guidance or showing deference to the decision by the national court.[64] In only one case, the CJEU did not get to this open question as a result of the answer to the preceding sub question.[65] Only in four cases an open question was followed by a ready-made decision.[66]

3.4.6 The Responsiveness of The CJEU to Provisional Answers

Whether a certain type of response by the CJEU to a provisional answer by a national court is sparked by the style of argumentation of the referring court cannot be proven via a simple case law analysis. What such an analysis can teach us, though, is whether the CJEU explicitly refers to provisional answers. In case the Luxembourg court does not do so, one may not automatically conclude that the reasoning of the national court has had no impact on the CJEU's decision because that impact may remain invisible due to the secrecy of the internal deliberations within the court and the absence of dissenting opinions.

[64] Case C-404/13, ClientEarth v. The Secretary of State for the Environment, Food and Rural Affairs [2014], ECLI:EU:C:2014:2382; C-121/15, Association nationale des opérateurs détaillants en énergie (ANODE) v. Premier ministre e.a. [2016], ECLI:EU:C:2016:637; C-477/13, Eintragungsausschuss bei der Bayerischen Architektenkammer v. Hans Angerer [2015], ECLI:EU:C:2015:239; C-148/13, A e.a. v. Staatssecretaris van Veiligheid en Justitie [2014], ECLI:EU:C:2014:2406; C-81/14, Nannoka Vulcanus Industries BV v. College van gedeputeerde staten van Gelderland [2015], ECLI:EU:C:2015:575 and C-432/15, Odvolací finanční ředitelství v. Pavlína Baštová [2016], ECLI:EU:C:2016:855.

[65] Case C-461/13, Bund für Umwelt und Naturschutz Deutschland eV v. Bundesrepublik Deutschland [2015], ECLI:EU:C:2015:433

[66] Case C-441-14, Dansk Industri (DI) v. Sucession Karsten Eigil Rasmussen [2016], ECLI:EU:C:2016:278; Case C-316/15, Timothy Martin Hemming e.a. v. Westminster City Council [2016], ECLI:EU:C:2016:879; C-6/15, TNS Dimarso NV v. Vlaams Gewest [2016], ECLI:EU:C:2016:555 and Case C-605/15, Minister Finansów v. Aviva Towarzystwo Ubezpieczeń na Życie S.A. w Warszawie [2017], ECLI:EU:C:2017:718.

The case law shows that the Court does not directly and openly enter into a debate with the referring courts about their provisional answers. As just mentioned, this does not imply that the CJEU is ignoring the signals it receives from the referring national courts. It could be that the arguments from the national court have played an important role in the internal decision-making process of the CJEU, despite the fact that it does not show in the final ruling. Sometimes the opinion of an Advocate General may reveal that it was influenced by the provisional answer(s) of the referring court. However, opinions from Advocates General usually suffer the same faith as references by national courts, namely: that the CJEU rarely respond to the arguments being provided.

The latter does not mean that the CJEU always remains silent with regard to provisional answers. What we found is that the Court, from time to time, touches upon the provisional answers in the section in which it describes 'the dispute in the main proceedings and the question referred for a preliminary ruling'. This is not standard practice though. If we take the nine cases in which the German Federal Administrative Court provided a provisional answer, the CJEU only referred to the position of the Bundesgerichtshof in four cases.[67] Something similar applies to the Czech cases. In the six cases with provisional answers from the Czech Supreme Administrative Court, the CJEU only hints at the position of the national court in half of the cases, although it does not refer to the provisional answers directly.[68] Only in two Polish cases, an exception appears to be made to this general rule of not explicitly referring to provisional answers. In one case, the CJEU signals that referring court got the answer wrong,[69] whereas in another case it explicitly agrees with the referring court on one particular point.[70]

[67] See Cases C-477/13, Eintragungsausschuss bei der Bayerischen Architektenkammer v. Hans Angerer [2015], ECLI:EU:C:2015:239; Case C-47/13, Martin Grund v. Landesamt für Landwirtschaft, Umwelt und ländliche Räume des Landes Schleswig-Holstein [2014], ECLI:EU:C:2014:2248; Case C-148/14, Bundesrepublik Deutschland v. Nordzucker AG [2015], ECLI:EU:C:2015:287 and Case C-395/14, Vodafone GmbH v. Bundesrepublik Deutschland [2016], ECLI:EU:C:2016:9.

[68] See cases C-80/13, ACO Industries Tábor [2014], ECLI:EU:C:2014:2011; Case C-508/14, Český telekomunikační úřad v. T-Mobile Czech Republic a.s. and Vodafone Czech Republic a.s. [2015], ECLI:EU:C:2015:657 and Case C-43/14, ŠKO–Energo s. r. o. v. Odvolací finanční ředitelství [2015], ECLI:EU:C:2015:120.

[69] See case C-277/14, PPUH Stehcemp sp. j Florian Stefanek, Janina Stefanek, Jaroslaw Stefanek v. Dyrektor Izby Skarbowej w Łodzi [2015], ECLI:EU:C:2015:719, para 31 and further

[70] See case C-276/14, Gmina Wrocław v. Minister Finansów [2015], ECLI:EU:C:2015:635, para 39

The general picture that our case law analysis provides is that the CJEU is hesitant to engage in a dialogue about the interpretation of EU law with national courts, which take the effort to substantiate their position with regard to what they believe should be the outcome of the preliminary reference. In the majority of the cases (44 out of 78) the supreme administrative courts do not provide the CJEU with provisional answers, despite the fact that the Court itself has argued that: 'the referring court may, if it considers itself able, briefly state its view on the answer to be given to the questions referred for a preliminary ruling'.[71] This appears to be an open invitation for national courts to take position. If that is the intention, one wonders why the CJEU does not respond more actively and openly to provisional answers offered by national courts. Not only, would that be a sign that the co-actorship of national courts in the preliminary reference procedure is taken seriously, it could also encourage courts that shy away from sharing their view about what is supposed to be the correct interpretation of EU law to share their view with the CJEU. This would give meaning to the preliminary reference procedure as a dialogue between national courts and the CJEU.

This leaves us with the question why the CJEU is so reluctant to respond explicitly to the provided answers. We believe that the explanation cannot always be found in a lack of internal consensus or in unwillingness from the side of the Court. One reason could be that the Court avoids referring to the provisional answers because it does not want to embarrass the referring court in case of disagreement. Another explanation could be that the CJEU does not want to give preference to national courts that provide provisional answers over the ones that refuse to do so. Last but not least, it might be that the CJEU does not want to be placed in the position of an appellate court reviewing the provisional answers of the referring court. Our interviews (hereafter in Chapter 4) can shed more light on this matter.

3.5 Implementing the Decision of the CJEU

In the first paragraph of this chapter, we roughly discerned between three different stages in the communication between the CJEU and the referring courts. The third and final stage concerns the time after a decision is taken by the CJEU until the final decision of the referring

[71] Information note on references from national courts for a preliminary ruling (2009/C 297/01), article 23.

court: here the latter court gets a chance to implement the preliminary ruling into its own decision of the case that led to a reference and inform the CJEU about the outcome. Especially in cases where the CJEU did not come up with a ready-made (outcome) decision for the referring court, there is room for interpretation and possibly extended dialogue. What exactly do we know about the communication that takes place in this third stage of the preliminary reference procedure?

Do national courts always neatly obey to the CJEU's ruling or do they bend the rulings by the Court in the application phase if they feel this is necessary? Unfortunately, the answer to this question is very hard to give. In our case law study it appeared to be impossible to systematically compare the final decisions of the referring courts with the preliminary rulings of the CJEU since the decisions of the national courts implementing the Court's decision are often not available via the EUR-Lex database. Moreover, our communication with the Court learned that the CJEU does not systematically collect the final decisions from national courts. Even if a national court does send (a summary of) its final decision to the CJEU this decision is usually not translated in the working languages of the Court (French/English). As a result, the attention for these final decisions by the CJEU and by court watchers is low. The fact that national courts frequently only provide a summary of their final decision to the CJEU also does not help because one does not know how these summaries are being made. Consequently, we cannot tell to what extent national courts comply faithfully with the CJEU's preliminary rulings. More surprising is that the CJEU apparently also does not systematically follow-up on its own preliminary rulings to find out what is done with them.

At the same time, there are reasons to believe there might be a cause for further research on this point. The literature indicates that certain monitoring and enforcement problems do occur.[72] In the Melloni case, for example,[73] the Spanish Constitutional Court showed that it is not self-evident that a referring court will always comply with the CJEU's preliminary ruling. Although the final ruling in itself did not violate EU law, the court refused to accept the CJEU's interpretation as grounds for

[72] Falkner and Treib argue that within the EU a group of Member States including – but not limited to – the Czech Republic, Hungary, Slovakia and Slovenia and referred to as the 'world of dead letters' faces problems that prevents these countries from putting EU law in practice and enforcing it, *see* G. Falkner and O. Treib, 'Three Worlds of Compliance or Four? The EU-15 Compared to New Member States' *Journal of Common Market Studies*, 46 293 (2008).

[73] Case C-399/11, Stefano Melloni v. Ministerio Fiscal [2013], ECLI:EU:C:2013:107.

its national ruling.[74] A more explicit example of non-compliance we found in our sample of cases, concerns the Danish Ajos case.[75]

Karsten Eigil Rasmussen was dismissed by Ajos A/S in May 2009. According to paragraph 2a(3) of the Danish Law on salaried employees no severance allowance shall be payable if, on termination of the employment relationship, the employee will receive an old-age pension from the employer and the employee joined the pension scheme in question before reaching the age of 50. Mr. Rasmussen had reached the age of 60 and was entitled to such an old-age pension from Ajos A/S under a scheme he had joined before reaching the age of 50. In its reference, the Danish Supreme Court asks in essence whether Mr. Rasmussen can invoke the general principle of EU law prohibiting discrimination on grounds of age directly against Ajos A/S. The CJEU held that 'the requirement to interpret national law in conformity with EU law entails the obligation for national courts to change its established case law, where necessary, if it is based on an interpretation of national law that is incompatible with the objectives of a directive . . .'.[76] Thus the Danish Supreme Court 'could not validly claim that it was impossible to interpret the national provision at issue in conformity with EU law by the mere reason that it had consistently interpreted that provision in a manner incompatible with EU law'.[77] The Danish Supreme Court, however, decided to disregard this judgment of the CJEU. A majority of eight out of nine judges found that the Danish Accession Act does not allow unwritten general EU law principles, such as the prohibition against discrimination on grounds of age, to be applied directly and take precedence over national law in a dispute between private parties.[78]

Holdgaard, Elkan and Krohn Schaldemose have argued that both the decision of the CJEU as the judgment of the Danish Supreme Court are legally sound and understandable. However, what is regrettable, in the opinion of these authors, is that both courts failed in carrying out a judicial dialogue in the spirit of good faith: '(. . .) the preliminary reference procedure was used in a way that gradually built up tensions and ended in a clear clash'.[79]

[74] A. Torres Pérez, 'Melloni in Three Acts: From Dialogue to Monologue' *European Constitutional Law Review* (2014), 323.

[75] Case C-441/14, Dansk Industri (DI) v. Sucession Karsten Eigil Rasmussen [2016], ECLI:EU:C:2016:278.

[76] Para 33. [77] Para 34.

[78] Decision of the Danish Supreme Court of 6 December 2016, Case 15/2014. See www.supremecourt.dk/supremecourt/nyheder/pressemeddelelser/Documents/Judgment%2015-2014.pdf, accessed on 19 January 2019.

[79] R. Holdgaard, D. Elkan and G. Krohn Schaldemose, 'From Cooperation to Collision: The ECJ's *Ajos* Ruling and the Danish Supreme Court's Refusal to Comply' *Common Market Law Review*, 55, 17–54 (2018).

Although we do realize that this is just one example of non-compliance and that does not allow us to draw broader conclusions, it shows that it is not self-evident that supreme administrative courts will automatically comply with the judgments of the CJEU. Examples like the Ajos case make us realize that the CJEU could perhaps have avoided a clash with the other highest courts by engaging in a dialogue that makes it possible for referring courts to explain more in-depth why certain preliminary rulings will presents serious problems for the internal constitutional order of a member state.[80] In the Ajos case, this concerned a long-standing tradition with regard to the primacy of parliament. The Danish Supreme Court was reluctant to simply overrule the democratically elected legislature on the basis of an unwritten principle of law, developed by the CJEU in its case law, where at the time of the accession, the Danish legislature could never have foreseen that this would be a consequence of joining the Common Market. Actively engaging in a judicial dialogue with national courts is one of the few tools that the CJEU has at its disposal to convince national court to comply with its decisions even in politically and constitutionally sensitive cases.[81]

3.6 Conclusions

It takes two to tango and for a judicial dialogue to function. So much is clear from the case law analysis we presented above. From the side of the referring courts the way preliminary questions are being formulated can be more or less inviting for the CJEU to engage in a dialogue. Closed-questions to the Luxembourg court that force it into a yes or no answer might be used to pinpoint the CJEU on a certain issue, but the downside is that the leave very little room for a dialogue with the CJEU. The same holds true for compatibility questions that basically ask the CJEU to declare whether certain national rules, principles or decisions are complying with EU law. The preliminary reference procedure is not meant to answer these types of questions, but still national (highest) courts raise them on a regular basis as we have shown. Compatibility questions can be a way for national courts to avoid responsibility for painful decisions that can put the legislature in a difficult situation. In such a case, it can

80 A.M. Slaughter, 'A Typology of Transjudicial Communication' *University of Richmond Law Review*, 29, 99, 115 (1994).

81 See already G. Federico Mancini, 'The Making of a Constitution for Europe' *Common Market Law Review*, 26 595, 605–606 (1989), at 597.

be the easy way out for courts to ask the CJEU to declare 'a certain kind of national provisions' incompatible with EU law. In other situations, national courts simply want to facilitate the litigating parties in receiving a clear answer to their questions. In case the referring court is afraid that the CJEU may come up with a catalogue of criteria to answer whether a certain national legal construction is legitimate in light of EU law, it may seem attractive to formulate it as a compatibility questions and seduce Luxembourg to provide a solution.

A positive way to stimulate dialogue with the CJEU by the referring court could be to make use of the possibility to offer provisional answers to the questions being referred. This not only shows that national courts are prepared to think along with the CJEU about issues concerning the interpretation and validity of EU law, but it also informs the Court what possible consequences different answers to preliminary questions may have. Interestingly enough, though, our case law reveals that the CJEU almost never (explicitly) responds to the provisional answers given by the referring courts. Hence, these courts do not know whether going through the effort to inform the Court about what they believe should be the correct interpretation of EU law has any impact at all. The non-response by the CJEU could even be seen as a discouragement for national courts to position themselves as co-actor in the process of judicial law making since active courts that offer provisional answers are not treated differently from inactive courts that leave everything to the CJEU.

At the same time, we have seen that the CJEU is quite active when it comes to reformulating preliminary questions, often without a prior request for clarification to the referring court about whether the CJEU understands what the Luxembourg court meant to ask. Furthermore, there appears to be a correlation between closed questions and ready-made answers from the side of the CJEU and more open questions that result in decisions providing guidelines for the referring courts about how to decide the dispute that resulted in preliminary questions. Perhaps the most surprising is that the CJEU appears to be quite eager to answer compatibility questions with an answer that clearly indicates whether national law is in compliance with EU law, although the official position is still that compatibility questions are supposed to be for the national court to decide. Whether the CJEU does this to present itself as a citizen's court or as the arm of the law of national courts cannot be determined on the basis of a case law analysis. Nevertheless it does seem striking that, on the one hand, the CJEU almost seems to operate as an appellate court when it comes to preliminary questions that basically deal with matters of (in)compatibilities between national law and EU law, while, on the other hand, the Court seems to show little interest in what happens with preliminary rulings in the aftermath of its decision. Does the CJEU have blind faith in national courts when it comes to implementing preliminary rulings or is the Luxembourg court not really interested in whether national courts show loyalty in the process of applying preliminary rulings to national disputes?

4 Results from the Interviews

4.1 Introduction

After finishing our case law analysis, we interviewed two judges of ten supreme administrative courts covered by the case law study, as well as five judges and two advocates-general of the CJEU.[1] The interviews were meant to get information from judges and advocates-general about their personal experience with the "dialogue" between supreme administrative courts and the CJEU. In addition, we wanted to verify the outcomes of our case law analysis and to find out whether the concept of a judicial dialogue is viewed by judges as a fruitful concept in the course of the preliminary reference procedure. Does the concept accurately express the mutual responsibility and co-actorship between courts for the interpretation and application of EU law as proclaimed by the CJEU and do judges on both sides have the same take on this?

The interviews not only deepened our insights with regard to the style of communication between these courts, but also enabled us to ask questions about things that could not be taken from the literature or case law analysis, such as: how do judges feel about the formal and informal possibilities for information exchange and mutual cooperation regarding the interpretation of EU law before submitting a reference, during the proceedings in Luxembourg, and after the CJEU's ruling?

In order to avoid misunderstanding, we are certainly not only interested in theoretical debates about dialogue concepts, constitutional relationships between courts in a multilevel legal order, and questions of power, but also in the practicalities of the information exchange within

[1] We had one additional interview with a judge from the CJEU, but were not allowed to record it and decided to leave it aside. See the methodology paragraph hereafter.

the preliminary reference procedure, such as language barriers, exchange of case law between courts, research and documentation issues.

Finally, we want to learn how and where, if necessary, the communication between national supreme administrative courts and the CJEU might need (further) improvement. Hence, we also asked judges on both sides where improvements may be possible in the preliminary reference procedure.

4.2 Interview Methodology

4.2.1 Individual, Semi-Structured and In-Depth Interviews

The interviews we have done took the form of individual, semi-structured and in-depth conversations.[2] This technique allowed for flexibility and a conversational way of communication and it provided the possibility gather in-depth knowledge as to what drives judges to take certain decisions, e.g. why and when do national courts choose to give a provisional answer or adopt a particular style of communication with other courts? As Jaremba and Mak argue, qualitative interviews have the advantage that they enable participants to express themselves with far more nuance than would have been possible in for example an anonymous digital questionnaire. Using open interviews as a method also makes it possible to ask follow-up questions, which may help to better understand the obtained answers and allows exploring topics more in-depth.[3]

In order to prepare for the interviews, a list of open questions was designed based on the draft literature review and the case law analysis and sent in advance to the participating judges. The interviews usually took between an hour and a half and two hours. All judges of the supreme administrative courts gave their consent to record the interviews for internal purposes (e.g. to transcribe and code the interviews, verify our own notes and listen back certain parts of the conversation afterwards to see whether our memory regarding certain highlights of the interviews proved to be correct) after the guarantee from our part that interviewees would not be quoted in the final report. Unfortunately,

[2] S. Jones, '*Depth Interviewing*', in C. Seale (ed.), *Researching Society and Culture* (Thousand Oaks, CA: Sage Publications, 2003) pp. 257–260.

[3] U. Jaremba and E. Mak, 'Interviewing Judges in the Transnational Context', *Recht en Methode*, 5, 6 (2014), available at: www.bjutijdschriften.nl/tijdschrift/lawandmethod/2014/05/RENM-D-13-00002.pdf.

one judge of the CJEU did not agree with recording the interview. As a result, this interview was not involved in the research. Afterward transcription of the interviews took place and finally the interviews were hand-coded and analysed with the aim to find possible common patterns in the answers that were given to our questions.

4.2.2 *Selection of Interviewees*

Regarding the representativeness and reliability of the obtained information, it needs to be said that the selection of the interviewees took place within the body of the participating supreme administrative courts themselves. Assisted by a letter of introduction and recommendation from the Dutch presidency of ACA-Europe – the presidents of the supreme administrative courts had the opportunity to select judges from their court for the interview. Since the aim of the research project is to trace the way judges perceive their relationship with the CJEU, we asked for an opportunity to speak with judges who are particularly involved in EU-law and have experience with preliminary references. Of course, we acknowledge the fact that leaving the choice of who was going to be interviewed to the presidents of the national courts might influence the outcomes due to 'selection bias'.[4] It is, for example, rather unlikely that the presidents have selected judges who are critical towards their own court's style of judicial law making or who otherwise might express views that are not supported by president or the mainstream opinion in the court.[5] Moreover, one has to realize that we only spoke to two judges per court and that the interviews took place in English, which may have also limited the representativeness of the answers by our interviewees. For the CJEU, something similar applies. After president Lenaerts had promised us full cooperation, he asked the Dutch judge on the CJEU, Ms. Prechal to select the interviewees. She provided us with the names of the five judges and two advocates-general we have ultimately spoken to.

4.2.3 *Representativeness of the Data*

As already mentioned, interviews with a couple of members from each court cannot guarantee a fully representative picture of the view of

[4] S. Brinkmann, *Qualitative Interviewing* (New York: Oxford University Press, 2013), p. 57 ff.

[5] At the same time, this could also be a guarantee that we did speak with judges representing the mainstream view of their court.

courts as a whole.[6] In an interview with the Austrian court, one respondent even explicitly argued that if we had spoken to the younger generation of judges in that particular court, we might very well have received different answers to some of our questions. Still, the interviews show that both judges with a positive and a more critical view on the idea of a dialogue between national courts and the CJEU were represented. Furthermore, our main aim with the interviews has been to describe and analyse different possible perceptions concerning the idea of a judicial dialogue between the different courts. Hence, diversity was more important than representativeness. Important was to get a feeling about the different perspectives on the preliminary reference procedure and to learn about the possibilities and constraints for further improving the communication process between courts both horizontally (between national courts) and vertically (between the CJEU and national courts). The ACA-questionnaire that was sent by the organizing Dutch Council of State in preparation of the ACA-workshop in The Hague on 7 November 2016 offered an opportunity to compare the outcomes of our interviews with the results from the questionnaire that was distributed among the ACA members.[7]

4.2.4 *Openness of the Interviewees*

Although we were warned by fellow researchers that judges can be very difficult interview partners because they are used to 'speak' through their decisions and would not always like to talk about themselves or the institutions they are part of, we genuinely felt the interviews usually took place in an open atmosphere without much suspicion from either side. Not only did we learn a lot about the questions we raised, but quite

[6] We did compare the outcomes to our interviews with the 2016 ACA questionnaire on the preliminary reference procedure though, which was discussed at the ACA seminar on the preliminary ruling procedure on 7 November 2016 in The Hague, which we attended. Where there are important differences between our findings and the survey outcomes, we will notice these in (the footnotes to) this chapter. The same goes for important supplementary information not mentioned in our interviews. See for the ACA General report on the survey: www.aca-europe.eu/index.php/en/seminars/511-seminar-in-the-hague-on-7-november-2016. Hereafter we will refer to the report as: 'ACA General report 2016'.

[7] In a certain way, the ACA questionnaire shows similar limitations to our interviews because the questionnaires are answered collectively on behalf of separate supreme administrative courts and not individually by each and every judge sitting on the court. On the one hand, this guarantees that the answers represent the "official position" of the court(s). On the other hand, it makes it impossible to detect possible differences of opinion between individual judges in the court or between (some) judges and the court's management.

often, the interviewees also proved to be willing to share views and ideas we did not explicitly ask for, especially where it came to possible ways to improve the communication in the preliminary reference procedure. Only in a few cases, we felt that judges were perhaps not always willing or able to talk openly about some controversial issues.[8] Apart from that, language barriers sometimes made it somewhat difficult to have an entirely spontaneous conversation. In case the conversation in English proved to be burdensome, judges often offered to provide additional information in writing after the interviews in case we felt that might be valuable. In other words, we were positively surprised by the general willingness to cooperate.

4.2.5 *Data Analysis: Three Stages in the Procedure with Different (Sub)themes*

Different analytic strategies have emerged for interpreting our in-depth interviews. For the purpose of this research project, we have adopted a commonly used approach that relies on using codes for segments of text with similar content, which enabled us to systematically develop separate categories for arguments made throughout the interviews and distil them into major themes.[9]

First, we followed a chronological approach distinguishing between three different stages in the communication within the preliminary reference procedure:

1. The preparatory phase in which the reference is designed up to the submission of a preliminary question, where national courts can inform each other and the CJEU about whether similar legal problems with the explanation of EU law exist in other Member States and about what sort of consequences alternative preliminary rulings could have for the national legal orders.
2. Information exchange during the procedure before the CJEU, where the Court has certain procedural means to request

[8] Interesting is that the judges from the Danish Supreme Court did not mention the upcoming Ajos decision where the court rejected to follow a preliminary ruling from the CJEU even once, although this case clearly represents some of the tensions in the cooperation with the CJEU and it must have been on the minds of the judges when we spoke to them.

[9] See: J. Ritchie, L. Spencer and W. O'Connor, 'Carrying out Qualitative Analysis', in J. Ritchie and J. Lewis (eds.), *Qualitative Research Practice: A Guide for Social Science Students and Researchers* (London: SAGE Publications, 2003), pp. 219–262.

information from referring courts but can also amend preliminary questions.

3 Communication after a decision is taken by the CJEU. Continuation of the dialogue could, for example, happen when the referring court raises new similar questions in case it feels its original questions have not actually been answered (well) or when the CJEU takes the initiative to inform whether and how its preliminary ruling is being applied in the national practice.

Next, we coded the transcripts of the interviews looking for distinct (sub) themes and for discovering possible patterns in the answers.

4.2.5.1 Does the Reference Leave Room for Debate?

The first main theme we discovered for the preparatory phase (Ad 1), is the way in which the *style and structure of preliminary references offers room for 'debate' from the side of the CJEU*. Within this theme, we discern three subthemes. The first one is about whether a successful vertical dialogue with the CJEU does not presuppose coordination between highest administrative courts about the way in which preliminary questions are framed. The second subtheme concerns the use of provisional answers informing the CJEU and inviting it to respond. The third subtheme is about the relationship between references put forward by lower courts and references submitted by supreme administrative courts.

4.2.5.2 The Proceedings before the CJEU: Opening the Black Box?

For the communication during the procedure at the CJEU (Ad 2), the overarching theme is: *CJEU proceedings: black box or open book?* Based on the case law analysis, little can be said about the communication between the CJEU and national highest administrative courts during the proceedings in Luxembourg. During the coding of the interviews, however, again three themes came up. Firstly, the way in which requests by the CJEU for clarification of the reference could stimulate a dialogue with national highest courts. Secondly, whether there are other (informal) possibilities for information exchange to keep referring courts at least updated about the progress of the case at the CJEU. Thirdly, what the advantages and disadvantages could be of giving national court a formal role in the hearing by the CJEU.

4.2.5.3 Acceptance or Disobedience of Preliminary Rulings

Finally, we discussed the potential for dialogue after the CJEU has ruled (Ad 3). The general theme here is to what extent is there, apart from the decision itself, any: *formal or informal communication between CJEU and national highest courts to stimulate acceptance or disobedience of preliminary rulings*? A first subtheme here, concerns the style of argumentation by the CJEU and the extent to which the Court tries to convince referring courts by going into their arguments. Second, the supreme administrative court judges made critical remarks as to the autonomous approach of law making by the CJEU that sometimes provides national highest courts with hardly any margin of appreciation. Thirdly, we were interested in the way the supreme administrative courts communicate with the CJEU: do they have informal meetings where they can discuss problems with the CJEU and is there for example a communication channel for national courts to ask for follow-up questions in case the preliminary ruling is unclear? Fourth and finally, we discussed the way the CJEU monitors the follow-up of its preliminary decisions by the national courts.

4.3 The Preparatory Stage

From the case law analysis, we have already learned that highest national courts are not always very clear about why they sometimes deliberately refuse to send certain questions to the CJEU. Interviews with supreme court judges learned us very little about the reasons for (not) referring questions to Luxembourg, although for example both the Belgian and the UK judges as well as Dutch judge A argued that they believe the CILFIT criteria should not be interpreted too strictly, because if taken literally, the CJEU would be flooded with references.

As to the content of references, most judges seem to have a strong preference for closed questions to the CJEU, which often leave the Court little room for manoeuvre. The main reason for this, according to the interviews, is that the referring courts are interested in a specific answer to decide the case at hand and do not want to give too much room to the CJEU to deviate from the problem as they see it. Simultaneously, judges from the CJEU (as we will explain hereafter) stress the fact that highest administrative courts could probably produce better references that would enable the CJEU to provide more generalized answers that may satisfy not only the referring court, but also other courts that may have similar problems with EU law–related issues.

The latter presupposes that referring courts communicate with other (foreign) supreme administrative courts before submitting preliminary questions about the content of their questions in order to find out to what extent courts in other Member States can identify with the questions. In that sense, a 'horizontal dialogue' precedes an effective 'vertical dialogue' with the CJEU. This has important consequences for the style and structure of preliminary questions, which should then be formulated in a way that transcends, as much as possible, the specific national context and formulates the problem(s) with regard to the validity and/or interpretation of EU law in a more abstract way. This would probably also help the judges of the CJEU to better understand what the essence of the problem is and how it could affect different Member States.

Regarding the question whether horizontal communication between highest courts could result in coordinated action to avoid certain references, the interviews taught us there is only a minor chance the CJEU would notice this. As CJEU judge D asserted, the real test would be to trace all cases where a national judge for no good reason has not referred a case to Luxembourg. However, the CJEU does not monitor this and the European Commission is not actively monitoring this either. As both advocates-general on the CJEU argued, the CJEU lacks time to do so and the European Commission, in turn, seems to be reluctant to take action against deliberately non-referring national courts at least as long as there is no evident systematic pattern. Despite the lack of systematic research, there is, as advocate-general A said, a tacit acknowledgement that in a European Union of 24 languages, the likelihood that any national judge would be able to check whether the meaning of a term is equally clear in all the languages of the EU is quite unrealistic. Therefore, this advocate-general argued, we just know that actually the CILFIT criteria are not respected. However, the extent to which this is the case remains unclear.

4.3.1 *Dialogue with Other National Courts: No Vertical Dialogue without a Horizontal Dialogue?*

What would a horizontal dialogue between highest administrative courts look like? The bottom line seems to be that supreme administrative courts inform each other as soon as they intend to submit preliminary questions. It requires that national courts on a regular basis inform each other about their experiences with EU law in a certain area and about their own case law, including decision in which they did *not* decide to submit a request for a preliminary ruling.

4.3.1.1 Practicalities and Career Judges vs Parachuted Ones

Whether judges take the effort to look into in the case law of other (foreign) highest courts and inform themselves about the experiences of other supreme courts, depends largely on practical issues. A frequently heard complaint was that contacting other supreme courts and carrying out a comparative analysis is too time consuming.[10] To mention an example: both Polish judges told us that because of the enormous caseload they actually only have a three weeks period to draft preliminary questions. Such a short period would make it almost impossible to dive into the case law of other supreme courts.

However, there also appear to be different 'types' of supreme court judges with different views on preliminary references. On the one hand, there are judges (mostly typical career judges) who are mainly focused on dispute resolution and on clearing the backlog of cases.[11] On the other hand, there are judges with, for instance, an academic background that have not climbed the same career ladder to end up in the Supreme Court. They seem to feel more responsibility for the EU law making process embodied in the preliminary reference procedure and who see the need to engage with other highest courts in order to prepare references even in case there is little time to do so.[12] Actively communicating with other supreme courts is impossible, though, without a solid organisational (digital) infrastructure was one of the topics that frequently came up.

4.3.1.2 The Infrastructure and Language of the Horizontal Dialogue

That brings us to a second point: the complaint that there is no system to track down the case law of the other supreme courts in a fast and reliable manner. One of the instruments developed to support supreme administrative courts in the application and interpretation of European Union law and, if necessary, in referring a preliminary question to the CJEU is the ACA-Europe-forum and database. This system does not seem to work optimal in practice.[13] A recurring remark in the

[10] We heard this from Czech judge A, German judge A and both Polish judges.

[11] For example, Czech judge A, German judge A, both Polish judges and both Belgian judges.

[12] Czech judge B, German judge B, UK judge A and French judge B.

[13] The ACA General report 2016 under topic 1, question 4, mentions in particular four problems/needs for improvement: (1) need for more regular updates of information; (2) more flexibility; (3) greater ease of use and (4) improvement in the combined efforts of member institutions aimed at maintaining the Forum.

interviews is that one often has to wait too long before receiving an answer to a question that has been posted on the ACA-forum. Frequently, questions are only answered by a few (mostly the same) sister courts.[14] A further complaint is that it is unknown on whose desk the questions will land. In some supreme courts, questions are answered by a competent judge in the relevant field of law, whereas in others, the questions are dealt with by sometimes unexperienced law clerks. This raises questions as to the reliability of the information flow on the ACA-forum.[15]

Some judges add that language is also a problem.[16] It would be difficult to effectively communicate with other judges who are not fluent in English or French.[17] Given these obstacles, a large majority of the interviewees feel the ACA-forum does not function as it should. The same applies to the ACA-database, which should contain the references of all supreme (administrative) courts as well as the decisions in which these courts decided not to file a request for a preliminary ruling because the question would entail an acte clair or an acte éclairé.[18] The interviewees are worried about the reliability of the database since only a selection and often only a (translated) summary of the decisions of the referring courts are accessible via the database. According to some interviewees from Denmark, Germany and France, nobody really feels responsible for keeping the database up to date and the way in which the database is fuelled differs from court to court.[19]

4.3.1.3 Informal Judicial Networks

At the same time, we heard many judges say they feel the need to obtain information about the way foreign supreme administrative courts are

[14] We heard this from Czech judge A and both the German, Polish and French judges.

[15] That is what we very explicitly took from German judge A, German judge B and French judge B.

[16] This is confirmed and extended in het ACA General report 2016 under topic 1, question 5, where many rapporteurs mention that references to relevant foreign judgments are usually only made to decisions available in the languages known to the judges and their assistance. Consequently, ACA member refer predominantly to foreign case law in English, French and German. Moreover, lack of resources would often limit and extensive search for possible relevant foreign case law.

[17] Czech judge B, UK judge A, French judge B and both the Polish judges. We cannot agree more, since language sometimes also proved to be an obstacle during our interviews with some judges.

[18] French judge B the founding father of this database, told us so.

[19] Both the Danish judges, German judge B and French judge B.

dealing with certain questions of EU law.[20] That is why some judges developed their own mechanisms to exchange information. Informal networks of judges have, for example, been developed in certain areas of law. Czech judges A and German judge B, for example, told us they attend meetings of a network involved with migration law. Similarly, the German judge A participates in a network on environmental law and the French judge B, together with both Polish judges, takes part in a network on tax law. Simultaneously, both Belgian judges we interviewed seemed to be unaware of the existence of these informal networks.

Next to these specialized networks in certain fields of law, we were told that supreme and constitutional courts of some of the bigger countries within the EU: the German Constitutional Court, the French and Italian Council of State and the Supreme Court of the United Kingdom also get together on a biannual basis.[21] Moreover, there appears to be a network of Scandinavian Supreme Courts who meet regularly.[22] Finally, we noticed that some Supreme Court justices have a strong focus on the case law of certain (bigger) sister courts. The Austrian judges and the judges from the Czech Republic, for instance, indicated to focus quite heavily on the jurisprudence of the German Bundesverwaltungsgericht. These patterns of information exchange are partly ex post and partly ex ante, but they normally lack a question and answer system for ad hoc questions, although some judges admitted that these informal networks lowered the threshold for them to call or email individual colleagues in other Member States to acquire information.

The CJEU also has regular meetings with the General Court, the European Court of Human Rights (ECHR) and the Civil Service Tribunal. Moreover, the CJEU maintains frequent relationships with the US Supreme Court, occasionally with the Benelux Court of Justice, and with national judiciaries on a country-by-country (appointment) basis. What is interesting that the CJEU biannually meets with the German speaking constitutional courts and the ECHR in a so-called meeting of the six.[23] Finally, the CJEU also has the annual two-day Forum for members of the judiciary, which are geared in alternate years towards members of the lower echelons and the higher echelons of the judiciary. They include

[20] Czech judge B, UK judge A, German judge B, Dutch judge B, both French, Polish and Spanish judges.

[21] See UK judge A.

[22] We took that from the interview with the Danish judges

[23] ACA General report 2016, under topic 1, question 8.

attending a hearing and a briefing on the case being heard and a number of workshops.

4.3.1.4 Need for Hands-On Information Exchange and Learning

Several interviewees indicated they feel there is a need for a rapid task force or helpdesk to assist judges with finding reliable information about the case law, references, and experiences of other supreme courts. ACA could serve as a platform here, but it would need a more permanent structure with a larger supporting staff. A suggestion made by the French judges was that every supreme administrative court appoint one qualified person to provide input to the ACA-forum and ACA-database.

The Danish judges suggested building a central ACA research and documentation centre, although many other interviewees believed this would probably become too expensive.[24] Interesting is that a number of interviewees signalled that the general meetings of ACA-Europe, are too little 'hands on' to assist individual judges with real-life problems they have to deal with in daily practice. As an example, French judge B said about the ACA meetings: 'we all know how the preliminary reference procedure is working, we need something more specific'. Organizing workshops of judges in areas like asylum, environmental and tax law to discuss problems with regard to preliminary references and subsequent rulings by the CJEU would probably be more effective.[25] Those kind of networks might be facilitated by ACA-Europe, although, for example, not all supreme tax courts are members of ACA. Almost all judges acknowledged the importance of informal meetings where one could get to know each other during coffee or lunch in order to exchange views and lower the threshold to contact foreign colleagues in day-to-day working relations whenever the interpretation and validity of EU law might be at stake.

Regarding the horizontal dialogue between highest courts, there appears to be consensus among members of the CJEU that cross border information exchange is very important and may contribute to a better working preliminary reference procedure. This sense of importance has led to the establishment of a 'European Judicial Network'.[26] This network is designed to promote the exchange of information on

[24] Both Czech judges A and B, German judges A and B and French judges A and B.
[25] We heard this from for example Czech judge A, German judge B and French judge B.
[26] See www.ejn-crimjust.europa.eu/ejn/EJN_Home.aspx.

jurisprudence between the participating national courts and the CJEU. On a site with limited access, the participating national courts and the CJEU publish information on their jurisprudence concerning EU law, on questions, which the national courts referred to the CJEU for a preliminary ruling as well as on notes and studies. This network is managed by the CJEU. However, a true horizontal dialogue might also serve to improve the coordination of preliminary references. Especially in important pilot cases, it could be worthwhile to refer the question in its full extent to the CJEU. Therefore, it might be sensible to join cases coming from different (highest) courts all dealing with the same kind of issue. On the national level too, it is held to be important that preliminary references are being coordinated.[27]

4.3.2 *Providing Provisional Answers*

Our case law analysis in the previous chapter learned that some courts systematically provide the CJEU with provisional answers, or at least with arguments for alternative decisions, while other courts merely use the CJEU as a post-box where difficult questions regarding the interpretation and validity of EU law may be dropped. An obvious question, resulting from this is: why do some supreme administrative courts quite frequently take position towards the preferred outcome of the preliminary ruling, while other courts refuse to do so? What sort of criteria, if any, are applied and why?

4.3.2.1 Practical Reasons for Abstaining from Provisional Answers

An important explanation why some of the courts systematically refuse to offer provisional answers has to do with practical difficulties, such as: a high caseload and worries about delaying the procedure. In particular Czech judge A and both Polish judges argued that providing provisional answers is time consuming and conflicts with the expectations from the government that courts should decide without undue delay. As previously mentioned, we also discovered that judges have quite different views on the role of their court in developing the law. Some judges clearly lean towards a pragmatic decision-making model in which the dominant role of the court is to solve legal problems and 'get things done'.[28] These judges tend to see law making as a 'luxury good' their

[27] We took that from CJEU judge A and both advocates-general on the CJEU.
[28] Both judges A and B of the Belgian, Austrian, Spanish and Danish courts expressed this view.

court often cannot afford in practice. This may also have to do with how judges perceive the constitutional role of their court. French judge A, for example, argued that the Conseil d'Etat still predominantly presents its role as 'la bouche de la loi'. According to him, the court wants to avoid the impression the Council of State is creating new law as that would run against the principle of legal certainty.

4.3.2.2 Judicial Law Making Also a Role for National Courts

Other judges have a quite different view in which law making is an increasingly important part of the role of supreme courts in today's globalizing multi-level legal order (e.g. judge B in Germany and judge B in the Czech Republic).[29] These judges feel that interpreting and further developing EU law cannot and should not be left to supranational courts only. The difference between the role model of the 'judge referee' and the 'judge law maker' runs across national lines. Sometimes we even saw striking differences within one court. Perhaps these can partly be explained by the background of the judges. As we already indicated, those who have made a judicial career moving up the ladder from being a district court judge to finally ending up at the supreme court seem to be more pragmatic and result-oriented than, judges with, for example, an academic or policy background who were 'parachuted' into the supreme administrative court.

4.3.2.3 No Provisional Answers to Avoid Looking Biased

Another reason for deference towards the outcome of the preliminary reference procedure is that judges want to avoid being perceived as biased. Taking position with regard to the outcome of the preliminary ruling, could damage their appearance of impartiality, which might be harmful once the case returns to the national court. This argument was given by both judges from the Austrian, Danish, Spanish and Belgium court. French judges judge B acknowledged this risk, too, but felt that it could be avoided by describing different possible answers (or 'scenarios') to the CJEU, while describing the potential consequences for the national legal order(s). We also heard some judges saying that they refrain from giving provisional answers because they do not like 'to get it wrong'. The Czech judge B and the Spanish judges A and B were quite open about this and argued that, although most colleagues probably would not want to

[29] Like the both judges A and B of the British, the Polish and the Dutch courts do.

admit it, avoiding a position is also a matter of risk aversion. Some judges (both judges from the Belgian Council of State and the Danish Supreme Court and judge B of the Austrian Supreme Administrative Court) even viewed it as inappropriate to give a provisional answer because they felt the CJEU is better equipped to decide about the correct interpretation of EU law. Finally, Austrian judge A and Dutch judge B stated that they had once provided a provisional answer but were disappointed by the lack of responsiveness from the CJEU. This would make them hesitant to do it again.

4.3.2.4 How Does the CJEU See Provisional Answers?

How do the judges of the CJEU feel about this? One of the judges started by saying that providing a provisional answer is a possibility for the national courts, but it is not compulsory and it is not even recommended.[30] Another judge argued, though, that although not compulsory it is a strong recommendation to provide a provisional answer.[31] The origin of the provisional answers according to CJEU judge B is found in cases on security issues as a means to facilitate a decision of the CJEU within a short time period. It was certainly not meant as a tool to be used frequently outside the realm of this special kind of preliminary rulings procedures.[32] However, if a national court wants to provide a provisional answer it must feel free to do so.

Are the judges and the advocates-general on the CJEU pleased if a national court makes use of the possibility to come up with a provisional answer? Here we found roughly two different answers. On the one hand, there was a judge who seemed to be very sceptical about national judges providing provisional answers.[33] This judge explicitly asked the question: 'what's the advantage for us'? His answer: 'not very much'.[34] Others, are more enthusiastic. As one of them said, the advantage of a provisional answer is not that the CJEU cannot interpret EU-law itself but that it forces the referring judge to explain how he sees the interplay between EU-law and national law.[35] Another judge added that the national judge is better placed to understand and to outline the context and the circumstances of the case in relation to the national legal system.[36]

Both judges were of the opinion that national courts should be invited more actively to provide the CJEU with provisional answers.

[30] CJEU judge B. [31] CJEU judge D. [32] See CJEU judge B. [33] CJEU judge B.
[34] CJEU judge B. [35] CJEU judge D. [36] CJEU judge A.

Nevertheless, as one of the advocates-general argued,[37] it should not become mandatory because it also depends on the legal tradition of the Member State whether the national judge is entitled to provide a provisional answer. Therefore, as both advocates-general argued, the CJEU might recommend the national courts to use a standard form with boxes that need to be filled in with the name of the parties, the date, the question, factual background, legal background, what type of procedure you want (ordinary, emergent, accelerated, priority, etc.), with the possibility to share a provisional answer or opinion to the preliminary question. The majority of the CJEU judges we interviewed, seem to be against such a proposal because they feel it would frustrate national courts freedom if the Court would start to send standard forms to fill in, even without making this mandatory. These judges appreciate national courts to provide a provisional answer, but feel they should not be obliged to do so.

4.3.2.5 Non-Response by the CJEU

Meanwhile, one way of encouraging national courts to provide provisional answers could be to explicitly respond to these answers in the judgment by the CJEU. This would reward courts that have taken the effort to share their view on how the preliminary ruling should read. CJEU judges, however, have different takes on this. All of them argued that the fact that the Court does not explicitly respond to provisional answers does not imply that these answers do not play a role in the internal debate within the CJEU.[38] As one of the judges said,[39] the response to provisional answers should follow from the reasoning of the judgment. The fact that some judges of supreme administrative courts told us they do not come up with provisional answers because the CJEU does not explicitly respond to them, is according to one CJEU judge a kind of opportunism.[40] These judges would probably not be interested in giving their opinion at all. One reason why the CJEU does not explicitly address the provisional answers, we heard, is that it would bring the Court in the position of an appellate court that may go against the decision of referring courts. This would not fit the preliminary

[37] CJEU A-G A.

[38] The ACA General report 2016 under topic 2, question 16, mentions one rapporteur who claims that provisional answers by the referring court are frequently reflected the CJEU's reasoning.

[39] CJEU judge D. [40] CJEU judge A.

reference procedure, according to one judge.[41] Another reason, brought up by one of the advocates-general,[42] is that the CJEU would be in a 'catch 22 situation': if the Court feels the relationship with national courts is meant to be a partnership based on dialogue, it is quite likely that national judges would be rather upset if the CJEU told them publicly that they 'got it wrong'. Not responding to provisional answers could, at least to some degree, also have to do with a kind of politeness. Both advocates-general, however, indicated they also sometimes felt frustrated when the CJEU does not explicitly respond to their opinions.

4.3.3 *Risks Concerned with Leapfrogging*

The way national judicial systems are structured differs. In the UK, for example, there is a single supreme court, whereas France and Germany have multiple supreme (administrative) courts and regional courts are hierarchically integrated into one or more of these supreme courts. The preliminary reference procedure may disturb this sometimes-delicate national hierarchy because lower courts can directly address the CJEU in case of a dispute that also touches upon the validity or interpretation of EU law.

4.3.3.1 No Formal Procedures to Keep Lower Courts Aligned

For supreme administrative courts, the question may be how to keep the lower courts somehow aligned. Is there any coordination in the interpretation and application of EU law and how could one prevent that multiple lower courts too easily refer similar questions, with perhaps even different provisional answers to the CJEU?[43] Mak argues from her interviews with judges in the French supreme courts that informal mechanisms do exist in order to establish a coordination in relation to European norms.[44] Our interviews make clear that in countries with multiple supreme courts, there usually seem to be no formal coordination mechanisms concerning the application and interpretation of EU law and regarding the process of referring questions to the CJEU. At the same time, members of supreme administrative courts do seem to have informal contacts with judges from other supreme courts within their

[41] CJEU judge B. [42] CJEU A-G A.

[43] Concerning the French situation, Bell has argued that there is a sense of rivalry between the different French national supreme courts Bell, J., "Living with Five Supreme Courts" (2015) 21 (1) European Journal of Current Legal Issues.

[44] E. Mak, *Judicial Decision-Making in a Globalised World* (Oxford: Hart Publishing, 2013), pp. 90–94.

country (e.g. Council of State and Supreme Court in the Netherlands or the Conseil d'Etat and Conseil Constitutionnel in France).

4.3.3.2 Lower Courts Have the Right to Bypass Their Supreme Court

Another question concerns the relationship supreme administrative courts have with their lower courts.[45] Statistically, the latter have been responsible for a large majority of the preliminary questions in the past, although supreme courts have lately caught up with lower courts in this respect.[46] From the Rheinmühlen judgment, we learned that lower courts could refer preliminary questions to the CJEU even when the highest national court has already provided an interpretation over the same legal matter.[47] This raises questions about the impact this leapfrogging by lower courts might have on the relationship with their supreme courts and on the relationship between highest courts and the CJEU. We asked supreme court judges how they envisage their relationship with the lower courts and to what extent (informal) contact with them take place concerning the timing and substance of preliminary questions. It is difficult to draw far-reaching conclusions from what we heard in the interviews, especially now that we have not spoken to lower courts about the reasons for bypassing their supreme court.[48]

4.3.3.3 Informal Alignment in Spain

All this being said, we touched upon some striking things. In Spain, for example, a lot of this leapfrogging has taken place. A notorious example is the Azis case,[49] where a lower court successfully bypassed the Supreme Court and the national legislature with regard to the validity

[45] Although it is not an obligation, lower courts can refer a preliminary question concerning the interpretation of EU law. If the question concerns the validity of EU law though all national courts have the obligation to refer that question to the CJEU. Case C-314/85, *Foto-Frost v. Hauptzollambt Lübeck-Ost* [1987], ECLI:EU:C:1987:452.

[46] A. Dyevre, A. Atanasova, and M. Glavina, 'Who Asks Most? Institutional Incentives and Referral Activity in the European Union Legal Order' (August 25, 2017). Available at SSRN: https://ssrn.com/abstract=3051659 and http://dx.doi.org/10.2139/ssrn.3051659.

[47] Case C-166/73 *Rheinmühlen-Düsseldorf v Einfuhr- und Vorratsstelle für Getreide und Futtermittel* [1974], ECLI:EU:C:1974:3.

[48] The ACA General report 2016, under topic 1, question 2 mentions that Supreme Administrative Courts are, in general, hesitant to communicate with lower courts over preliminary references because consultations could undermine the autonomy and independence of judges and even affect the secrecy of deliberations.

[49] Case C-415/11, S Aziz v. Catalunyacaixa [2013], ECLI:EU:C:2013:164.

of certain terms in mortgage loan agreements in light of the unfair terms directive. Cases like these might explain why in Spain an EU law network of courts has been established. According to the Spanish judges, this network serves as a tool to safeguard the uniform interpretation and application of EU-law. This network consists of judges that are specialized in the field of EU law and is divided into different sections: civil law, criminal law and administrative law. As the Spanish judges told us, this network works quite well when it comes to the coordination of preliminary references.

Spanish judges can raise practical questions concerning preliminary references to each other and ask members of the supreme courts for advice. The judges emphasized the informal nature of the network. The answers to questions that have been raised are non-binding. However, the Spanish Supreme Court is part of this network and is able to answer questions that lower courts are dealing with in relation to EU law, which could be a practical way to avoid lower courts too easily approaching the CJEU regarding questions their own highest court could solve. At the same time, the CJEU seems to oppose every attempt from the side of national highest courts to prevent lower courts from bypassing them in case they disagree about the validity or correct interpretation of European legal rules. According to the CJEU judges, the national courts should have the widest discretion in referring matters to the Luxembourg court if they consider that a case pending before them raises questions involving interpretation, or consideration of the validity of EU law.[50]

4.3.3.4 Specialized Judicial Networks

In some other Member States, the supreme administrative court and the lower courts also inform each other about preliminary questions in order to streamline the flood of questions and prevent unnecessary references by lower courts.[51] Dutch judge A told us that in the field of asylum law, the Council of State has regular meetings with judges of the regional courts informing each other on questions of EU law.[52] In the

[50] CJEU judges A and D, as well as both CJEU A-G´s.

[51] The ACA General report 2016, under top 1, question 2, also mentions the involvement of judicial networks (within the Council of the Judiciary) that sometimes even seem to help individual courts with the drafting of preliminary questions. On national Supreme Administrative Court mentions the existence of a national database that contains all preliminary references in the field of administrative law.

[52] We took this from the interview with Dutch judge A.

Czech Republic, judges and law clerks of the Supreme Administrative Court and of the lower courts meet each other on a regular basis in seminars on various topics involving EU law organized by the judges themselves.[53] In other countries, though, there seems to be far less contact and coordination. German judge B for example complained he is not kept up to date about what other regional courts are doing. The reason would be that the bureau of the representative of the government, responsible for coordinating the information flow, is severely understaffed.

The French and UK judges indicated their situation is quite different from the one in most other Member States. As one of the UK judges stated:[54] '(. . .) lower courts in the UK are less willing to refer than lower courts on the continent (. . .)' and '(. . .) they are certainly entitled to, but usually they prefer to send it up through the system'. According to this judge: 'we are quite a coherent system, we are on very good terms with judges at all levels and although we are in form hierarchical, on a personal level we are not and we are also quite a small system'. In France too, there appears to be little fear for leapfrogging by lower courts. This mainly has to do with the centralistic French system. As one of the French judges told us, the lower courts first look to the jurisprudence of the Council of State and would not easily dare to disagree with that if they think the CJEU may have a different opinion.[55]

4.3.3.5 How Does the CJEU View Leapfrogging?

One CJEU judge[56] and both advocates-general stressed the importance of a coordination mechanism on the national level to monitor and streamline preliminary questions where possible. Simultaneously, they emphasized that coordination may never result in lower courts losing their freedom to refer a case to Luxembourg. Courts within one Member State may share best practices and exchange information but as soon as a lower court decides to bypass its own supreme court and refer the question to the CJEU, it should have full freedom to do so. One judge of the CJEU said the lower courts are increasingly using the preliminary rulings procedure as a means to circumvent their own supreme court.[57] To the question if this might not disrupt the national legal system this judge answered that the temptation of supreme courts in some Member States to try to control lower courts is simply wrong from a community

[53] We heard this from Czech judge A. [54] UK judge B. [55] French judge B.
[56] CJEU judge A. [57] CJEU judge B.

law perspective. Interestingly enough, though, one of the advocates-general stressed the importance of some coordination by supreme courts, for example, when it comes to the selection of good test cases to bring to the CJEU.[58] One CJEU judge explicitly referred to the Dutch practice of regular meetings between the Supreme Administrative Court's judges doing migration law and judges from lower courts or between the Supreme Court's judges doing tax law with their lower courts in order to align preliminary references.[59]

4.4 Dialogue during the Proceedings before the CJEU: Black Box or a Shared Responsibility?

In the academic literature, the stage between sending a preliminary question to the CJEU and the final decision by the Luxembourg court is often qualified as the 'black box'. During this stage, the case is out of the hands of the referring court. An obvious question for the interviews was of course: does no formal or informal communication take place during this period? In case there is no communication in practice, do both courts never feel the need to communicate with each other during this stage?

In case the CJEU would see the interpretation and application of EU law as a shared responsibility, one would expect the Court to engage in a conversation with the referring court when it is not perfectly clear during the proceedings what the national court meant to ask. This would probably also apply when other issues regarding the facts of the case or relevant particularities with respect to national law would come up. In the interviews, we wanted to learn, among other things, why the CJEU frequently chooses to reformulate questions without reaching out to the referring courts to clarify things.

Another possible way of information exchange between the referring court and the CJEU might consist of taking part in the proceedings before the CJEU. In the interviews, we have asked how judges on both sides feel about suggestions in the literature to give national courts a more active role during the hearings before the CJEU. In case a more active role of the referring courts during the oral hearings in Luxembourg is considered too far-reaching, would there be other ways to at least get informed about relevant facts of the case or about the national legal context? Do

[58] CJEU A-G B. [59] CJEU judge A.

national courts, for instance, communicate informally with their 'own' judge or advocate-general on the CJEU during a preliminary reference procedure or is there any other contact with the representative of their own government defending the case before the CJEU?

4.4.1 *Requests for Clarification*[60]

In the case law, we have not found a single case where the CJEU has explicitly mentioned in its decision to have applied article 101(1) of the Rules of procedure of the CJEU in order to request the referring court to clarify its preliminary question or to provide additional information about other aspects of the case. That such 'requests for clarification' are rarely mentioned in the case law, does not necessarily provide evidence for the fact that the CJEU has not used the instrument.[61] However, one would expect some traces of such requests in case the CJEU wanted to signal the sort of information it values from referring courts in order to moderate the decision making process.

The interviews confirmed the CJEU rarely makes use of its power to issue a request for clarification from the referring court. The judges of the supreme administrative courts we interviewed told us they have never experienced the CJEU filing a request for clarification. With regard to the reasons for this non-use of article 101 of the Rules of Procedure, interviewees claimed this probably has to do with negative experiences in the past. An example that was given by an advocate-general concerned the fact that in a Greek case, the CJEU asked the referring court to explain why it had submitted these preliminary questions.[62] After the CJEU had waited for three months, the CJEU received a very short answer of the Greek court. As this advocate-general stated:

60 Interesting is that the ACA General report 2016 mentions under topic 2, question 10, that a small majority of the participating courts in the survey claim they do not see the need to have other forms of communication with the CJEU outside the preliminary reference procedure. However, several courts argue that the CJEU could make better use of the instrument of a request for clarification of article 101 of the Rules of procedure of the Court.

61 The ACA General report 2016, under topic 2, question 19 mentions that between 1 January 2009 and 30 October 2012, 21 requests for clarification have been made and between 1 November 2012 and 30 April 2016, 35 request for clarification would have been made. The question is of course how 'rare' does these numbers make the request for clarification. What is more important, though, is that several rapporteurs mention that the CJEU could make more frequent use of it and/or simplify the procedure for requesting clarifications.

62 CJEU A-G A.

> The national court said, thank you for your question. In order to answer it, we would need to reopen the proceedings and hear the parties. We do not want to do that and we are not going to do it. Please get on with the reference.

In other words, the CJEU got nowhere and lost three months. Against this backdrop, it does not come as a surprise that the CJEU will not easily decide to go down the same path again. Simultaneously, one may wonder how convincing it actually is that the CJEU relies its use of an official request for clarification on one (or even a few) bad experience(s). Applying article 101 of the Rules of Procedure may indeed be time consuming – although that also depends on the period the CJEU leaves the national courts to respond[63] – and on how national procedural laws deal with such requests. It is certainly not impossible that the CJEU could have send signals to the national legislators in case the latter would obstruct a quick and efficient information exchange with the Court.[64] However, this presupposes a more frequent and longer lasting experience with this instrument before dismissing it.

One may also not forget that applying requests for clarification could prevent the CJEU from answering preliminary questions that were not meant to be raised or reformulating such questions in a way that make them unrecognizable and useless for the referring court. Nevertheless, as one of the judges of the Dutch Council of State argued, requests for clarification might also withhold the CJEU the opportunity to unilaterally reformulate the preliminary questions, thereby losing the chance to answer the questions the CJEU itself likes to answer or which it sees as the most important ones it should be able to answer.[65] Although it sounds somewhat paradoxical, using requests for clarification in a systematic way in order to find out what the referring court actually wants to learn in a way limits the CJEU's power to reformulate preliminary questions in a way it finds the most appealing. After all, by reserving the power to reformulate preliminary questions, the CJEU also takes some control over the answers to these questions. From a strategic perspective, this might be attractive.

[63] Article 101 enables the CJEU to give the referring court or tribunal a time limit to answer to a request for clarification.

[64] In the ACA General report 2016, the CJEU emphasizes that the instrument of the request for clarification should not be used as a stopgap for orders of references that do not meet the basic criteria of Article 94 of the Court's rules of procedure.

[65] Dutch judge A.

4.4.1.1 Do National Courts Feel the Need to Be Consulted Before Their Questions Are Reformulated?

An important question remains, of course, how the referring courts envisage the possible use of article 101 of the Rules of Procedure by the CJEU. For example, do they actually feel the need to be consulted in case their questions are reformulated by the CJEU? What is interesting is that quite a number of judges indicate that the CJEU frequently reformulates preliminary questions, for instance, by way of saying that 'the referring court is asking in essence'.[66] Some of them added they have experienced that by rephrasing the question the CJEU sometimes lost essential elements from the original question.[67] One of the French judges pointed out a case in which the CJEU did not answer the question that it was explicitly asked to address by the French Conseil d'État.[68] A member of the UK Supreme Court very critically asserted that they have had difficulty with the CJEU reformulating questions, which it does and thereby sometimes completely failing to answer the critical question.[69]

Against this background, some of the interviewed judges indicated they sometimes felt the need to be consulted by the CJEU before the latter starts reformulating the preliminary question.[70] Even some judges, who claimed to never have had the experience that by reformulating their question the CJEU changed the direction of the decision, argue that the CJEU should consult the referring court as soon as it feels the need to reformulate the question. One of the German judges said that for psychological reasons alone a consultation of the referring court in these situations is to be welcomed.[71] According to this judge, the referring courts may from time to time get the impression that in the eyes of the CJEU they are too silly to formulate a good preliminary question, whereas a request for clarification would express the vulnerability of the CJEU in fully understanding the question in its legal and factual context.

Most judges agreed that a consultation of the referring court is needed in case the CJEU intends to reformulate the preliminary question in a way that could possibly result in losing essential elements of the original

[66] Like Czech judges A and B, UK judge B, French judge A, Dutch judge B, both Spanish and Polish judges.

[67] UK judge B, French judge A, Dutch judge B and both Polish judges.

[68] French judge A.

[69] UK judge B. See also Czech judge B and Dutch judge B.

[70] See Czech judge B, German judge B, Dutch judge B, UK judge A and French judge B.

[71] German judge B.

question. One judge added that a consultation of the referring court is also needed in case the CJEU decides not to answer the question.[72] From a Czech,[73] a Dutch[74] and a French judge,[75] we have heard that questions about the relevance of the preliminary question as well as about the factual and legal context of this question should not be answered by the CJEU without consulting the referring judge. Another Dutch judge agreed on this point,[76] but added that the referring judges have less reason to deviate from the preliminary decision of the CJEU if the latter has consulted the referring court beforehand about the actual meaning of the preliminary question. In the opinion of this judge, courts would usually feel less constrained to deviate from the preliminary rulings of the CJEU in case the answers are unclear or the CJEU gives an answer to a question that was not raised or had a different meaning for the referring court.

4.4.1.2 Informal Requests to Clarify Questions without Hearing Litigants

Most interviewees in favour of requests for clarification from the CJEU before amending preliminary questions wished to keep the consultation of the referring court by the CJEU rather informal.[77] As one of the French judges said, the consultation needs to be a light, informal and transparent instrument.[78] A Dutch judge argued that consultations by the CJEU should be dealt with in a quite pragmatic way, but added to have no idea how other courts would see this.[79] An interesting question that came up during the interviews is whether the referring court indeed needs to hear the parties when being consulted by the CJEU. From some interviews, we got the impression that even in the stage of formulating the preliminary question the supreme administrative courts seldom give the parties the opportunity to respond to the intention to submit a reference and to the actual formulation of the preliminary question.

[72] Czech judge A. [73] Czech judge A. [74] Dutch judge B.
[75] French judge B. [76] Dutch judge A.
[77] The ACA general report 2016, under topic 2, question 10 mentions that national courts for example have quite different views of and experience with an exchange of letter with the (registry of the) CJEU. One rapporteur is against the use of letters because letter from the CJEU would not be public and non-binding. Another rapporteur mentions his court did send letters to the CJEU but never received answers and a third rapporteur sees a role for exchanging letters between the filing of a preliminary question and before the Court has handed down its ruling, for instance, to discuss the refining or reformulation of questions.
[78] French judge A. [79] Dutch judge B.

In case the decision to raise preliminary questions and to determine the content of the questions is viewed as the prerogative of the referring courts, it is hard to see why the latter should automatically give litigants the opportunity to respond to a request for clarification by the CJEU. After all, the litigating parties will also have the opportunity to share their view on the case at hand during the oral hearing in Luxembourg.

4.4.1.3 How Does the CJEU Feel about Requests for Clarification?

As regards the reformulation of preliminary questions, one of the CJEU judges was very outspoken: in the vast majority of the cases, the reformulation of the preliminary question by the CJEU is a means to save the question.[80] According to this judge in at least 90 per cent of the cases the reformulated question is better that the initial one. However, even if this percentage would be correct, the question remains whether it might not be sensible to ask the referring court for clarification in cases where the CJEU has the impression that the question is not precise enough or badly drawn.

Three CJEU judges and one advocate-general seem to be very sceptical about launching a formal request for clarification.[81] They point at the procedural complications when the referring court is asked for a clarification. In some legal systems, the referring court needs to reopen the case and provide the parties with the opportunity to respond. Either way launching and answering the request for clarification takes some serious time – about four or five months. These sceptics remind us that the CJEU tried the request for clarification once, but the result was according to one of the advocates-general disappointing: the referring judge refused to take action and persevered with the original preliminary question.[82]

One of the advocates-general added that a request for clarification may foreshadow what the CJEU is going to answer.[83] For that reason, it would not be appropriate to say to the national court: 'what we think what you are asking us is this', if that may already reveal to the national court in what direction the answer will go. Another advocate-general, however, was less sceptical and saw the request for clarification as an instrument that deserves to be used more frequently.[84] Interestingly, this interviewee claimed it would be preferable if the advocate-general instead of

[80] CJEU judge A. [81] CJEU judges A, B, D and E as well as CJEU A-G A.
[82] CJEU A-G A. [83] CJEU A-G A. [84] CJEU A-G B.

the CJEU uses the power to issue requests for clarification. The advantage would be that it could clear-up things already earlier in the procedure and hence save time. The reason why this advocate-general would like to have the opportunity request for clarification is to get more information about the national legal context of the preliminary question rather than to discuss a possible reformulation of the preliminary question.

4.4.2 *Keeping the Referring Courts Updated about the Proceedings in Luxembourg*

The time between submitting a reference until the preliminary ruling of the CJEU is usually characterized as the 'black box'. Our interviews with judges from the supreme administrative courts confirmed this metaphor and indicate that from the moment they submit a request for a preliminary ruling, the case is out of their hands and that there is no further contact with the CJEU.[85] As both Danish judges said, the referring court is only informed about the upcoming decision of the CJEU in the case that was referring just before the Court decides the case.

We asked judges whether this radio silence is problematic. On this point, the answers varied. We can say, though, the picture for all referring courts as to the period of silence is roughly the same: after having sent the question to Luxembourg the file of that case ends up in a drawer and it will not come out until the CJEU gives its decision. In the meantime, other cases require the attention of the national courts. Several of the interviewees indicated they would like to somehow be kept updated about the proceedings in Luxembourg by the CJEU.[86] According to them, the CJEU fails to do this. An alternate route for the referring courts of getting information about 'their Luxembourg case' is by contacting their 'own' judge or advocate-general on the CJEU or by getting in touch with the representative of the government who participates in the CJEU hearing. We wanted to know: does this happen?

[85] The ACA General report 2016 under topic 2, question 13 does mention that a number of rapporteurs state that the practice of the CJEU of transmitting the written observations of the Member States and institutions to the national (referring) court is perceived as very useful. Two rapporteurs mention that it would be desirable if the referring court could respond to this in particular when it feels the facts of the case or the national legislation is presented in another way as in the preliminary reference. They add that the parties should be notified about this. Some rapporteurs feel it would also be helpful if the CJEU could send a transcript of the hearing to the national court.

[86] See for example Czech judges A and B, German judge B, UK judge B, French judge B and Dutch judge B.

4.4.2.1 Informal Contacts between Referring Courts, CJEU Judges and AGs?

What we took from the interviews is that informal contacts between judges from the referring court and CJEU judges or advocates-general rarely take place and do not concern information on the case that has been referred by the respective administrative court. Only both British judges confirmed to have informal contacts from time to time with an advocate-general. They immediately added, though, that this person has only been contacted if the UK Supreme Court was not sure whether to make a reference or if it had heard about a reference in another case in order to find out: is it worthwhile also referring a question or should we just wait for the decision in the pending case? Regarding the relationship with the representative of the government, all judges of the supreme administrative courts were very outspoken: the courts have no contact with the representative of their government concerning the individual case during the proceedings. As French judge B and both Danish judges asserted: the government has a different constitutional role to play and takes a different position in the proceedings before the CJEU, which makes it difficult to engage with this representative into a dialogue. Only one of the Czech judges confirmed that he is from time to time in informal contact with the representative of the government,[87] although he admits that it conflicts to a certain extent with the impartial role the court is supposed to play.[88]

4.4.2.2 Other Means to Be Kept Informed

A number of interviewees have mentioned the limited supply of information to the referring courts about the proceedings before the CJEU and some made suggestions for improvement. One of the most obvious things is that referring courts want to stay up to date about the case they referred. One could, for example, think of a digital track and trace system that shows the progress of a case before the CJEU.

Interesting is the suggestion of Czech judge B, who indicated to have a problem with the CJEU in the sense that it publishes far less information

[87] This corresponds with the answers to the ACA 2016 survey on the preliminary reference procedure. See the General Report under topic 1, question 1, where it is mentioned that one court mentions annual meetings with the representatives of the government, who 'are always available for individual consultations and it is possible to address a specific question to them if necessary.'

[88] Czech judge A.

about the proceedings than for instance the US Supreme Court. He wondered why the CJEU does not publish the opinions of the intervening Member States online. He also questioned why the transcripts of the oral hearings are not available, like in the United States. This judge believed it would be useful to have these documents, not only to understand why the CJEU has taken a certain decision in a particular case, but more generally to get a better insight in the decision-making process of the CJEU. The most obvious reason why the CJEU does not provide the texts of the interventions and the transcripts of the hearings might have to do with the quantity of the cases and the related translation problem. According to this Czech judge, these are not convincing arguments for not releasing these documents. It would still be better to have those sources only in English or French, instead of having no documents at all.

4.4.3 *Referring Courts Playing a More Active Role in the Proceedings and Oral Hearings before the CJEU?*

Some interviewees go even further in finding ways to get better informed about the proceedings before the CJEU. They argued, for example, that the referring court should be given an active position during the proceedings before the CJEU. What this more active role should look like is still a matter for debate. None of our interviewees believes that referring courts should have a role as a party in the proceedings before the CJEU. This would not match with the neutral position the referring court is supposed to take.

The Polish judges and their Czech colleagues argued, as one of them (Czech judge B) said, 'we should not be a party but we would like to react to what is happening in the proceedings'. They want to have the opportunity to respond to what litigating parties have brought up in relation to national law because they see it as their exclusive role to interpret national law. Both Polish judges would also like to have the opportunity to respond to the opinion of the advocate-general in case the (legal or factual context of the) preliminary question is misunderstood. An interesting idea was launched by the German judge B. As it is very important for the CJEU to be well informed about the consequences its decision might have for the law in every Member State, the question is whether this can be left solely to the intervening governments. Governments have political interests. Moreover, when it comes to questions such as: do you have any similar cases in your country or what would be the legal consequences of different kinds of decisions, these would be best answered by national supreme courts, according to this judge. That is why he proposes that the supreme courts should be giving the opportunity to inform the CJEU on the consequences that a decision in a particular case might have for the national legal system. This should not only be the case when the reference was made by the supreme court itself, but also when it came from a lower court and perhaps even when it came from a foreign court. This kind of information on the factual and legal context of the preliminary question could be provided either written or verbally.[89]

Most judges do not see a role for the referring court during the oral hearings before the CJEU in Luxembourg.[90] It would not only be confusing to the parties, but also very costly and time consuming. The Czech and Polish judges, however, do feel the need to attend the oral hearings and have the opportunity to participate in the debate. As far as time and financial burdens are concerned, the Polish judges suggested video conferencing instead of traveling to Luxembourg to attend the oral hearing.

The Luxembourg judges and advocates-general were very outspoken as it comes to referring judges participating in the hearings before the CJEU. They rejected this idea for the reason that they do not see what these national judges should defend before the CJEU and what it would add to the already existing way of providing the CJEU with information via the reference for a preliminary ruling.[91] One judge indicated, though, that if the parties to the proceedings before the CJEU disagree on the interpretation of national law, the CJEU is quite powerless.[92] In that case, it might be helpful to ask the national court about the interpretation of national law. Moreover, CJEU judges want to be kept informed whether, for example, a case that is referred is not withdrawn by one of the parties, because it could mean that the preliminary question would have become a hypothetical one. In the ACA survey, the CJEU rapporteur emphasizes that the CJEU should be informed at the earliest possible

[89] The ACA general report 2016 mentions under topic 2, question 14, that 'the involvement of the national court that a considerable number of rapporteurs perceive as beneficial (and not inappropriate), relates mostly to the clarification of the aim and purpose of the referred question, the intentions of the national court, the specific points of national law and the facts of the case'.

[90] The ACA General report under topic 2, question 14 mentions several reasons, most notably that is would create tensions to the independent and impartial role of the referring court towards the litigating parties, personalize the debate, and disrupt the already delicate institutional balance.

[91] For example, both CJEU A-G´s and CJEU D and E.

[92] CJEU judge D.

convenience about these kinds of things because it could affect pending cases before the Court. At the same time, the CJEU rapporteur stresses that the Court cannot continue to answer the preliminary question in such a case even if this could be helpful for a large number of other pending cases in the Member States.[93] Why is it so important to inform the CJEU about the relevance of preliminary questions for other courts in situations where a (referred) case is no longer pending before the national court, in case the CJEU cannot answer hypothetical questions anyway? Is the only reason to inform the Court in such circumstances that it can drop the case as soon as possible?

4.5 The Preliminary Decision and Its Follow-Up: Acceptance or Disobedience?

When the CJEU has spoken, it is up to the referring court to implement the preliminary decision in the case pending before it. In order for the CJEU to be able to count on an effective implementation of its decision in the national legal orders of the Member States, it is important that the decision may count on support from the national courts. However, do the preliminary decisions of the CJEU indeed find broad acceptance among the supreme administrative courts and to what extent does the CJEU actually know about the follow-up of their decisions? Based on the interviews we can distinguish between four different issues in relation to this final stage of the preliminary reference procedure.

Firstly, there are complaints among the supreme administrative court judges about the style of reasoning and the relating lack of responsiveness of the CJEU. Secondly, the supreme administrative court judges made critical remarks as to the methodology underlying the decisions of the CJEU. Thirdly, we were interested in the way the supreme administrative courts communicate with the CJEU: do they have informal meetings to discuss the outcomes of a preliminary ruling with the CJEU? Is there, for example, a possibility to ask for clarification in case the preliminary decision contains some ambiguities? Fourth and finally,

[93] ACA General report 2016, topic 2, question 20. It is striking that here, the CJEU rapporteur underlines that the Court needs to be informed at the earliest possible convenience but that in case national courts send letters to the Court to inform it on urgent matter, the register of the Court sometimes does not even respond that is has received such letters because they do not fit the format of the preliminary reference procedure.

we discussed the way the CJEU monitors the follow-up of its preliminary decisions; what does the CJEU actually know about the implementation of its preliminary answers?

4.5.1 *Useful Answers but Badly Motivated*

According to most supreme court judges, the CJEU is doing quite a good job and its decisions are normally useful to help resolving the dispute before the referring court. At the same time, based on their own experience, several interviewees pointed to decisions from the CJEU that have not been sufficiently tailored to the legal problem at hand. Sometimes the Court would even have overlooked the consequences its ruling could have for the national legal orders.[94]

A shared point of criticism among most supreme administrative court judges is that the CJEU's decisions could be better motivated. Many interviewees expressed their dissatisfaction with the style of reasoning by the CJEU, which would be quite apodictic and unpredictable.[95] One of the UK Supreme Court judges argued the CJEU sometimes behaves like a Delphic oracle, which requires you to read between the lines to ascertain or to guess the significance of what it says.[96] In addition, some judges view the way the CJEU motivates its judgements as concealing.[97] The CJEU would often make it look like decisions almost automatically follow from the applicable EU law and from its earlier case law, while this would actually not be true. In such cases, the CJEU would hide the element of judicial creativity in deciding on way or the other.[98] In this regard, the Polish judges even called the decisions of the CJEU a form of 'patchwork'. Every single case forms a composition consisting of earlier case law of the Court, but often without a compelling storyline that would logically end-up in the final decision. Some interviewees complained about the lack of openness about the arguments that led the CJEU to its decision. This would make it difficult to test the validity and truth-value of the underlying assumptions.[99] The fact that the CJEU almost never explicitly comes back from its earlier case law does,

[94] For example, both French judges A and B, German judge B, UK judges A and B and Dutch judge A.

[95] For example, German judge B, Czech judge B, Dutch judge A, French judge B and both the Polish and the UK judges

[96] UK judge B.

[97] Both UK judges and Czech judge B as well as the German judge B.

[98] Very explicitly about this: Czech judge B and UK judge B.

[99] Czech judge B who speaks of falsifiability

according to one of the judges, also provide an example of this concealed style of reasoning.[100]

Some even go further by claiming that style of reasoning adapted by the CJEU sometimes lacks frankness.[101] One example mentioned in this respect was the Berlusconi case in which the CJEU applied the principle of lex mitior, which it claims to form part of the constitutional traditions of the Member States, whereas it does not even exist in common law jurisdictions. How could it then ever be part of the constitutional tradition of the Member States? This incorrectness would also have been pointed out in the conclusion of advocate-general Kokott, but the CJEU would nevertheless have maintained its claim. Another element concerning the motivation of the CJEU's decisions has to do with the lack of responsiveness. As mentioned earlier, the CJEU almost never explicitly responds to provisional answers provided by the referring courts and quite rarely refers to domestic case law. Even both advocates-general said to sometimes have difficulties with the CJEU completely ignoring their written opinions without in any way explaining why the advocate-general's arguments would be irrelevant.

4.5.1.1 What Explains the Lack of Discursiveness?

What might be the explanation for this style of reasoning of the CJEU? The administrative court judges had their own explanation for that. We heard three main reasons for the lack of discursiveness.

First, the CJEU would always be aware of the fact that their judgments will apply in all 28 Member States and thus in a great variety of legal systems. Therefore, a certain amount of vagueness and veiled argumentation would sometime be attractive in order to avoid unnecessary legal problems for one or more of the national courts.[102] Secondly, at least in hard cases, the CJEU consists of 15 judges with very different legal backgrounds raised in different judicial cultures.[103] The collegial decision-making at the CJEU and the absence of dissenting and concurring opinions urges them to find a compromise that forces the CJEU towards a particular style and format of reasoning. A third, more practical explanation – and we heard that quite often – is that the CJEU has a longstanding francophone tradition of judicial law

[100] The German judge B mentions the Dublin-3 case as an example
[101] UK judge A. [102] That is what for example Czech judge A said.
[103] We heard that from for example Dutch judge B.

making.[104] The French official language of the Court, which would sometimes be difficult to master for new (young) judges and the dominance of French speaking clerks and supporting staff would result in a very sober style of judicial reasoning. During the interviews, we often heard that judicial dialogue has to do with openness, frankness and responsiveness in the motivation of the decisions of the CJEU. The sobriety in the style of reasoning seems to be a major issue among the supreme administrative court judges. As one judge claimed, the CJEU will not carry the judiciaries of Europe with it unless it maintains and improves the quality of reasoning.[105]

What we took from the Luxembourg interviews is that most judges and advocates-general share the opinion that the style of reasoning of the CJEU is quite minimalistic.[106] Some say this is a matter of efficiency reflecting the enormous caseload of the CJEU,[107] while others claim it goes back to the same reason the CJEU does not explicitly respond to the opinions of advocates-general.[108] The Court would not want to be impolite.[109] What has also been mentioned is that reaching consensus, especially in grand chamber cases, is sometimes difficult enough in itself and would not succeed without a certain amount of 'deliberate ambiguity'.[110] One advocate-general said that the style of reasoning of the CJEU is a self-referential system, although there would be a tendency towards more principled answers lately.[111] Moreover, only a limited number of judges on the CJEU would have actually had experience of being a national trial court judge.

Even though CJEU judges seem to recognize and share some of the criticism of the national judges with regard to the style of reasoning, it does not seem to cause a sense of urgency on their side, also to get more grip on the follow-up of preliminary rulings.

4.5.2 *Autonomous Method of Law Making: Shifting from a Bottom-Up to a Top-Down Approach?*

One of the things that came up during the interviews is that some of the judges claim the CJEU's methodology of judicial law making has gradually shifted from a bottom-up approach built on the legal traditions of

[104] We heard that from for example both the UK judges, the Czech judge B and the German judge B.
[105] UK judge B.
[106] CJEU judges A and B and both advocates-general.
[107] CJEU judge B and CJEU A-G B.
[108] CJEU judge A and CJEU A-G A.
[109] Very outspoken on this was CJEU A-G A.
[110] CJEU A-G A.
[111] Also CJEU A-G A.

the Member States to a more autonomous top-down approach. Typical for the latter approach is that the Court derives its main arguments from the treaties and from its own previous case law.

UK judge B argued there could be no doubt the CJEU's law making approach has become more autonomous. According to him, there appear to be fewer references to principles of national law. The other UK judge A argued that the teleological style of interpretation of the CJEU is an expression of this more autonomous way of law making. CJEU judges would look at what they regard as overarching objectives and give a directive a meaning, which will better achieve the Treaty objectives, rather than reflecting the compromise that was actually reached in the Council. This judge felt that the more CJEU judges do this, the more the idea of acte clair becomes unworkable. Some judges from Denmark, France, the Czech Republic and the Netherlands seemed to recognize this.[112]

There may very well be an explanation for this approach of the Court. The introduction of the Charter of Fundamental Rights may, for example, contributed to a more top down method of law making in human rights cases. One UK judge warned that if the CJEU choses to base its decisions on treaty provisions or on the Charter of fundamental rights, this would make them virtually immune for legislative override.[113] One of the French judges explicitly stated that in his opinion, the CJEU has in VAT-cases gone too far by basing its decisions directly on the Treaty. According to UK judge B, all this may form an explanation for the pushback of the German Constitutional Court, saying 'CJEU you must recognize that there are some lengths to your jurisdiction'.

4.5.2.1 A Margin of Appreciation?

Another side effect of a more autonomous approach by the CJEU is that it bears the risk that the process of EU law making is slowly drifting away from the law in the Member States. German judge B even seemed to argue that the CJEU has sometimes lost a little bit the contact with what happens on the ground. UK judge A added that it would be helpful if the CJEU was more sensitive to domestic political and constitutional implications that may be affected by the way the CJEU decides cases.

One of the things that came out of the interviews is that the CJEU lacks a margin of appreciation doctrine like the one the ECHR has. Czech judge

[112] Both Danish judges, French judge B, Czech judge B and Dutch judge A.
[113] UK judge B.

B argued he has tried to convince the CJEU in one of his references to leave some margin of appreciation for the national government and for national institutions, including national courts However, the CJEU did not go along with this proposal. UK judge B also asserted that the judicial law making by the CJEU is often too isolated and remote from the national legal systems. One explanation for this would be that national courts are generally staffed with career judges who have worked in the system for quite some time and who know how the system works, whereas you tend to get a much higher proportion of lateral-entry judges (e.g. academics, high-ranking government officials, state councillors, etc.) in the CJEU.

A suggestion by this judge was to select CJEU judges on merit instead of on nationality. As an example, he pointed at the doubling in size of the General court. The original proposal was to select an additional nine judges from across Europe, which would have been selected purely on merit, but this was voted down by the smaller countries who said they would not be able to supply judges that could compete with judges from larger Member States purely on merit. This judge wondered whether it might not have been a good idea to work with a selection process that is closer to the system in Strasbourg, where you sometimes have an ad hoc judge from a Member State sitting on the ECHR.

4.5.3 *The Follow-Up of the Preliminary Decisions*

After the CJEU has delivered its preliminary decision, it is up to the referring court to implement the Court's answer. The premise is that the referring national courts will simply follow the CJEU's ruling.[114] In the vast majority of cases, this is probably how it goes. Sometimes, though, national courts do not comply with a preliminary ruling. A striking example is the aforementioned Ajos case of the Danish Supreme Court. This was of course a high-profile case. What we do not know is how often preliminary rulings are implicitly watered-down by the referring court in practice because national courts often do not send their final decisions to Luxembourg, as we were told.

[114] The ACA General report 2016 under topic 2, question 16 mentions that generally the rapporteurs feel there is no need to contact with the CJEU after a preliminary ruling has been given by the Court. Again, this would run against the (perceived) independence of the courts and the secrecy of the deliberations. One rapporteur, however, sees the need to able to ask the CJEU for clarification in case of doubt as to the interpretation of the ruling.

Even if the follow-up of a preliminary ruling by the referring court is send to the CJEU, these decisions are very often not translated into English or French. Some courts only send a (translated) abstract. CJEU judges told us, there is no systematic oversight mechanism in Luxembourg to monitor the referring courts compliance with the preliminary ruling of the CJEU. As advocate-general A stated, the CJEU does not have the resources to track what has happened with cases after they have been decided by the Court. One might perhaps expect the Commission to monitor the implementation of CJEU preliminary rulings, because then an infringement procedure could be started whenever a national court fails to comply. The Commission does not do this, though, not only because it would require a huge effort, but also since this could run against the separation of powers doctrine. According to advocate-general A, the commission is nervous about bringing infringement proceedings that have to do with the way national courts behave. It would only be prepared to do so if there is a systematic pattern of non-compliance. This begs the question: how would the Commission do this, if the follow-up of preliminary ruling is not systematically monitored?

With regard to the implementation of preliminary rulings, some judges from supreme administrative courts have indicated they sometimes have trouble understanding the CJEU's rulings. This point is also related to the reformulation of the preliminary questions and to the veiled style of argumentation. Against this background, some judges indicate they sometimes feel the need to launch immediate follow-up questions regarding how a preliminary ruling should be understood.[115] One might draw inspiration here from French administrative law where the administration, according to article R. 931-1 of the Code de justice administrative, has the possibility to ask a division of the Council of State for clarification about the decision. This so-called service-après-vente would meet the need of judges who have indicated to appreciate more formal or informal contact after the CJEU has provided its decision.

Two advocates-general argued that it would be impossible for the Court to monitor the implementation of its preliminary rulings, because the CJEU would not have the resources to do so and would require more active cooperation from the side of national highest courts, starting by systematically sending translated versions of follow-up decisions to the CJEU. They hinted to a task for the European Commission here, but they

[115] Both Polish judges and Dutch judge B.

immediately added that infringement procedures are time-consuming exercises. Moreover, the European Commission would probably be reluctant to take action against national courts. This would only emerge in case of a systematic pattern of non-compliance.

4.6 To Dialogue or Not to Dialogue?

At the end of our interviews, we asked the judges how they felt about characterizing the preliminary reference procedure as a 'judicial dialogue'. Moreover, we wanted to learn in case judges on both sides would see it as a dialogue, for what problem a judicial dialogue should be the solution. In case our interviewees would not want to portray the preliminary reference procedure as a dialogue, it raises the question: why does the CJEU itself repeatedly picture it as such?

The bottom line in the interviews was that a judicial dialogue presupposes a two-way communication style that goes beyond the current Q&A procedure. We discovered that different views exist about whether the relationship between the supreme administrative courts and the CJEU needs to have a more dialogic character. The differences depend to a large extent on how judges see their role in the law-making process. Some judges clearly lean more towards a pragmatic decision-making model, in which the dominant role of the court is to solve legal problems and 'get things done'.[116] Judges adhering to this view, tend to see law making as a 'luxury good', which their court often would not be able to afford in practice. There are, however, also judges for whom law making is an increasingly important part of the role of supreme courts in today's globalizing multi-level legal order.[117] They believe EU law making cannot and should not simply be left to supranational courts. The difference between the role model of the 'judge referee' and the 'judge law maker' runs across national lines. Sometimes we even saw striking differences within one court. To some extent, the different backgrounds of the judges may explain these differences. Although our sample of

[116] Both judges A and B of the Belgian, Austrian, Spanish and Danish courts expressed this view.

[117] Like the both judges A and B of the British, the Polish and the Dutch courts do. It is interesting to note that a recent survey shows a tendency towards an even greater focus on the law-making task of the supreme courts. See M. Feteris, 'Development of the Law by Supreme Courts in Europe' *Utrecht Law Review*, 13, 1, 155–169 (2017). DOI: 10.18352/ulr.401.

interviews is too small to draw strong conclusions, career judges who have moved up the ladder from being in a district court, an appellate court, an finally a supreme court, seemed to be more pragmatic and result-oriented than judges who did not have such a career.

The first category of judges seemed to be less interested in developing a judicial dialogue with the CJEU. What they are mostly looking for is useful and ready-made answers to solve the cases pending before their court without undue delay. Career judges appreciate informal contacts with CJEU judges, but do not feel the need to be engaged more actively in the preliminary reference procedure. For the 'judge law maker' this is different. They view the idea of a judicial law making more as a means to, not only contribute to the quality of preliminary rulings, but also as a way to improve the legitimacy of the European law-making process. One of the UK judges said the CJEU would eventually lose the national courts if it does not adopt a reciprocal method of law making.[118]

Interestingly, judges and advocates-general from the CJEU also seemed to have different views on the idea of judicial dialogue. What we heard from two judges was that most CJEU judges see their relationship with the referring courts as a form of cooperation rather than as a dialogue.[119] Asked about the difference between dialogue and cooperation one of them claimed that cooperation would be a more technical term dealing with the relationship between two separated competencies, not representing a shared responsibility.[120] The interpretation of EU law would be the sole responsibility of the CJEU and the implementation of the preliminary decision into the national legal system would be the exclusive competence of the national courts. This is also the opinion of both advocates-general. As one of them argued the inter-court relationship lacks a dialogical character because it is the CJEU that takes a decision that needs to be respected by the referring court.[121]

According to another CJEU judge, a judicial dialogue is possible even in a hierarchical relationship, but the term 'dialogue' should be seen more as a description of what actually takes place between national courts and the CJEU, than as a normative framework guiding the inter-court relationship.[122] As it comes to strengthening the cooperation and communication with national courts, CJEU judges and advocates-general seem to believe more in strengthening informal contacts than in the formal instruments like responding to provisional answers, issuing requests

[118] UK judge B. [119] CJEU judge A and B. [120] CJEU judge A.
[121] CJEU A-G B. [122] CJEU judge D.

for clarification or, more generally, moving to a more discursive style of reasoning. Informal contacts are generally seen as valuable, not only because of the possibility to talk about problems, but also as a means to grow mutual understanding and trust.[123] As one of the advocates-general called it, informal contacts function as a lubricant. It is the oil in the judicial engine.

4.7 Conclusion

Perhaps the most important lesson to be taken from the interviews is that there is a gap between the rhetoric on judicial dialogues, cooperation and co-actorship between national highest courts and the CJEU and what actually takes place in practice. The majority of judges on both the CJEU and supreme administrative courts, seem to realize there is at the moment little room for a judicial dialogue that goes beyond one party asking questions and the other party answering them. Procedural mechanisms that could be used to facilitate a dialogue between both courts, such as requests for clarification, provisional answers and leaving more leeway for highest courts to scrutinize potential preliminary questions before they are send to the CJEU, are relatively unpopular.

In theory a better horizontal communication between national courts about the necessity to raise questions, about formulation of preliminary questions, and about the consequences that different possible answers may have for the national legal orders could certainly be used to inform the CJEU much better. However, this horizontal communication process is troubled by language barriers, practical constraints, such as too heavy caseloads, and by the absence of a solid (digital) communication infrastructure. Such an infrastructure could help courts to inform each other about relevant foreign case law, about pending preliminary questions in other jurisdictions and about different possible views regarding the interpretation of EU law. Moreover, there are different attitudes towards the idea of a judicial dialogue involving a more shared responsibility between the CJEU and supreme courts. From the side of the national courts there are two categories of judges. The first one is primarily interested in deciding cases without undue delay, offering legal effective legal protection for citizens and receiving ready-made answers from the CJEU. These judges are not waiting for more responsibility for the

[123] CJEU A-G A.

development of EU law. They view the CJEU as better equipped for this job. On the other hand, there are 'judge law makers', who seem to believe that in a modern multilevel legal order, the interpretation of EU law should be a mutual responsibility in which preliminary references should be more than a matter of questions and answers. These judges view themselves more as European judges, who are responsible for the fact that EU law does not drift too far off from the laws, principles, and legal traditions in the Member States. Some of these judges even seem to be worried about the risk of an increasing strive for autonomy from the side of the CJEU, which would make the Luxembourg court gradually immune for criticism.

From the side of the CJEU, there are certainly judges who encourage a horizontal dialogue between national highest courts, let alone because this could enable them to give broader answers and facilitate judicial law making without running the risk of unnecessarily disturbing national legal orders. Some CJEU judges also appear to be in favour of a better streamlining of preliminary questions by highest courts in order to keep their workflow on a reasonable level and improve the quality of preliminary questions. Simultaneously, though, all CJEU judge warn that a filtering of especially lower court references by the national supreme courts, should not result in blocking the right of the former courts to refer. Behind this appears to be a fear to lose the references from lower courts, which could hamper the enforcement of EU law, in particular in case highest courts are not willing to refer.

Somewhat paradoxical is that CJEU judges do not appear to be worried about the fact that what happens after the CJEU has delivered a preliminary ruling is often unclear. The CJEU does not systematically follow-up on what referring courts have done and the latter courts sometimes do not send their final decision that is supposed to implement the preliminary ruling to the CJEU. What the CJEU does with the decisions that are being sent, apart from publishing them online in usually the national language, is unknown to CJEU judges and advocates-general. Last but not least, it seems fair to say that CJEU judges do not seem very keen to envisage the preliminary reference procedure as a judicial dialogue in which they share more responsibilities with national highest courts or give them a broader margin of appreciation concerning when to refer cases and how to apply the rulings from the CJEU within the national context.

5 Trust and Dialogue

5.1 The Preliminary Reference Procedure as a Dialogue?

The foundations of the preliminary reference procedure were based on the idea of cooperative federalism. Craig and De Burca have argued that the original conception of the preliminary reference procedure in the Treaties reveals an allocation of roles in which the CJEU and national courts had separated but equal authority. They acknowledge, though, that the relationship between the Luxembourg court and the national (highest) courts has steadily become more vertical and multilateral.[1] It has become more vertical because of cases, such as CILFIT, Köbler, and Welthgrove,[2] which have put a penalty on a refusal to refer or withdraw preliminary questions. In this vertical relationship, especially lower national courts seem treated as watchdogs for the enforcement of EU law by the CJEU in case highest national courts refuse to refer. As we will argue hereafter, this watchdog role may be useful to protect the *effet utile* of EU law but could also affect the spirit of cooperation between highest national courts and the CJEU.

The procedure has become more multilateral and focused on law making in the sense that, even though the Treaties are silent about this, preliminary rulings received erga omnes effect. They do not only bind the referring court, but also affect the courts in all the other EU Member States, which implies that CJEU's decisions go far beyond the case at hand. The question is whether this has also led to changes in the style of communication by the Court as one might expect that a stronger focus

1 P. Craig and G. De Burce, *EU law, Text, Cases and Materials* (Oxford: Oxford University Press, 2011), p. 443.

2 P. Wattel, Köbler, 'CILFIT and Welthgrove: We Can't Go on Meeting Like This' *CMLR* 41, 177–190, 2004.

on law making and erga omnes effect of preliminary rulings would result in a more argumentative and persuasive style of reasoning to convince a wider audience of national courts. Strangely enough, though, some authors argue that the relationship between the CJEU and national courts has shifted from being cooperative and nonconfrontational towards becoming more hierarchical, even though the CJEU holds on to a language in which national courts are presented as 'partners'.[3] We wonder: what is behind this? The rhetoric of framing the preliminary reference procedure as a 'judicial dialogue' may fit very well with a desire to keep peace with each other. However, this does not mean that is has any truth-value.[4] After having presented our case law analysis and interviews, it is now time to answer the question to what extent there is a dialogue between the CJEU and national highest administrative courts. Moreover, is the interchange something more than a relationship in which one party asks the questions and the other one provides the answers to these questions or to the reformulated versions thereof?

5.2 Dialogue Concept

In previous chapters, we have tried to stay away from providing a definition of a judicial dialogue that might serve as a benchmark against which the case law and interview results could be assessed as being more or less 'dialogical'. The reason is that we do not believe it is up to us to determine what the relationship between the CJEU and highest national administrative courts should be. At the same time, we cannot entirely avoid the question what could be seen as dialogical about the current preliminary reference procedure and how that procedure works out in the relationship between the CJEU and national highest administrative courts in practice.

Even if one does not want to associate the dialogue between courts as something that comes close to a Habermasian speech situation, in which participants would be able to evaluate each other's assertions solely on the basis of reason and evidence in an atmosphere completely free of any

[3] T. de La Mare and C. Donnely, 'Preliminary Rulings and EU Legal Integration: Evolution and Stasis' in P. Craig and G. De Burca, *The Evolution of EU Law* (Oxford: Oxford University Press, 2011), p. 377

[4] Very clear that this is not the case are D. Kochenov and M. van Wolferen, The dialogical rule of law and the breakdown of dialogue in the EU, EUI Working Paper LAW 2018/01, p. 15, who even talk about a Ciau?eschian monologue from the CJEU vs national highest courts.

coercive influences ('herrschaftsfreier Kommunikation') where the participants are motivated by the desire to obtain consensus,[5] there is probably a threshold below which it does not make sense to still talk about a judicial dialogue. In the first chapter, we have raised three questions that point to the position of the CJEU, which has been most active to claim it wants a dialogue with national courts. Does this dialogue imply that (a) the CJEU is actually prepared to share power and responsibility with national highest administrative courts concerning the validity and correct interpretation of EU law; (b) the CJEU is willing to enable national courts to talk back at the Court to inform it about the potential consequences of preliminary rulings and (c) is the CJEU prepared to show accountability towards national courts regarding the way in which it has taken into account their views of how EU law should be interpreted, applied and enforced? During the course of our research, we have seen that these questions can be matched with similar ones focused on the national highest administrative courts, such as (a) are these courts prepared to submit relevant questions concerning the interpretation of EU law to the CJEU and leave the Court some discretion regarding the type of answer that may be given? (b) are supreme administrative courts willing and able to think with the CJEU regarding the (provisional) answers that could be given to these questions? (c) what about the accountability of national highest administrative courts towards the CJEU with regard to, for example, providing reasons for not raising questions where this might be expected or showing compliance with preliminary rulings by informing the Court about how these are implemented in the case that was referred?

Previous chapters have already indicated that the preliminary reference procedure is currently perhaps not more than a situation in which national courts raise questions and the CJEU tries to answer them. This, without there being much room for sharing power and responsibility, for actively showing how the views of the other party in the dialogue have been taken into account and for being transparent about how rulings have come about or have been implemented at the national level. We will nevertheless go into this again in order to summarize our most important findings. What we have not looked into before, however, is how the current rather minimalistic interpretation of the dialogue

[5] J. Habermas, Discourse ethics: Notes on a programme of philosophical justification, in J. Habermas, *Moral Consciousness and Communicative Action* (Cambridge, MA: MIT Press, 1999), p. 43ff.

between the CJEU and highest administrative courts could be explained. This is also what we will try to do hereafter. Our point of departure here is that just as in everyday dialogues between people, both partners in a judicial dialogue have a responsibility to contribute to the quality of the discourse so that the debate goes beyond one side asking questions, which the other side answers. Of course, this does not exclude that, in the end, one of the partners may carry a greater responsibility for cutting the Gordian knot with regard to how EU law should be interpreted, let alone because there are obvious differences in terms of time, resources, supporting staff et cetera between courts on both ends. This does not exclude, though, that national highest courts and the CJEU both fuel the substance of a preliminary ruling.

5.3 Outline

After we summarize the most important aims of the preliminary references based on article 267 TFEU (§ 5.4), we can link these to different possible forms of cooperation and communication between courts (§ 5.5). Next, we move to the joint outcomes of our case law analysis and interviews in order to look for signs of dialogue in which national highest administrative courts and the CJEU attempt to talk back at each other (§ 5.6).

Following the order we have taken for the interviews, we will first look into the *formal* possibilities built into the procedure to enhance communication concerning the formulation of preliminary questions, such as requests for clarification (§ 5.6.1) and the use of provisional answers (§ 5.6.2). After having observed that the application of these procedural mechanisms is suboptimal at best, we are going to compare this with the apparent eagerness from both national courts and the CJEU to address questions of compatibility of national law with EU law (§ 5.6.3), which supposedly belong to the exclusive domain of the former courts and should officially lead to inadmissibility of these questions. Surprisingly enough, though, this is frequently not the case. This begs the question: how come?

Subsequently, we are going to focus on *informal* communication channels. The interviews have taught us that both the CJEU and national highest courts also value transnational judicial networks, such as the ACA network, in which preliminary questions can be discussed. However, the information exchange in these networks is not without problems (§ 5.6.4) and we wonder: what do national courts receive in return from the CJEU for attempts to coordinate preliminary questions with sister courts abroad (§ 5.6.5)? Once a preliminary question has arrived at the CJEU, there is communication between the litigating parties, external interveners (e.g. governments and the Commission) and the CJEU, but the referring court is completely out of the picture. Some national judges are not pleased with this, which is why we ask ourselves (§ 5.6.6): what role might be left for national courts during the proceedings in Luxembourg? Finally, we will briefly address the possibilities for dialogue after the CJEU has given a ruling (§ 5.6.7). Is there a need from the side of the CJEU to communicate with national courts about the follow-up of its rulings or do the latter perhaps feel a need to get additional information from the CJEU?

After reiterating the outcomes from our case law analysis and interviews it is time for an evaluation, which will show that the dialogical features of the preliminary reference procedure at the moment are quite meagre to say the least. This calls for an explanation: how is it possible that the preliminary reference procedure is still pictured as the 'jewel in the crown' of the existing regime of judicial review in the EU,[6] when the communication and cooperation between national courts and the CJEU shows very few signs of actual co-actorship? There are several existing theories that could explain this, but we believe there is one major factor that has so far been underestimated by almost all authors, namely (§ 5.7) a lack of trust between national highest (administrative) courts and the CJEU. In the remaining part of this chapter we are going to zoom in on this by looking closer at the way in which the CJEU motivates its decisions (§ 5.7.1), the opportunity provided to lower courts to bypass their supreme courts in addressing the CJEU (§ 5.7.2), which is detrimental to the faith that highest administrative courts have in the CJEU. Linked to the empowerment of lower courts, there is the opaqueness of the purpose of the preliminary reference procedure. It seems to be in a constant flux between warranting legal unity and protecting individual citizen's rights.

We will conclude (§ 5.8) by arguing that choices need to be made in order to prevent more serious communication problems in the future.

5.4 Purpose of the Preliminary Reference Procedure

As we have seen in the previous chapters, there are different kinds of dialogues between different kinds of actors (e.g. between highest

[6] P. Craig, *EU Administrative Law* (Oxford: Oxford University Press, 2006), p. 285.

national courts and the CJEU, between the CJEU and ECtHR, but also between lower courts and the highest national courts and/or the CJEU. In practice, these dialogues fulfil a variety of aims, ranging from informal information exchange and coordination of rulings until the borrowing of each other's legal concepts. We believe it is fair to say, though, that the dialogue between the CJEU and national highest administrative courts should always be seen in light of the aims the preliminary reference procedure serves.

First, the preliminary reference procedure has originally been established to warrant a uniform interpretation and application of EU law by national courts and in doing so safeguarding the uniformity of EU law. Second and strongly related to this task of safeguarding the uniformity of EU law, the preliminary reference procedure serves as a proper venue in order to incentivise the process of judicial law making by allowing the CJEU to develop core doctrines of EU law (e.g. direct effect, supremacy, and state liability). Finally, the preliminary reference procedure, indirectly aims to guarantee an effective protection of rights provided to citizens under the Treaties.

How do these potential goals influence the actual functioning of the preliminary rulings procedure? We can fairly say that the preliminary rulings procedure is largely animated by the concern for the uniformity of EU law in the Member States. As the CJEU sees it[7]:

> Any weakening, even if only potential, of the uniform application and interpretation of Community law throughout the Union would be liable to give rise to distortions of competition and discrimination between economic operators, thus jeopardizing equality of opportunity as between those operators and consequently the proper functioning of the internal market. One of the Court's essential tasks is to ensure just such a uniform interpretation, and it discharges that duty by answering the questions put to it by the national courts and tribunals. The possibility of referring a question to the Court of Justice must therefore remain open to all those courts and tribunals.

In order to safeguard the uniformity of EU law the CJEU relies on the CILFIT doctrine, backed up by the Köbler jurisprudence in case of unlawful refusals to raise preliminary questions. As Komarek has rightfully argued, though, the question here is what the CJEU actually means by uniformity:[8]

[7] Report of the Court of Justice on certain aspects of the application of the Treaty on European Union, 1995, point 11.

[8] See: J. Komarek, 'In The Court(S) We Trust? On the Need for Hierarchy and Differentiation in the Preliminary Ruling Procedure' *E.L. Rev.* 32, 4, 467–491 (2007), at 470.

'Is it an absolute "sameness", suggested by the warning that even a potential weakening of the goal of uniformity could have disastrous consequences for the internal market?' Although the quest for absolute uniformity is, to a certain extent, understandable from an EU perspective, we could fairly say that no legal system may ever achieve it. Therefore, this dogma of uniformity has started to be questioned. As some scholars argue it may be the time to reflect on whether we need the Court of Justice to give a ruling on the interpretation of every provision of EU law that we can think of or whether its role should be more that of a genuine Supreme and Constitutional Court of the Union.[9]

Second, we see a tension between safeguarding the uniformity of EU law and another aim of the preliminary rulings procedure, namely, advancing the process of judicial law-making. Although the goal of advancing the judicial law-making process, on the one hand, and the pursuit for uniformity of EU law, on the other hand, are strongly related, they can be clearly separated. The search for uniformity serves as a justification for the CJEU's intervention even in cases of minor importance for the EU legal order as a whole. Although we cannot deny that the CJEU has played a very important role in the development of the law of the EU, it is still reluctant to recognize its law-making role. To cite the words of its current president of the CJEU: 'If courts go beyond their duty of saying "what the law is", they lack legitimacy as they intrude into the political process'. One may wonder, though, whether this argumentation is not a bit concealing: we all know that courts including the CJEU engage in the law-making process. The problem is perhaps not so much that the CJEU engages in law making via the preliminary reference procedure, but more that it is often not transparent about it and lacks a methodology to support rulings that go well beyond applying existing law. Furthermore, as soon as one accepts that developing new law via preliminary rulings (also) belongs to the core business of the CJEU, this raises questions with regard to the legitimacy of these rulings. How does the Court ensure these rulings are going to be supported by national courts and governments? Is a judicial dialogue perhaps not an instrument to facilitate trust and support, at least from the side of referring courts?

The third potential purpose of the preliminary rulings procedure – protecting individual rights – appears to be somewhat at odds with the idea of safeguarding uniformity and enhancing judicial law-making.

9 Ibid., at 478 and J.

This third goal is about protecting individual interests of litigants, whereas the first and the second goal transcend the level of the individual case. Nonetheless, the aim of protecting individual rights, also causes some controversy.

On the one hand, the focus on citizen's rights in the preliminary reference procedure may be seen as compensation for the lack of opportunities for individual applicants to address the CJEU directly. These opportunities are limited in order not to flood the Court with 'appeals' from EU citizens who are dissatisfied with certain parts of the national law and seek a possibility to overturn decisions of domestic courts. Allowing local courts to bring practical questions of EU law in the dispute between litigating parties to the CJEU via preliminary references also ensures that possible violations of EU law are decided as close as possible to citizens.[10]

On the other hand, there are at least two major objections against this focus on citizen's rights. The first objection is that CJEU within the preliminary reference procedure is only allowed to make judgments with regard to the interpretation and validity of EU law. The Court is simply not competent to review national law and to solve individual cases.[11] This is the prerogative of the national courts. Empirical research by Van Alphen seems to point in the direction of preliminary references, in particular by lower courts, shifting towards a citizen's infringement procedure. Lower courts can use references not only to get some clarification on the proper interpretation of EU law, but also to learn whether they could disregard or even annul national legislation as interpreted by a higher national court in case that legislation runs against EU law.[12]

[10] See: S. Bogojević, 'Judicial Dialogue Unpacked: Twenty Years of Preliminary References on Environmental Matters Initiated by the Swedish Judiciary' *Journal of Environmental Law*, 29, 263–283 (2017), at 268–269.

[11] C.W.A Timmermans, 'Looking Behind the Scenes of Judicial Cooperation in Preliminary Procedures', in F. Caffagi and S. Law (eds.), *Judicial Cooperation in European Private Law* (Edward Elgar Publishing 2017), p. 40; M. Broberg and N. Fenger, *Preliminary References to the European Court of Justice* (Oxford: Oxford University Press, 2010), p. 156; Paul Graig and Gráinne de Búrca, *EU Law: Text, Cases, and Materials* (Oxford: Oxford University Press, 2011), p. 474.

[12] T. van Alphen, 'Legal protection by the European Court of Justice: an empirical study on the use of the preliminary reference procedure as a citizen's infringement procedure', Master Thesis Tilburg University (2018), p. 62. See also: B. de Witte, 'The Preliminary Ruling Dialogue: The Types of Questions Posed by National Courts' in Bruno de Witte et al. (eds.), *National Courts and EU Law: New Issues, Theories and Methods* (Cheltenham: Edward Elgar, 2016), pp. 15–25.

A second objection is that the preliminary reference procedure is not suited to (continue to) provide effective judicial protection for individual citizens and at the same time function as a beacon for national courts and legislatures with regard to the validity and interpretation of EU law(s).[13] As Weiler has argued, the attachment to the preliminary rulings procedure in its current form is detrimental to the CJEU wanting to be the most authoritative interpreter of EU law that watches over the unity, coherence and effectiveness of European law.[14] As Advocate General Jacobs already put it in 2002:

> [T]he Court's primary task in preliminary rulings is not to decide specific cases on the basis of narrowly distinguished facts, or to solve a problem for the national court in the particular case, but to state clearly and coherently for the benefit of everyone in the Community what the correct understanding of the law is, and to give rulings of general significance. It is only that broader function which justifies the system of preliminary rulings and explains the unique procedure whereby Member States and the Commission are systematically invited to submit observations and indeed why the judgment of the Court and the Opinion of the Advocate General in every case are published in no fewer than 11 languages.[15]

With an increasing caseload, the CJEU will at some point have to decide what kind of court it wants to be. If it wants to be a court that provides more general guidance for national courts regarding the interpretation (and hence) development of EU law, there is a need for a change in the architecture of the preliminary reference procedure. In that case, the CJEU should stay more away from offering legal protection in individual cases. In addition, it presupposes that CJEU should not only argue convincingly, but also needs to stay away from pulverizing its authority by answering to each and every preliminary question – notwithstanding how detailed and insignificant they may sometimes be – resulting into hundreds of preliminary rulings every year that cannot remain coherent.

[13] J. Komárek, supra note 8, at 484.

[14] J.H.H. Weiler, 'Epilogue: Judging the Judges: Apology and Critique', in M. Adams, H. de Waele, J. Meeusen and G. Straetmans (ed.), *Judging Europe's Judges: The Legitimacy of the Case Law of the European Court of Justice* (Oxford: Hart publishing 2013), p. 252.

[15] Opinion of AG Jacobs in C-136/00, *Danner* [2002] ECR I-8147, ECLI:EU:C:2002:558, para. 38. Currently, the official languages of the EU are (in English alphabetical order): Bulgarian, Czech, Danish, Dutch, English, Estonian, Finnish, French, German, Greek, Hungarian, Italian, Irish, Latvian, Lithuanian, Maltese, Polish, Portuguese, Romanian, Slovakian, Slovenian, Spanish and Swedish (Article 1 of Council Regulation EEC No 1/58). See J. Domingues, 'The Multilingual Jurisprudence of the Court of Justice and the Idea of Uniformity in European Union Law' *UNIO – EU Law Journal*, 3, 2, 125–138 (2017).

5.5 Different Aims of the Preliminary Reference Procedure May Require Different Forms of Cooperation and Communication

Each of the aims of the preliminary reference procedure may rely on different forms of cooperation and communication between national courts and the CJEU.

Protecting the *uniformity of EU law*, for instance, would be impossible if national courts refused to raise preliminary questions on a larger scale. Lower courts, on their turn, would not be able to function as 'guardians of the Treaties', in case they adhere to their own highest courts (e.g. supreme courts or constitutional courts), when they believe these courts misinterpret EU law and should have raised preliminary questions to the CJEU. This explains why the Luxembourg court has been very lenient, especially towards courts of first instance, in case national courts produced preliminary questions with minor procedural flaws.

The CJEU undoubtedly realized that declaring preliminary questions inadmissible too easily might discourage national courts to bring important flaws in the interpretation of EU law to its attention, which could easily hurt the *effective enforcement* of community law. Being too lenient in providing lower courts access to the CJEU, however, could lead to a flood of preliminary questions, which the Court would ultimately be unable to handle. This could perhaps explain why the CJEU is no longer so mild towards smaller procedural errors by lower courts while referring questions.[16]

Grimbergen has rightfully argued that changes in the 'assessment-intensity' of references adopted by the CJEU comes with a responsibility from both sides. The CJEU has a duty to actively inform national courts with respect to how it assesses references in order to guarantee legal predictability of the preliminary reference procedure. National courts, on their turn, are responsible for providing the CJEU with sufficient information on facts and national law, on the necessity of the preliminary reference, and on the relevance of the questions being raised.[17] Grimbergen has shown that, as a result of an ever-increasing caseload and more complex questions, the CJEU has begun to examine the

[16] N. Wahl and L. Prete, 'The Gatekeepers of Article 267 TFEU: On Jurisdiction and Admissibility of References for Preliminary Rulings' *CMLR*, 55, 511–548 (2018).

[17] R. Grimbergen, 'How Boundaries Have Shifted: On Jurisdiction and Admissibility in the Preliminary Ruling Procedure' *Review of European Administrative Law*, 8, 2, 39–70 (2015).

necessity of preliminary references and its content more closely. Consequently, the Court encroached upon the assessment domain of referring courts. This is not necessarily problematic as long as the CJEU is predictable in how it assesses the necessity and relevance of preliminary questions but unfortunately this is not always the case.[18] National courts, on the other hand, should not complain about unpredictability of the CJEU regarding refusals to answer preliminary questions in case they, for instance, knowingly ask hypothetical questions or questions they are supposed to answer themselves.

Regarding the latter, courts are under an obligation of allowing citizen's access to justice in order to *protect their rights* under EU law. Opinion 1/09 reiterates this. Although the preliminary reference procedure offers a remedy that is only available to Member State courts, the truth is that a majority of the references stem from proceedings where a private party challenges the validity of certain national legal provisions in light of EU law.[19] Just think of the Sunday trading cases, where British retailers tried to attack UK laws prohibiting shops to open on Sundays by claiming that the free movement of goods would require this.[20] In such cases, the referring courts often do their best not to frame the question as a matter of enforcement, but present it as a problem of interpretation of EU law and protection of individual rights because they want the CJEU to address the question.

In the end, the CJEU should make as clear as possible how relevant EU provisions need to be understood to provide guidance as to how, for example, free movement rules in the basic Treaties need to be interpreted so that not only the referring court, but also courts in other Member States, know how to deal with problems like legislative provisions to prohibit shops to be open on Sundays. It is needless to say, that this requires a balancing act that presupposes a transparent, faithful, and open way of communication between national courts and the CJEU. This is important in order to avoid that: citizen's rights are ignored, courts in different Member States are triggered to issue follow-up

[18] Ibid., 69. According to Grimbergen the CJEU, for example, often does not discern between questions of not having jurisdiction and inadmissibility of preliminary questions.

[19] M. Broberg, 'Judicial Coherence and the Preliminary Reference Procedure: Article 267 as a Private Party Remedy for Ensuring Judicial Coherence in Europe', *Review of European Administrative Law*, 8, 2, 9–37 (2015), at 12.

[20] H.W. Micklitz, *The Politics of Judicial Co-operation in the EU – Sunday Trading, Equal Treatment and Good Faith* (Cambridge: Cambridge University Press, 2005), pp. 274 and 462–463.

questions, and the CJEU overtakes the responsibility from national courts for the application and enforcement of EU law.

If the preliminary rulings procedure is primarily seen as a means to safeguard the uniformity of EU law or as an instrument to protect the individual rights of EU-citizens, the need for a dialogue seem to be rather absent. In a model that is aimed at safeguarding the uniformity of EU law the national courts are particularly seen as 'the eyes and the ears' of the CJEU responsible for bringing cases to the attention of the Luxembourg court in order to make sure that the latter can continue to play its role as the engine of the further integration of the EU legal system. In citizens infringement cases the supreme (administrative) courts take up the role of a lower court leaving the final say to the 'supreme court' in Luxembourg. In these two models there is not much room and no need for sharing power and responsibility or national courts actively sharing their views on the interpretation, application and enforcement of EU law with the CJEU and for the CJEU to show accountability towards national courts regarding the way in which it has taken into account their views. The need for a more dialogical communication pattern increases though if we take the view on the preliminary rulings procedure as an instrument that is primarily aiming at the development of EU law by the CJEU. From the interviews it is striking that in particular those judges believe in the concept of a judicial dialogue between the CJEU and the supreme administrative courts who explicitly recognize supreme courts having a role that goes beyond simply applying the law and who feel that these courts have a responsibility in the law-making process. The focus on judicial law making within the preliminary rulings procedure gives rise to a constructive interaction between the legal order of the EU and those of its Member States. This may serve as an explanation why supreme administrative courts' judges who emphasize this law-making task see themselves as co-actors in the 'law making business' and favour a dialogical paradigm in which the CJEU and the supreme (administrative) courts have a shared responsibility for the further development of EU law.

5.6 Dialogical Patterns Derived from Our Case Law Analysis and Interviews

Although the case law analysis and interviews are not fully synchronized (e.g. one cannot obtain information from the case law about the horizontal communication between national courts prior to a reference or about the communication between the CJEU and national courts after a preliminary ruling) there is certainly overlap between both studies. On most topics, our interviews confirmed the outcomes of the case law analysis.

5.6.1 *Non-Use of Requests for Clarification before Reformulating Preliminary Questions*

One of the first things that come to mind after combining the outcomes from the case law with the interviews is the limited use of procedural instruments in the preliminary reference procedure that could, in theory, facilitate dialogue.

The CJEU, for instance, rarely seems to apply article 101 of the Court's rule of procedure in order to file a request for clarification in case the preliminary question by a referring national court is considered to be unclear. The CJEU seems to have no problems, though, to reformulate such questions even when it is in the dark about the motives of national courts to refer it to Luxembourg. National courts, on the other hand, appear to have a strong preference for closed (binary) questions, offering the CJEU little discretion as to the sort of answers that may be given, which could give an additional incentive to reformulate questions that otherwise be held inadmissible for being unclear.

Sometimes a different technique is used to 'save' preliminary questions. Langer recalls an opinion of Advocate General Jääskinen in a Dutch tax case. The case concerned a reference from the Dutch Supreme Court. The Advocate General voiced strong criticism about the quality of the reference order. He suggested that the reference at hand was on the verge of being inadmissible. However, in order to rescue the reference Jääskinen obtained additional information by requesting the opinion delivered by the Dutch Advocate General to the Supreme Court in the national proceedings, which did contain the necessary information. Although this action by Jääskinen may be applauded, it also reveals how vulnerable references can be in case not the entire decision, including addendums, is translated and send to the CJEU. In such a case it may depend on coincidence and, in this case, tenacity from the side of the Advocate General at the CJEU, whether the necessary information is obtained and the question is not declared inadmissible.[21]

[21] J. Langer, 'The preliminary ruling procedure: old problems or new challenges?', Inaugural lecture held on 31 March 2015 on acceptance of the Professorship of European law and the national legal order (2015), p. 4. Available at SSRN: https://ssrn.com/abstract=2885256 or http://dx.doi.org/10.2139/ssrn.2885256. Here, we are talking about a different dialogue, namely between the Advocate General at the CJEU and the Advocate General at the Dutch Supreme Court. It may even suppose a third dialogue. After all, who or what triggered Jääskinen to request the opinion of the Dutch Advocate General? How did he know the relevant information might be in this opinion if he was not tipped by somebody?

According to the interviews, the main reason for not using requests for clarification from the CJEU seems to be that it could delay the procedure (e.g. due to the fact that referring courts might need to reopen the procedure and consult with litigating parties) and that requests are not always very helpful to the Court because national courts sometimes refuse to provide relevant additional information. Hence, the CJEU basically seems to view the use of article 101 as a waste of time. We certainly do not want to argue that a request for clarification is useful in each and every case, but especially with regard to complex issues where the referring court has a good track record with regard to formulating proper preliminary questions or has shown initiative (e.g. by providing provisional answers or other attempts to inform the CJEU, such as by adding translated relevant documents to the reference), it should not be too much to ask the referring court for clarification of its question within a limited period (e.g. the CJEU may add a deadline to the request for clarification).

However, in the interviews, it was also suggested that taking the possibility to issue a request for clarification more seriously could limit the CJEU's possibilities to reformulate questions the way it seems fit. After all, once the CJEU starts to consult referring courts about the intentions behind the reference, it will also become more difficult to ignore these. For strategic reasons it might be unattractive to issue requests for clarification because that would make it more difficult for the CJEU to self-determine the scope of the case. On the other hand, as one interviewee argued: if the CJEU reformulates questions in a way referring courts do not recognize, national court judges will probably also feel freer to afterwards interpret preliminary rulings the way they like best. What the Luxembourg court may gain on the front end by reformulating the questions, it may lose at the rear end when the Court's ruling needs to be implemented and enforced by the referring court and other national courts.

5.6.2 Provisional Answers and the Lack of Response from the CJEU

Referring courts are often apparently still unwilling to share with the CJEU how they think the answer to their question should read, even though the CJEU's Preliminary Ruling Proceedings Recommendations (PRPR) explicitly offers the possibility to share provisional answers with the Court. Currently there is certainly no legal obligation for national (highest) administrative courts to provide provisional answers, but if national courts want the CJEU to exchange views with them beyond what is strictly required legally and show accountability and responsiveness towards the opinions of referring courts, the latter cannot keep silent and passive. Whatever definition of dialogue one takes, it must be a two-way operation.

The other side to this story is that the CJEU almost never responds to provisional answers, even when the referring court is not trying to push and persuade the Court there is only one Dworkinian 'right answer' possible regarding the referred preliminary question. Slovenian high court judge Zalar wrote about this:

> The problem that the highest national courts are not sufficiently encouraged to refer more cases to the CJEU lies partly with the CJEU itself: the CJEU does not invite referring courts to provide an opinion on the legal questions referred and it never engages in discussion regarding the opinion of the referring court on the relevant question, although to my knowledge, some courts have offered such opinions and included answers to the questions in referrals and have cited case-law and interpretations of other national courts in their referral. Instead, the CJEU cites extensively the opinions on the interpretation of European Union law given by the governments.[22]

It is striking, to say the least, that the CJEU apparently has more attention for the opinion of national governments on EU law than it has for the views of national highest courts, although the latter are supposed to be more independent. With regard to these highest courts, however, we can also observe two schools of thought, namely:

(1) Judges who feel it is not up to them to provide provisional answers to their own questions, because (a) there are practical obstacles, such as an already heavy caseload and too short throughput terms to think about provisional answers; (b) judges arguing that if they knew the answer, they would not have raised questions to the CJEU; (c) the idea that the CJEU is by definition better equipped and more knowledgeable to answer questions about interpretation and validity of EU law than national courts; (d) giving a provisional answer could backfire in the sense that litigating parties might feel the referring court is biased because it has taken position even before the CJEU has ruled and (e) provisional answers would not match with the

[22] B. Zalar, 'Basic Values, Judicial Dialogues and the Rule of Law in the Light of the Charter of Fundamental Rights of the European Union: Judges Playing by the Rules of the Game' *ERA Forum*, 14, 319–333 at 330 (2013).

constitutional division of powers between national and supranational courts.

(2) Judges who feel it makes perfect sense to provide provisional answers because it offers referring courts a great opportunity to share their views about the interpretation or validity of EU law and also signal to the Court what the most likely consequences for the national legal order will be of different possible answers to preliminary questions, which might contribute to a higher level of precision and clarity of the CJEU's rulings. These judges usually also have a more active view on judicial law making in which national courts have a responsibility as co-producers of EU law.

Judges and advocates general at the CJEU, on their turn, also have different takes on provisional answers. They argue that it is not always unwillingness or lack of internal consensus that prevents them from engaging with provisional answers. The CJEU would also avoid responding to provisional answers, because it does not want to embarrass the referring court in case of disagreement in case the answers are not thought through. Some CJEU judges go further than that, though, by stating that provisional answers can show bias from the side of the referring court towards the parties and would sometimes not be much more than an expression of opportunism or wishful thinking by the referring court. From that perspective, it does not make much sense to respond to these answers. Certain judges and advocates general also refer to the general (French) style of argumentation by the Court that is by nature less discursive and argumentative than, for example, the style of decision making of Anglo-Saxon courts where there is a system of dissenting and concurring opinions that would be better suited to deal with provisional answers.

In particular, the fear from national courts of 'getting it wrong' and the CJEU's non-response to provisional answers in order to avoid 'embarrassment' by the national highest courts and the reference to 'national opportunism' as a reason behind provisional answers, could also point in the direction of a lack of trust between courts on both sides to share views beyond what is legally required (see hereafter § 5.5). It is hard to see why national highest courts would otherwise be afraid of decisions from the CJEU that deviate from the interpretation they had in mind. Moreover, to what degree would supreme administrative courts risk embarrassment if the CJEU is willing and able to explain the reasons for any differences of opinion to the national courts? Is the idea that even highest national courts could get it wrong not inherent to a system in which there are supranational courts? It is hard to believe that national courts would not realise that the CJEU cannot only take their view into account, but also has a responsibility for the unity of EU law as a whole. Notwithstanding this, they will probably assess whether the CJEU's reasoning includes:

> a certain reflexivity that takes into account the differing legal cultures and traditions that underlie the pluralistic EU legal community. It would be realistic to describe the dialectical relationship between the ECJ and national courts as constituting a forum where different normative views meet and compete. It follows that in order for ECJ interpretations to gain acceptance, they should be based on a shared understanding of underlying values of the legal order.[23]

National judges will have less faith in the CJEU when they perceive the Luxembourg court is deaf to problems that certain preliminary rulings may cause for the coherence and functioning of the national legal order, for certain sensitive national interests or for the faith that citizens have in national institutions responsible for upholding the rule of law.[24] An interesting case in point is the Diageo Brands ruling of the CJEU.[25]

In this case, the Dutch company Diageo Brands obtained an order from the Bulgarian court for the seizure of bottles of whisky bearing the 'Johnny Walker' brand on the basis that their importation into Bulgaria from outside the European Economic Area infringed its trademark. That order was subsequently overturned and Diageo's appeal to the Bulgarian Supreme Court was unsuccessful. Diageo failed at first instance in its substantive claim for infringement of its trade mark and did not appeal that decision, which therefore became final. Simiramida, a Bulgarian company, started proceedings in the Netherlands for compensation for the damage it claimed to have suffered as a result of the seizure, relying on the decision of the Bulgarian courts. In its defence, Diageo argued that the Bulgarian judgment should not be recognised as it was

[23] E. Paunio, 'Conflict, Power, and Understanding – Judicial Dialogue Between the ECJ and National Courts' *Journal of Extreme Legal Positivism*, 4, 7, 5, 14–15 (2010).

[24] L. Azoulai, 'The European Court of Justice and the duty to respect sensitive national interests', in M. Dawson and B. De Witte (eds.), *Judicial Activism at the European Court of Justice* (Chelthenham: Edward Elgar, 2013), p. 167 ff.

[25] Case C-681/13, *Diageo Brands* [2015], ECLI:EU:C:2015: 471.

manifestly contrary to public policy within the meaning of article 34(1) of Regulation, No 44/2001.[26] The Dutch Supreme Court asked in a preliminary question to the CJEU whether the fact that a judgment of a court of a Member State is manifestly contrary to EU law and was delivered in breach of procedural safeguards, constitutes a ground for refusal of recognition under Art 34(1). The CJEU denied this. The rules of recognition and enforcement are based on mutual trust, and judicial decisions in one Member State should be recognized automatically in another Member State. The CJEU concluded that "just" because a judgment sought to be recognized may be contrary to EU law does not automatically mean that it would be contrary to public policy to recognize or enforce it, where the error is not a manifest breach of a rule of law regarded as essential in the EU legal order and (therefore in) the Member State order or of a right recognized as being fundamental in those legal orders. The CJEU ruled here that the mere fact there were three dissenting opinions in the Bulgarian Supreme Court specifically pointed out the alleged breach of EU law does not yet prove that this court has knowingly ignored European law.[27]

Krommendijk and Loth have argued that the Dutch Supreme Court believed the Bulgarian courts to have consciously ignored Article 5(3) of Trademark directive 89/104/EEC. They ask themselves why, even if the CJEU does not share the Dutch Supreme Court's allegations regarding abuse of law by the Bulgarian courts, it did not respond in a less formal way in order to address the obviously serious concerns of this court.[28]

[26] Now article 45(1)(a) of the recast Brussels Regulation, No 1215/2012.

[27] The three dissenting opinions to the decision of the Bulgarian Supreme Court referred to established case law with which the majority opinion contravenes. That this must be recognized by the Bulgarian Supreme Court is also supported by a later decision of the Bulgarian Supreme Court dated April 26, 2012, with a dissenting opinion of its President and five justices, which confirmed its decision of June 15, 2009 in a new interpretative decision, notwithstanding the Canon/IPN decision of the CJEU and a letter dated December 21, 2010 from the European Commission to the Association des Industries de Marque in which the Commission states that the Bulgarian judges are not allowed to follow the interpretative decision of June 15, 2009. On top of this, the Dutch Supreme Court considered that, although the wrong application of Community law may lead to liability of the Bulgarian State according to the Francovich case (CJEU November 19, 1991, case C-6/90), recognition of the decision of the Bulgarian court, may result in an order for Diageo by the Dutch court in the proceedings on the merits to pay an amount of damages of at least ten million Euros. The Dutch Supreme Court argues that this would put serious pressure on the principle of sincere cooperation of Community law.

[28] J. Krommendijk and M. Loth, *Europese Rechters in Gesprek* (Den Haag: Boom Juridische Uitgevers, 2018), p. 81.

Although Diageo Brands tried to convince the Dutch Supreme Court to ignore the CJEU's preliminary ruling, it finally ruled that it is simply not entitled to assess the correctness of the CJEU's preliminary ruling or replace it by its own decision. This will certainly not have increased the confidence of Diageo Brands in the Dutch court system where it comes to trade mark protection.

The risk for the CJEU to take such a formal position is that at some moment national courts might lose interest in a cooperation and open communication with the CJEU when they perceive the underlying values and legal principles of EU law, as interpreted and communicated by the CJEU, become alien to their own legal system or when the Luxembourg court is not even prepared to engage with the arguments and concerns of referring courts. The latter corresponds with a study by Taal, who has investigated the knowledge-sharing practices between national courts and discovered that the preparedness to share information correlates with the social trust and collegial closeness between judges.[29] It is hard to see why this would be any different for the communication between national courts and the CJEU.

5.6.3 *Compatibility Questions and Response from a 'Citizen's Court'?*

In sharp contrast to the way in which national courts and the CJEU deal with provisional answers, stands the approach towards compatibility issues. National courts are apparently willing to regularly raise questions concerning the compatibility of national legislation with EU law and the CJEU is often willing to answer them even though answering questions about the compliance of national law with EU law belong to the prerogative of national court.

At first sight this might be seen as a sign of great confidence in the CJEU's ability to enter into a dialogue with national courts. One may doubt, though, whether this is a correct interpretation.

Firstly, one should not rule out the possibility that especially lower courts are more focused on offering individual legal protection for citizens, whose rights are impaired by national laws that appear to be violating EU laws, than on communicating with the CJEU about the validity or correct interpretation of EU law per se. Our interviews have

[29] S. Taal, *Working Separately Together: A Quantitative Study into the Knowledge Sharing Behaviour of Judges* (Bern: Stämpfli Verlag, 2016), pp. 88 and 106.

shown that even judges from highest administrative courts sometimes appear to be more interested in deciding cases than in judicial law making and in receiving an authoritative interpretation of EU law. Secondly, as Broberg and Fenger have concluded, some national courts are more than happy to shift the blame for decisions regarding incompatibility of national legislation with EU law to the CJEU,[30] especially in case of politically sensitive topics which are dealt with by courts that are not used to set aside national legislation for violating EU law.[31] Thirdly, for lower courts, asking compatibility questions can be an attempt to use the CJEU as leverage to overturn decisions by higher courts (or legislators) they disagree with. In that case the preliminary reference procedure empowers them to challenge decision of higher courts. That this actually happens in practice is hardly disputed, although there is debate about the extent to which this 'empowerment doctrine' explains the increase in preliminary questions to the CJEU now that national highest courts are more prone to refer questions than in the past.[32] Whatever position one takes in this debate, it seems to have little to do with cooperation of getting the interpretation of EU law right.

What is more difficult to understand is why the CJEU is prepared to answer compatibility questions where it could formally declare these inadmissible and leave them to be decided by national courts. After all, this would not only decrease the Court's case load but probably also increase the CJEU's popularity with Member State governments. Instead, the CJEU seems to be quite eager to answer questions regarding the compatibility of national legal provisions with EU law. Sometimes the CJEU is even willing to answer hypothetical questions, such as:

[30] A recent and interesting example is the reference from the Polish Supreme Court on whether or not the forced retirement of most of its senior judges and other infringements of judicial independence are compatible with EU law. See: S. Biernat and M. Kawczyńska, Why the Polish Supreme Court's Reference on Judicial Independence to the CJEU is Admissible after all, VerfBlog, 2018/8/23, https://verfassungsblog.de/why-the-polish-supreme-courts-reference-on-judicial-independence-to-the-cjeu-is-admissible-after-all/, DOI: https://doi.org/10.17176/20180823-162630-0.

[31] G. Butler, 'Standing the Test of Time: Reference for a Preliminary Ruling' *Irish Journal of European Law*, 20, 1, 112 and 1 (2017) M. Broberg and N. Fenger, *Preliminary Questions to the European Court of Justice* (Oxford: Oxford University Press, 2014), p. 51.

[32] See: A. Dyevre, A. Atanasova, and M. Glavina, 'Who Asks Most? Institutional Incentives and Referral Activity in the European Union Legal Order' (August 25, 2017). Available at SSRN: https://ssrn.com/abstract=3051659 or http://dx.doi.org/10.2139/ssrn.3051659.

> Must Articles 12 and 13 of [the authorisation directive] be interpreted as precluding the introduction, for budgetary purposes, by legislation of a national or local authority, of a tax on mobile communications infrastructures, installed on public or private property, used to carry on activities provided for in the general authorisation?[33]

The fact that the CJEU is willing to respond to questions focused on whether national laws are in compliance with EU law, could perhaps be explained by the fact that the Luxembourg Court wants to present itself as 'citizen's court', especially since the possibility for citizens to have direct access to the CJEU to complain about infringements of EU law are very limited.[34] Another reason might be that the CJEU prefers to come up with ready-made answers as a service to referring courts that need to decide a particular dispute. Nonetheless, it could also be that the CJEU sees answering compatibility questions as an opportunity to stress the importance of the enforcement of EU law and does not want to discourage in particular lower courts to refer questions.

The latter could even be sparked by a desire from the side of the CJEU to monitor and control the enforcement of EU law. After all, it enables the Court to keep a certain amount of control over highest national courts reluctant to refer questions to Luxembourg, by putting them under 'surveillance' from lower courts, which might have less trouble challenging national legal rules via a reference to the CJEU. This could be relevant in case certain national highest courts would still be hesitant to refer questions to the CJEU. As we will explain hereafter, this strategy might even have a negative effect on the dialogue between national courts and the CJEU because it could feed distrust. The main reason, however, for not labelling the questions and answers with regard to compatibility issues as a judicial dialogue is that it has little to do with exchanging views or sharing responsibility regarding the way in which EU law should be interpreted. Compatibility questions match best with ready-made answers.

5.6.4 *Horizontal Dialogue between Highest Administrative Courts to Inform the CJEU*

One of the topics where there appears to be quite a bit of overlap between the views of judges of the CJEU and of the highest administrative courts,

[33] Case C-454, Proximus SA v. Commune d'Etterbeek [2015], ECLI:EU:C:2015:819. In other cases, the referring court is flat-out asking whether a certain application of national law in the case at hand is compatible with EU law. See for instance Case C-322/13, Ulrike Elfriede Grrauel Rüffer v. Katerina Pokorná [2014], ECLI:EU:C:2014:189.

[34] J. Langer, ibid., p. 2.

is the need for improved horizontal information exchange about draft references between the referring court and other (foreign) courts that might have similar (pending) cases in order to be able to better inform the CJEU.

At first sight, this horizontal communication between national highest courts appears to have little to do with any dialogue between supreme administrative courts and the CJEU, but this appearance is misleading. The truth is that a better horizontal exchange of information between national highest administrative courts is a precondition for an improved dialogue on the interpretation of EU law between the CJEU and supreme administrative courts. The better referring courts are informed about whether the concerns regarding 'their' preliminary question are shared by foreign courts and the more they know about the potential effects that different preliminary rulings from the side of the CJEU could have, the better equipped they are to inform the Luxembourg court about the legal consequences of its potential decisions via provisional answers or via other more informal communication channels.[35] In this respect, knowledge is also power since the CJEU will need to pay more attention to a well-informed question from a supreme court from a small Member State, such as the Netherlands, Belgium or Denmark, as soon it knows that this court's views and concerns are shared by multiple highest courts in other Member States. On the positive side, the CJEU will probably also be more inclined to engage in judicial law-making and developing precedents that have a wider scope than the case at hand, when it is better informed about potential consequences of different possible rulings for courts in other Member States.

The CJEU itself holds the preliminary reference procedure to be crucial for the: 'preservation of the Community character of the law established by the Treaty. It aims at ensuring the coherence of European law across all the Member States.'[36] In a synopsis of the work of the CJEU in 1971, the Court added that participation by national courts in the preliminary reference procedure is: 'an index both of judicial cooperation between the Court of Justice and the national courts of the Member States and of

[35] Previous research by Mak has shown that Western highest courts increasingly look to the case law of sister courts abroad to find arguments and best practices to solve cases. See: E. Mak, *Judicial Decision-Making in a Globalized World: A Comparative Analysis of the Changing Practices of Western Highest Courts* (Oxford: Hart publishing, 2013), p. 137.

[36] Case 166/73, *Rheinmülen-Düsseldorf* [1974] ECR 33, ECLI:EU:C:1974:3, para 2.

the integration of European law into national law.'[37] As we said earlier, horizontal dialogue is of practical importance for the referring court because, apart from a short notice published in the C series of the official Journal with the name of the referring court and the questions asked, the outside world has no knowledge of other preliminary references pending before the CJEU (see hereafter in § 5.6.6), until the opinion of the Advocate General is issued or the Court has decided. The latter makes it extremely important for national highest courts to inform each other about references, let alone because it could prevent other courts from raising basically the same questions to the CJEU which would only lead to an even higher workload for the CJEU. The opposite is also true, though. In case a court doubts whether to refer questions to Luxembourg, it may help to be able to exchange views with other foreign courts to determine whether a reference is required according to the CILFIT criteria. After all, not referring questions without good reason could lead to liability, although this has rarely happened so far.[38]

Unfortunately, our interviews have revealed that the horizontal communication between national highest courts is currently hampered by different sorts of practical barriers and technical constraints, such as a lack of time due to a heavy caseload, language barriers, lack of a reliable and up to date database with relevant information on preliminary references. This is confirmed by the research of Jaremba, who also mentions a lot of these problems, such as language constraints, lack of knowledge of EU law, constitutional limitations in certain Member States to take EU law into account in certain situations, and so on. She sums it up by observing that most national judges have a common goal, namely:

> to be as efficient as possible and decide the cases without any undue delay. This implies that judges may tend to rely on heuristics and may tend to resort to the law which they are most knowledgeable of, and which is directly at their disposal, that is to say, national law. The daily backlog of cases, accompanied by the notorious lack of time may therefore effectively hamper the engagement of national judges with EU law, since overwhelmed judges can simply have not enough time at their disposal to deepen the EU-law-related matter, and/or resort to the preliminary ruling procedure and wait for the answer of the ECJ to their question. Finally, the Court of Justice needs to more closely examine the

[37] European Court of Justice, Synopsis of the work of the Court of Justice of the European communities in 1971, Luxembourg 1973, p. 16–17.

[38] See for an exception: Case C-416/17, Commission v. France [2018], ECLI:EU:C:2018:811.

uniformity and coherence of its own jurisprudence and it should be more open to the fact that local legal cultures may establish boundaries which the judges are not supposed to exceed.[39]

Apart from these practicalities, our interviews have learned, the information exchange with the CJEU is at the moment rather one-sided.[40] National courts are obliged to provide the Luxembourg court with all relevant information at the moment the preliminary question is submitted. Otherwise they risk their questions to be declared inadmissible. The CJEU, however, does not seem to provide much information in return. It puts no effort in making national cases that lead to a reference accessible online in a translated version and it does not keep the referring court posted about any progress in the case whatsoever. And as some of the interviewees have complained, it does not provide opinions of the Member States, nor the transcripts of the hearings. For a European court that claims to be interested in a judicial dialogue this is a rather peculiar position to be in. It may also explain why organizations, such as ACA Europe, have developed their own communication channels, not only for sharing cross boarder knowledge between judges about EU law, but also for the technical quality and focus of preliminary references.

The latter corresponds with existing empirical research which shows a positive correlation between transnational judicial networks and the confidence of judges in their own knowledge of, and familiarity with, EU law.[41] The same research also indicates that in administrative law, the acquaintance with EU law is probably already higher than in areas where the harmonisation process has developed much slower, such as in criminal law. This does not mean, though, there is no room for improvement. What we have learned is that the existing information databases, such as ACA's Dec.Nat, are not very reliable because they are not systematically updated, and the information is not checked for accuracy. As far

[39] U. Jaremba, 'The Role of National Courts in the Process of Legal Integration in the European Union: Retrospective and Prospective', in Flora A.N.J. Goudappel and Ernst M.H. Hirsch Ballin (eds.), *Democracy and Rule of Law in the European Union* (The Hague: T.M.C. Asser Press/Springer, 2016), p. 58–59.

[40] More in-depth about this: M. Bobek, 'Of Freasibility and Silent Elephants: The Legitimacy of the Court of Justice Through the Eyes of National Courts', in M. Adams, H. de Waele, J. Meusen and G. Straetmans (eds.), *Judging Europe's Judges: The Legitimacy of the Case Law of the European Court of Justice* (Oxford and Portland: Hart Publishing, 2013), p. 219 ff.

[41] See for instance: J. Mayoral, U Jaremba and T. Nowak, 'Creating EU Law Judges: The Role Of Generational Differences, Legal Education and Judicial Career Paths in National Judges' Assessment Regarding EU Law Knowledge', *Journal of European Public Policy*, 21, 8 (2014), 1120–1141.

as personal meetings are concerned, most judges seem to believe that informal judicial networks are quite useful as long as they organise hands-on meetings where specific (e.g. frequent) problems can be discussed between national supreme court judges and judges from the CJEU while there is no danger of interference with pending cases.

The majority of judges we spoke to, does not see a danger for judicial independence in such meetings. They believe that it will enhance mutual understanding and learning from each other as long as these meetings are held in good faith and the exchange of arguments is not directly used against each other in future cases. Some judges, however, also complained about the existing official (institutionalized) meetings between national highest administrative courts and the CJEU. The topics being discussed would often be too broad and abstract with little room for actual criticism and debate in a workshop type setting.

5.6.5 *Vertical Dialogue: What do National Highest Courts Get in Return?*

Taking into account the 'opportunity costs' of a horizontal dialogue (e.g. the time and effort it takes to consult foreign courts) and the burdens for litigating parties (e.g. delay of the outcome of the national procedure), one wonders what highest national courts will get in return for their attempts to coordinate preliminary questions with other courts.[42] As mentioned, in theory, a better horizontal communication between the referring court and sister courts in other Member States would lead to more coordinated preliminary questions that better inform the CJEU about the consequences of preliminary rulings for the national legal orders. This could enhance the CJEU's willingness to listen and take referring courts more seriously and may even lead to less case-specific preliminary rulings by taking into account the potential consequences judicial law-making might have for the national legal orders ('Folgenorientierung'). The more the CJEU is enabled to oversee the consequences of its rulings, the better it will be capable of protecting an uniform interpretation of EU law by providing decisions that serve not only the referring court's needs, but also offer guidance for courts in other Member States.

Nonetheless, it remains to be seen whether national highest courts would be willing to improve the coordination of preliminary questions to

[42] P. Craigh and G. de Burca (ed.), *The Evolution of EU Law* (Oxford: Oxford University Press, 2011), p. 375.

the CJEU, in case the latter would see this as an opportunity to limit the discretion of national highest courts to the benefit of an effective legal protection of EU law in light of article 19 TEU. It is exactly on this point that several of the judges we interviewed expressed their concerns. Some of them seem to believe that the CJEU has gradually shifted judicial law-making from a bottom up approach relying on a comparative legal approach and on discovering general principles of law common to the national legal orders of the Member States in order to facilitate a judicial dialogue or as Lenaerts has put it:

> From a structural perspective, it is safe to say that the comparative law method fits well with the preliminary reference procedure which 'by setting up a dialogue between one court and another, specifically between the [ECJ] and the courts and tribunals of the Member States, has the object of securing uniform interpretation of EU law', is the keystone of the [EU] judicial system. Firstly, by embarking on a comparative analysis of the laws of the Member States, the ECJ favours a judicial dialogue with Member State courts. If the ECJ decides to depart from the solution used by a particular Member State legal system, it must explain why that solution does not fit well with the needs of the EU or, as the case may be, why the solution favoured by the legal systems of other Member States is better suited to the problem with which EU law is confronted. Second, where the solution adopted by the ECJ mirrors that set out in the laws of the Member States the effectiveness of EU law is better achieved. Third, the use of the comparative law method gives rise to a constructive interaction between the legal order of the EU and those of its Member States. Initially, the dialogue between the ECJ and Member State courts may serve to highlight the advantages and disadvantages of the different solutions adopted at Member State level, thus enabling the ECJ to choose the approach that seems most appropriate. Subsequently, by highlighting, in some cases, the fact that the approach adopted by the ECJ does not achieve the outcome expected, Member State courts may invite the ECJ to reconsider its approach. This illustrates how the comparative law method and the judicial dialogue go hand-in-hand.[43]

Several judges we interviewed seem to believe that the CJEU is gradually moving from this comparative bottom up approach on judicial law making, towards a more top down approach relying on autonomous interpretation of Treaty law and on, for example, the EU Charter of fundamental rights. This way the Court would, not only make itself immune for overrides by the legislature, but also water down the obligation to pay respect to the national identities of the

[43] T. Perišin and S. Rodin (eds.), *The Critical Legal Studies Perspective on the Role of the Courts in the European Union* (Oxford: Hart Publishing, 2018), p. 74.

Member States, as enshrined in article 4(2) TEU.[44] It is difficult to definitely verify or falsify the claim that the CJEU has exchanged a bottom up approach to judicial law making for a top down one, because the case law of the Court shows examples of both a top down and bottom up approach. As Davies has argued,[45] there are enough cases where the CJEU has made concessions to national measures which are of a particular local sensitivity, and even a few cases where it may have bowed to the awareness of Member State anger, but probably not in fear of legislative overrides.[46] Interesting is that with regard to the way in which procedural law is regulated in the Member States, which is generally believed to be a matter of Member State autonomy, the CJEU tends to give more leeway to national legislatures than to national courts. On several occasions, the CJEU has held regarding the principle of sincere cooperation that the existence of discretion on the part of the national court provided by the national legislature, entails a duty to exercise that discretion of power in the way most conductive to the effective enforcement of EU law. This applies, even when the legislative rule itself does not run against EU law. This has led Wallerman to believe that, although the CJEU often stresses that the relationship with national courts relies on cooperation and dialogue: 'one might be inclined to infer that national courts are only trusted when little is at stake from the Union perspective'.[47]

As one of the Supreme Court judges mentioned in our interviews, what is lacking in the case law of the CJEU is a margin of appreciation doctrine that enables courts in the Member States to make their own

[44] See more in-depth about this duty to respect national identity: E. Cloots, *National Identity in EU law* (Oxford: Oxford University Press, 2015).

[45] G. Davies, 'Legislative control of the European Court of Justice', *CMLR*, 51, 1579–1608 at 1606. See also: A. Stone Sweet, *The Judicial Construction of Europe* (New York: Oxford University Press), p. 4. More positive about the chance that uncertainty about the risk of legislative override will affect the CJEU's decisions are O. Larsson and D. Naurin, 'Judicial Independence and Political Uncertainty: How the Risk of Override Affects the Court of Justice of the EU', *International Organization*, 70 (2016), 377–408.

[46] See: K. Lenaerts and J. Gutiérrez-Fons, 'The Constitutional Allocation of Powers and General Principles of EU Law' *CMLR*, 47, 1629–1669 (2010), at 1636: 'when engaging in gap-filling, the ECJ endeavours to find a compromise guaranteeing that the project of European integration is not put at risk, whilst making sure that its decisions are sufficiently close to the practice and values of national courts to enjoy recognition and credibility in the Member States.'

[47] A. Wallerman, 'Towards an EU Law Doctrine on the exercise of Discretion in National Courts? The Member States' Self-Imposed Limits on National Procedural Autonomy', *CMLR*, 53, 339–360 (2016), at 360.

choices within the boundaries set by the Treaties, the EU legislature and the jurisprudence of the CJEU. Putting it slightly differently: why would national highest courts tire themselves out to try to align preliminary questions with foreign courts to serve the CJEU's needs if the Court is not willing to show greater responsiveness towards them? De Burca has added to this that due to the introduction of the Charter of fundamental rights and the expanding of the CJEU's external (international) role beyond the scope of the Member States, the Court should adopt a more open, comparative, and responsive style. According to her, this should include the possibility of third party interventions, increase instead of decrease its references in CJEU decisions to opinions by the Advocates General and provide more leeway for national highest courts to enable them to effectively protect the coherence and legal unity of national law, let alone because of a greater learning ability and increasing need for legitimacy.[48]

5.6.6 *National Courts Totally Absent in the Procedure Before the CJEU*

Private parties have several ways to induce domestic courts to refer preliminary questions to the CJEU, such as by an agreement between parties to obtain a particular answer about a matter that is not acte claire or éclairé[49]; by designing the dispute in such a way that there is no possibility to appeal, whilst it is necessary to clarify a matter of EU law in order to decide the dispute[50]; by claiming an EU legal measure is invalid, etc.[51] In the end, however, it is the prerogative of the national court to decide whether or not to refer. National courts, on their turn, may have several reasons to avoid a reference even in case the parties agree a reference would be necessary. Perhaps the case at hand is not seen as the ideal pilot case for a referral because there are other similar pending cases better suited to refer or the dispute at hand can also be resolved without a reference. Paradoxical, however, is that as soon as the case lies before the CJEU, only the parties and interveners in the proceedings (e.g. national governments and the European Commission) are

[48] G. de Búrca, 'After the EU Charter of Fundamental Rights: The Court of Justice as a Human Rights Adjudicator' *Maastricht Journal of European and Comparative Law*, 20(2) (2013), 168–184.

[49] See for instance: Case C-379/98, *Preussen Elektra* [2001] ECR I-2099, ECLI:EU:C:2001:160.

[50] See already: Case C-6/64 *Costa/ENEL* [1964] ECR 585, ECLI:EU:C:1964:34.

[51] Case 3-34/10, Oliver Brüstle v. Greenpeace [2011] ECR I-9821, ECLI:EU:C:2011:669.

entitled to submit observations to the Court of Justice.[52] From then on, the referring national court is completely out of the picture, which eliminates almost every possibility to engage in any kind of dialogue with the CJEU, until the latter court has ruled. Langer formulates it as follows:

> The Court regularly invites the parties to the national proceedings and the Member States to answer written questions in the run-up to a hearing. During the hearing, it also routinely asks them to give further details about specific aspects of the case. What is striking is that these requests frequently concern the facts or the applicable national law. The Court obviously feels the need for additional information or considerations. Arguably, this is input which it cannot deduce from the reference order itself.[53]

Striking is that the CJEU appears to be interested in all sorts of input before and during the hearing in Luxembourg, but no longer in the opinion of the referring court with regard to the facts or applicable national law that cannot already be found in the reference itself. During our interviews, several judges have complained about the fact that they are voiceless during the proceedings. Not a single judge claimed that national courts should become a party to the procedure, but this does not mean there is no need for other possibilities to inform the Court. Especially in case of disagreement between litigating parties and/or the national government about the facts of the case, the correct interpretation of national law, or the consequences different possible preliminary rulings could have for the national legal order, it might be very useful when highest national courts could somehow participate in the proceedings in order to share their view with the CJEU because the referring court is the only independent actor in the dispute between the litigants.

When it comes to the consequences of potential rulings for the national legal order this task cannot be left to the governments because they usually have a certain (political) interest in the outcome of CJEU's decision, which makes the risk of bias realistic. In this regard Bobek has rightfully argued that the representation of Member States may be conceived as a holistic enterprise: there is one governmental agent representing a Member State as a whole. The governmental agent speaking on behalf of the Member State will be instructed by the government,

52 Article 23(2) of the Statute of the CJEU and articles 96(1) and 97 of the Court's rules of procedure.

53 J. Langer, ibid., p. 5.

i.e., by the executive, what the position of the Member States ought to be. There might be nobody, however, to speak on behalf of the internal, national dissidents.[54] It might be highly relevant though if highest courts could share their views with the CJEU. Just think of preliminary questions from lower courts, which are in apparent disagreement with steady case law from their own supreme court. In such a case, it is certainly not unthinkable that the lower court will frame its preliminary question in a way that favours the outcome it wishes the CJEU to reach.[55] In that case it seems not more than reasonable that the highest national court, who's jurisprudence is under attack, is given the opportunity to share its view with the CJEU. Something similar applies when two national courts try to use the preliminary reference procedure to settle a dispute they have amongst themselves, such as in cases like Melki and Abdeli and Landtová.

The Landtová case is interesting because the reference to the CJEU concerning the question whether a pension supplement based on nationality was in violation with EU law was made by the highest administrative court. However, the view of the Czech constitutional court which case law was under attack, was not represented during the proceedings before the CJEU. The constitutional court became aware of this through the opinion of the Advocate General and tried to share its views with the CJEU. However, the letter in which the Czech constitutional court requested to share its views after the reference had been made was refused by the registry of the Court saying that 'members of the Court do not correspond with third persons regarding cases that have been submitted to the court.' This formalistic reasoning may have been a major motive for the constitutional court to declare the preliminary ruling by the CJEU ultra vires.

Bobek has criticized the position taken by the Czech Constitutional Court because that court would have claimed unrightfully that its right to fair trial was violated by the CJEU, while that *human* right does not apply to courts but to citizens and the constitutional court could have also requested its own preliminary question to the Luxembourg court instead of playing the disproportionate ultra vires card.[56] Nevertheless, one might also argue that the CJEU could have

[54] M. Bobek, 'Landtová, Holubec, and the Problem of an Uncooperative Court: Implications for the Preliminary Rulings Procedure' *European Constitutional Law Review*, 10, 54–89 at 78–79 (2014).

[55] Bobek (2013), ibid., p. 224.

[56] Bobek (2013), ibid., p. 226.

prevented this overreaction by being more responsive to a fully understandable desire by the Czech constitutional court to share its view on a matter that directly concerned the legality of its own case law. Regarding the latter: which treaty provision or EU law prohibits the CJEU to be informed by a highest national court that wants to share its view on the framing of a question that has been referred by another highest court in the same country? If the rules of procedure of the CJEU (e.g. Article 96) do not allow for this; why not change the rules of procedure? Why not grant national (highest) courts, for example, the right to submit observations as amicus curiae, especially in case of intra-state judicial disagreements?

In Landtová this might have prevented a head-on confrontation between the CJEU and the Czech constitutional court, but it could also be helpful in cases where lower courts basically try to 'appeal' a decision by their highest national court via a certain framing of the preliminary question, which the highest court does not recognize and might want to comment upon. Not allowing such a form of information exchange by courts as 'third parties' puts a great, and probably unbearable, responsibility on the CJEU to find out for itself whether the referred question is not misrepresented in case there are differences of opinion between national (highest) courts concerning either the facts of the case or the correct interpretation of national law. Moreover, keeping the highest national courts on board when it comes to how preliminary references should be read in light of the facts and the national legal context also enhances the legitimacy of preliminary rulings by the CJEU. Being more open to the outside world during the proceedings is also relevant for the Court because there are frequently similar cases pending before other national courts that might not be referred if they knew about the pending case before the CJEU. It could save both national courts and the CJEU a lot of time if unnecessary references could be avoided. The likelihood thereof currently depends almost entirely on the effectiveness of the information exchange between national courts prior to the hearing in Luxembourg. Especially in case of references by lower courts, one may doubt to what extent these possess the capacity to inform themselves about preliminary questions from courts in other countries via a horizontal dialogue. If this is already very demanding for supreme administrative courts, may we not assume that for lower courts, a horizontal dialogue with other foreign courts should not be expected? If so, this calls into question why the CJEU is reluctant to provide more detailed information about pending references. Of course there may be practical reasons for this, such as translation costs, but it is hard to see why these problems could not be solved.[57] This is even more relevant now that access to information concerning requests for preliminary rulings would also result in greater compliance.[58]

5.6.7 *Dialogue after the CJEU Has Ruled*

Where the national courts seem to be absent during the proceedings before the CJEU, almost the opposite appears to be the case once a preliminary ruling is issued. Our interviews and contacts with the CJEU have learned that the Luxembourg court has limited attention for what happens after it has taken a decision. Almost any kind of dialogue appears to be missing there.

Although the referring court is normally asked to inform the CJEU about the follow-up of the preliminary ruling by sending a copy of its decision to the Court's registry, national courts often fail to comply with this request and the CJEU usually does not take any action in that case. Even if the final decision by the referring court is submitted to the CJEU, the decision is not fully translated. Only a number of keywords ('chaîne de descripteurs') are published on Eurlex with sometimes a translated summary of the core elements of the final decision made by the research and documentation staff of the CJEU and hence not by the referring court itself.[59]

See by way of example the final decision by the referring court as a follow-up of the ruling of the CJEU in case C-285/12. This search provides two results:

1. Conseil d'Etat (Belgique), section du contentieux administratif, 9e chambre, arrêt n° 228.760 du 14/10/2014 # Aboubacar Diakite / Commissaire général aux réfugiés et aux apatrides;
2. Conseil d'Etat (Belgique), section du contentieux administratif, 9e chambre, arrêt n° 219.376 du 16/05/2012 # Aboubacar Diakite / Commissaire général aux réfugiés et aux apatrides

This does not mean there are two final decisions in this case. The dates of the cases tells us that decision n° 219.376 of 16/05/2012 is the national reference and decision n° 228.760 of 14/10/2014 the final decision by the Belgium Council of

[57] E.g. by asking the referring court for a translation of the case or by providing a summary in English, which is undoubtedly the most accessible (second) language for the majority of the judges in national courts.

[58] Bobek (2013), ibid., p. 220.

[59] Open Eurlex, click on national law, select searching national case law, advanced search, and select reference for a preliminary ruling and add year and number. The results will show whether there is a summary available of the final decision by the referring court.

State. Clicking on the latter decision reveals the title and source of the follow-up decision. Clicking on the button Document information will then reveal all the available information, including in this case the descriptors (keywords) in English and a very brief summary of the final decision by the Belgium Council of State, only available in French.

It seems fair to say that the CJEU does not have an overview of whether a final decision by the referring court as a follow-up of its preliminary ruling actually comply with the Courts ruling, let alone that courts in third countries follow the ruling.[60] At first sight, this might be seen as a sign of trust from the side of the CJEU in the faithful execution of preliminary rulings by the national courts, but our interviews have learned that this would be a too optimistic and perhaps even naïve interpretation for several reasons.

First of all, according to both judges and advocates general from the CJEU, the Court simply does not have the time and resources to keep track of this. Moreover, as one advocate general rightfully argued, it would require an active and systematic cooperation from the side of referring courts where it comes to sharing their final rulings with Luxembourg. This cooperation is clearly absent. Two advocates general suggested a 'compliance check' would in the normal course of events lie more on the path of the European Commission. One of them, nevertheless, argued the Commission would not be very keen to do this. Not only would this monitoring of national court decisions create a tremendous amount of extra work, but the Commission would also not be eager to start infringement proceedings for disobedience by courts, because it touches upon the delicate balance of powers between the executive and judicial branch.

Secondly, the lack of attention for compliance of national court's decisions with the rulings by the CJEU cannot be justified by the fact that there is a low-risk of non-compliance. National courts play a decisive role in the decentralized enforcement of EU law.[61] A 2003 empirical study by Nyikos indicates that in the areas of free movement

[60] We realize of course that it would not be doable for the CJEU to follow whether courts in all Member States comply with the precedents set in preliminary rulings. More attention for how the referring court transposes the preliminary ruling in its final decision, however, might have an 'oil slick effect' once national courts start spreading the word amongst each other that the CJEU makes work of monitoring compliance with its rulings by the referring court.

[61] L. Conant, 'Compliance and What EU Member States Make of It', in M. Cremona (ed.), *Compliance and the Enforcement of EU Law* (Oxford: Oxford University Press, 2012), p. 23.

of workers and goods and equal treatment of men and women around 5 per cent of the domestic courts in Germany, France, United Kingdom, Belgium and the Netherlands appeared to be willing to avoid or circumvent 'unwelcome' preliminary rulings. This can be done in many different ways, for example, by reinterpreting the facts of a case, stretching the interpretation of the preliminary ruling in a way that leaves part of the national practice untouched, or simply by being vague about what the CJEU's ruling implies for the case at hand.[62] It is hard to see how the CJEU could put a stop to this since it does not have the necessary resources for systematic compliance monitoring. Moreover, in a situation of dialogue, national courts may also be looked upon to be transparent about how they follow-up on preliminary rulings from the CJEU.

What both the CJEU and the national courts would need in order to make the follow-up of preliminary references easier is a track and trace system in which at least the complete follow-up decision of the referring court is registered and made accessible. It would probably go too far to require that these decisions are translated in all official languages. At least making them accessible in English and/or French and German would help a lot. Not only would it enable the CJEU, the Commission and, for instance, academic court watchers, to get an idea about national court compliance, but it would also offer help to courts in third countries. Regarding the latter, it is important to realize that the CJEU does not always (explicitly) answer to all the questions that were raised by the referring court. In the follow-up, referring courts will nevertheless have to implement the entire preliminary ruling and where necessary fill-in the gaps with respect to questions that were not addressed by the CJEU. This should be done in good faith and without undermining the effect of the preliminary ruling. Courts in third countries would be able to learn from how the referring court does this in order to make up their mind regarding the consequences of preliminary rulings for similar cases in their jurisdiction. Making the final decisions of referring courts as a follow-up to preliminary rulings more easily digital accessible could hence have a tremendous learning effect and accordingly stimulate the dialogue between national courts. Even though the CJEU not strictly obliged to make follow-up decisions by national courts more accessible,

[62] S.A. Nyikos, 'The Preliminary Reference Process: National Court Implementation, Changing Opportunity Structures and Litigant Desistment' *European Union Politics*, 4, 397–401 (2003).

sticking to only being open about information that needs to be provided by law misses out on the very idea of sincere cooperation, partnership and dialogue. From a more practical perspective, it seems to make the most sense to use Eurlex as the central digital database where to find these translated versions of final decisions of the referring court. It will probably cost quite a bit of money to include these cases systematically, but one should not underestimate the spill-over effects this could have in terms of learning, enforcement, and finally legitimacy of CJEU decisions.[63]

5.7 Dialogue and Trust

As far as (lack of) cooperation, partnership and dialogue is concerned, an entire cottage industry of studies on the preliminary reference procedure has developed over the years. However, most of the studies in this 'industry' focus on explaining why certain courts refer more questions to the CJEU than others.[64] Variations in judicial participation in Article 267 proceedings have been explained via multiple theories,[65] ranging from approaches based on differences in judicial attitude and educational background (e.g. those national judges who are more familiar with EU law will be more keen to refer), transnational economic exchange (e.g. courts in countries that depend more heavily on the internal market will refer more), lower court empowerment (e.g. lower courts with limited possibilities to review legislation or appeal higher court decisions, will refer more), inter-court competition (e.g. national courts with higher ambition in terms of judicial law making, such as constitutional courts, will refer less cases), legal cultural explanations (e.g. courts in legal systems with more focus on primacy of the legislature will refer less), and so on.[66]

Fewer studies, for far, have explored what actually happens in the communication between the CJEU and national (highest) courts in order

[63] Just think about how academics could then use Eurlex to study how national courts implement and enforce preliminary rulings.

[64] See for an overview of these studies: A. Dyevre, A. Atanasova and M. Glavina, 'Who Asks Most? Institutional Incentives and Referral Activity in the European Union Legal Order' (August 25, 2017). Available at SSRN: https://ssrn.com/abstract=3051659 or http://dx.doi.org/10.2139/ssrn.3051659.

[65] M. Broberg and N. Fenger, 'Variations in Member States' Preliminary References to the Court of Justice: Are Structural Factors (Part of) the Explanation?' *European Law Journal*, 19, 4, 488–501 (2013).

[66] Ibid., p. 2.

to find out why the 'spirit of cooperation' that has made the preliminary reference procedure so popular since the days of Van Gend and Loos and Costa Enel,[67] now appears to be losing ground. Not only have we seen more cases recently where national highest courts push back at the CJEU, even by threatening to declare preliminary rulings ultra vires (Landtová, Gauweiler, Ajos), but also the integration project itself has become more contested due to the Euro crisis, the problems surrounding Brexit, and by the rise of nationalist governments in some EU Member States (e.g. Poland and Hungary).[68] The CJEU has increasingly been forced to adjudicate on politically sensitive issues partly because of this. Just think of the OMT case and other disputes concerning the supervision of banks and financial institutions by the European Central Bank or by agencies, such as the ESMA.

Criticism following rulings, such as: Viking, Laval, Mangold, Test-Achats, or Volkswagen Law, demonstrate that 'integration through law' probably faces more public outrage and political backlash than before.[69] Nevertheless, Werner explains the absence of really strong opposition and push-back against the CJEU's case law by pointing to three crucial factors: (1) the gradual development of the case law; (2) the signal sent by the Court, whereby a national provision that in principle contravenes European law can often still be (partly) upheld, and (3) the existence of fall-back solutions reducing the damage for Member States that lose their cases, which alleviates the immediate legal or political costs of its case law.[70] The fact that there is not more open

[67] See about this spirit of cooperation also: Case C-571/10, *Kamberaj* [2012], EU:C:2012:233, para. 41 and Joined Cases C-261/08 & C348/08, *Zurita García and Choque Cabrera* [2009], EU: C:2009:648, para. 36.

[68] See about the claim that the erosion of trust in the CJEU is derivative of a dramatic decline for the EU as a whole during the recent Eurozone sovereign debt crisis: M. Pollack, 'The Legitimacy of the European Court of Justice: Normative Debates and Empirical Evidence', in N. Grossman, H. Grant Cohen, A. Føllesdal and G. Ulfstein (eds.), *Legitimacy and International Courts* (Cambridge: Cambridge University Press, 2018), pp. 143–173.

[69] B. Werner, 'Why is the Court of Justice of the European Union not more Contested? Three Mechanisms of Opposition Abatement', *JCMS*, 54(6) (2016), 1449–1464, at 1450. See about integration through law: M. Cappelletti [et al.], *Integration Through Law: Europe and the American Federal Experience* (Berlin: De Gruyter, 1986), vol. 1, 'Methods, tools and institutions'; vol. 2, 'Environmental protection'; vol. 3, 'Consumer law, common markets and federalism in Europe and the United States'. See also: D. Augenstein, *Integration through Law Revisited: The Making of the European Polity* (Farnham: Ashgate, 2012).

[70] Ibid., p. 1461.

criticism from the side of (highest) national courts against the CJEU's case law in general, and preliminary rulings in particular, should not be taken as a token of silent agreement.

Both our case law analysis and interviews have revealed several indicators for a lack of trust between highest administrative courts in the CJEU. To repeat a few we have discussed in more detail earlier in this chapter and in previous chapters: the preference of national courts for closed questions that try to pinpoint the CJEU's decision making in order to prevent it from side-tracking or avoiding the issue at hand; the dissatisfaction with the CJEU's practice of reformulating questions without notification and communication; the unwillingness from some courts to provide the CJEU with provisional answers, because the Court does not seem to (visibly) do anything with that information; the frustration about the lack of possibilities to inform the CJEU about the facts of a case or the meaning of national legal provisions after a reference is made; the absence in Eurlex of translated versions of follow-up decisions by the referring court; the lack of more hands-on workshop type of meetings where Supreme Court judges and CJEU judges and/or Advocates General can discuss new trends and dilemma's regarding how to implement preliminary; the frustration by some highest courts about the prohibition by the CJEU to filter and synthesize preliminary questions from lower courts.

What is interesting is that criticism, from the side of CJEU often mirrors the disappointment from the side of national judges. CJEU judges, for example, often lament about the poor quality of preliminary questions and about the frequent need for the CJEU to reformulate these to make any sense of them; CJEU judges also complain about the fact that a request for clarification with regard to preliminary questions would often just delay the procedure and does not provide them with any relevant new information. Moreover, CJEU judges sometimes seem to lack faith in the competence of some highest national courts to provide useful provisional answers and even claim they want to avoid embarrassment for national courts by replying to provisional answers, because this could bring to light that the solutions that national courts had in mind are heavily flawed. CJEU judges are also mostly quite critical about a potential role for national judges during the proceedings in Luxembourg because it could affect the impartiality of referring courts and mix-up the responsibilities between different stakeholders (CJEU, litigants, national governments, Commission). Being accused of not showing an interest in the follow-up of preliminary rulings, CJEU judges argue they do not have the time and resources to monitor and correct follow-up decisions from the courts that have referred preliminary questions and also point fingers to national courts who fail to submit their rulings to the CJEU.

Finally, some CJEU judges appear to see lower courts as necessary 'compliance watchdogs' because certain supreme courts would still refuse to refer controversial questions to Luxembourg. This might also explain why the CJEU is reluctant to accept that highest courts collect, filter, and synthesize preliminary questions from their lower courts.

5.7.1 *Different Expectations Concerning the "Dialogue" and the "Purpose" of the Preliminary Reference Procedure*

Not all these mentioned points are perhaps crucial for a meaningful judicial dialogue. Certain technical difficulties probably also be overcome quite easily, such as an agreement on how to deal in a more predictable way with reformulating questions and when and how to answer to provisional answers. The same goes for working on ICT solutions to make national decisions which lead to a preliminary reference more accessible and also document what referring courts do in answer to a preliminary ruling. Even sticky problems, such as how to deal with language barriers and cultural differences (e.g. different styles of law making and motivating decisions) may be overcome.

What is probably far more difficult to deal with are differences in expectations about the purpose and meaning of a judicial dialogue. These differences do not only exist between national highest administrative courts and the CJEU, but also within both courts. Our interviews have clearly revealed that some national judges have no interest in a more encompassing judicial dialogue because they are primarily focused on dispute resolution, deciding within a reasonable time and avoiding a backlog of cases, whereas other judges clearly see a greater role for supreme administrative courts in the process of judicial law making to takes place within the preliminary reference procedure which they feel is too much dominated by the CJEU. Judges of the latter category have higher expectations about what cooperation and co-actorship with the CJEU in the preliminary reference procedure should entail.

To a lesser extent, we also see this on the side of the CJEU where some judges and advocates general, for example, stress the fact that a more discursive style of motivating decisions would not work due to the tremendous caseload of the CJEU and the need to keep the throughput time under control, whereas others have more substantive reasons for sticking to the current minimalistic style, such as the need to deal with differences between CJEU judges with very different styles and backgrounds (e.g. seeking for the lowest common denominator in order to reach agreement). What CJEU judges seem to share, however, is that there is little room for national highest administrative courts to share responsibility and co-decide about the interpretation of EU law. This idea would conflict with concepts, such as supremacy and direct effect of EU law.

This last point could also indicate different expectations regarding the (future) purpose of the preliminary reference procedure. In case the preliminary reference procedure would develop more in the direction of a citizen's infringement procedure in which the CJEU needs to be able to declare national legal provisions incompatible with EU law, it is quite clear that the CJEU needs the power to push through its decisions even against the will of national highest courts. As we will discuss hereafter, lower courts can in this scenario even leapfrog their highest court to enforce a certain interpretation of EU law that conflicts with the interpretation by the national supreme court. It becomes a different story, though, when the CJEU's preliminary rulings are placed in light of a law-making duty where the Court fills-in gaps in EU legislation and develops new rules and legal principles that steer the development of EU law. As, for example, the Ajos case has shown, national highest courts may not be automatically inclined to go along with each and every new rule or principle the CJEU develops, especially when national legislatures and other courts have had no influence at all on the CJEU's judicial law-making.

It seems likely that the more the preliminary reference procedure is going to develop into a motor for law making also in sensitive areas regarding criminal law and fundamental rights, the more national supreme courts are going to feel the need to have a say in this process of law-making. This becomes even more pressing where the CJEU may develop new laws or principles that Member States did not see coming, as was the case with the unwritten principle that prohibits age discrimination. Both Member State governments and national highest courts will probably want to prevent unpleasant surprises in this respect. This is only possible when the CJEU is willing to share information and responsibility.

5.7.2 Trust as a Non-Formal and Two-Sided Issue

What is hard to determine is whether a lack of trust between national highest administrative courts and the CJEU is the cause for the absence of a judicial dialogue that goes beyond a mere question and answers routine or that lack of a more meaningful dialogue is the reason for a lack of trust between courts on both sides. Mayoral seems to take the former position. He deserves credit for explaining that and why trust is a necessary (pre)condition for successful judicial cooperation between national courts and the CJEU. He has also rightfully argued that the importance of trust and trust-building between national and supranational courts is a topic that has been understudied, because (lack of) trust could, for example, help to explain: the acceptance of undesirable decisions, the willingness to show deference and vulnerability, or the preparedness to take risks in relationships based on uncertainty which purely self-centred actors would probably not accept.[71] However, the way Mayoral conceptualizes judicial trust between the CJEU and national courts seems to be flawed. This springs, among other things, from his definition of trust, which is: 'national judges' belief about whether the CJEU will follow an expected course of action under conditions of uncertainty'.[72] We believe this definition is too formal and one-sided. It is too one-sided because it puts too much emphasis on the role of the CJEU and on predictability as the primary indicator for trust. If the CJEU is, for example, predictably biased, partisan or politicized that would almost certainly never result in high-trust from the side of national courts. It is also too formal, because it says little about the content of what should be trusted.[73] According to Mayoral, the subjective belief of national courts creates trustworthiness via five features or indicators: (1) there is an individual assessment; (2) reciprocity (meaning: the belief is co-created by another actor with the capacity to create/betray trust); (3) consistency regarding the expected role one is supposed to fulfil (conditionality); (4) a situation of uncertainty, which links with risks regarding future actions; (5) a corporatist nature (e.g. esprit de corps) de connected to boarder attitudes towards the EU.

These factors are bundled by arguing that when the belief is strong enough it creates 'trustworthiness', which Mayoral defines as the *competence* to fulfil the role ascribed to CJEU by the Treaties in articles, like 267 TFEU.[74] Although we think there is much truth in what Mayoral claims, in our view he overlooks at least two important other features

[71] J. Mayoral, 'In the CJEU Judges Trust: A New Approach in the Judicial Construction of Europe' *JCMS*, 55, 3, 551–568 (2017).

[72] Ibid., p. 552.

[73] Hereafter we will see that Mayoral only mentions belief in the competence of the court(s), but we think this is not the only relevant factor.

[74] Ibid., p. 555–556.

that can be derived from the literature to determine trustworthiness. Next to the *competence* of courts in having the expertise to correctly interpret EU law, there is the commitment of courts to fulfil their legal obligations whenever possible in a *reliable* manner showing *honesty* in representing the law accurately and not arbitrarily.[75] Mayoral is not entirely consistent because he only talks about the competence of the CJEU, whereas trust in the relationship between highest administrative courts and the CJEU also depends in the faith the Luxembourg court has in the national supreme courts. This is exactly the element of reciprocity or relational meaning that he discerns but does not apply to his definition. As far as reliability is concerned, one cannot expect the case law of the CJEU to be (close to) a hundred percent predictable. Inherent to being a supranational court is that it deals with hard cases that have not come up before, which makes predictability by definition complex, at least substance-wise. Reliability in court behaviour means that one may expect that the CJEU at least strives for consistency and hence properly motivates decisions to change course in a transparent way because it takes Member State courts seriously.[76] Here the CJEU seems to have a bit of a problem with not living up to its commitment to exchange views with national highest courts. As we have repeatedly argued, the Court has, for instance, the possibility to issue a request for clarification in case preliminary questions are unclear, instead of immediately reformulating questions on its own and it does invite referring courts to provide provisional answers to their own questions but it does not (visibly) engage with the information that is put forward by these courts. This touches upon the reliability of the CJEU in the eyes of national highest courts.

Finally, honesty is a bit of a tricky term, because only people can be honest and not organisations, such as courts. Moreover, judicial decisions are collective decisions. It is not the honesty or dishonesty of an individual judge that determines the trustworthiness of a court's decisions, but the decision of the court as a whole. Accordingly, trust in courts has more to do with an expectation of fairness that it encapsulates

[75] See for an explanation of the relevance of competence, reliability and honesty: O. ONeill, *A Question of Trust* (Cambridge: Cambridge University Press, 2002).

[76] That this is a difficult task to fulfil for highest courts in general because using 'veiled arguments' is often a way to avoid showing that policy arguments have played a role in the decision-making process because a court wants to present itself rather as a law finder than a law maker. See J.B.M. Vranken, *Exploring the Jurist Frame of Mind* (The Hague: Kluwer Law International, 2006), chapter 3.

the interests of those relying on it.[77] Looking for answers for hard cases via a comparative approach to find general principles in the laws of the Member States fit with this, because it is a sign of looking for shared values and principles instead of just following one's own course of action. In case of the preliminary reference procedure, it is the national courts relying on the fairness of the CJEU and vice versa.

5.7.3 *Trust and the Style of Communication*

For the CJEU, this implies a willingness to motivate decisions and to take the arguments of the referring courts seriously and treat them as genuine co-actors in the process of law-making as promised in Opinion 1/09 of the CJEU of 2011. However, here Arnull has put his finger on a sour spot by stating that:

> The ECJ's judgments were originally modelled on those of the French Conseil d'Etat and Cour de Cassation. Although their form has since evolved, the ECJ continues to lack sureness of touch when dealing with its previous decisions and rarely engages in 'serious interpretive or policy analysis'. Its judgments are impenetrable to non-specialists and often make no real attempt to persuade a sceptical reader of the correctness of the result. In that sense, they provide support for Waldron's claim that judicial dialogue may be damaged where a court is confident that its view will ultimately prevail in any event. This approach has become unsuitable in a context where the Union is highly contested and national courts are growing restive. The ECJ might instead consider adopting a less formal and more discursive style, such as that of the European Court of Human Rights (minus any separate opinions). This would allow it to explore issues and set out its reasoning in greater depth.[78]

As both some of our interviewees and several legal scholars have argued, the style of reasoning by the CJEU is apodictic, non-discursive and concealing. What is often 'sold' by the Court as a stone-by-stone-approach to develop its case law into a steady jurisprudential course, is in fact much more often a patchwork of rather loosely related decisions that may at a certain moment in time transform into a more solid precedent, without being clear beforehand when and how this is going to happen.[79]

77 R. Hardin, *Trust* (Cambridge: Polity Press, 2006), p. 33.

78 A. Arnull, 'Judicial Dialogue in the European Union', in J. Dickson and P. Eleftheriadis, *Philosophical Foundations of European Union Law* (Oxford: Oxford University Press, 2012), pp. 132–133. See: www.oxfordscholarship.com/view/10.1093/acprof:oso/9780199588770.001.0001/acprof-9780199588770-chapter-5.

79 See for a debate on the style of reasoning of the CJEU: J. Bengoetxea, *The Legal Reasoning of the European Court of Justice: Towards a European Jurisprudence* (Oxford: Clarendon Press,

This makes the judicial law making by the CJEU unpredictable and unreliable and sometimes perhaps even a bit dishonest because the Court does its best to keep up appearances that because of the collegiality of decisions, the absence of separate or dissenting opinions, and the need for internal consensus-building, the current way of reasoning is the best way to go about.

However, Weiler has argued that collegiality and consensus-building within the parameters of the CJEU leads to an argumentative discourse that is limited to the essential but thereby also to a minimalistic and non-communicative approach when it comes to convincing referring courts. In his view, the current president of the CJEU, has:

> not answered the 'oft argued' critique against the quality of legal reasoning and the communicative style of the Court. What he demonstrated effectively is that the Court, like many prudent common law courts, moves from one question to another as they present themselves to the Court and does not give abstract answers. But as regards the quality of reasoning and communicative effect, all the cases he brings demonstrate the piling of one apodictic stone on top of another. In a way, what these cases prove is how a hugely important line of cases can be built on shifting sands when it comes to legal reasoning.[80]

It seems needless to say that such a stone-by-stone-approach to deal with preliminary questions maybe a very pragmatic way of going about, but it cannot gain trust on the side of the referring national courts. Simultaneously, however, national highest courts are no saints either. A legitimate question from the side of the CJEU would be how they can accuse the Court for not being discursive enough if one sees how many preliminary references are brought to the CJEU in an almost unreadable fashion without any attempt to describe the problem in the case at hand from a more abstract perspective freed from unnecessary national legal intricacies that do not really matter for understanding where the possible tension with EU law lies. In other words, from the side of the CJEU, one would expect especially national supreme court judges to understand that CJEU judges come from various countries and usually have little knowledge about the details of the legal system of the referring

1993); G. Beck, *The Legal Reasoning of the Court of Justice of the EU* (Oxford: Hart publishing, 2013); J.H.H. Weiler, 'Epilogue: The judicial Après Nice', in G. de Búrca and J.H.H. Weiler (eds), *The European Court of Justice* (Oxford: Oxford University Press, 2001).

[80] J.H.H. Weiler, 'Epilogue: Judging the Judges – Apology and Critique', in M. Adams, H. de Waele, J. Meeusen and G. Straetmans (ed.), *Judging Europe's Judges: The Legitimacy of the Case Law of the European Court of Justice* (Oxford: Hart publishing, 2013), p. 251.

court. This requires that in order to be able to have a successful dialogue, supreme court judges would need to try to describe the legal issue at hand from a less technical and national-oriented perspective in order to enable the CJEU to understand what the essence of the dispute is about and where the possible conflict with EU law lies.

It is of course difficult to speak about 'the' style of reasoning of national highest administrative courts because of the many differences between civil law courts and common law courts, Eastern European courts from former communist countries versus highest courts in old liberal democracies, and specialized supreme administrative courts and highest courts where administrative law is but one of the fields of law that is covered. It is nevertheless fair to say, though, that national highest administrative courts in general also have various difficulties with showing competence, reliability and honesty. To mention just a few: national courts are frequently not open about the reasons for not referring cases to the CJEU, for not offering provisional answers or not sending their final decisions after a preliminary ruling to the CJEU. Furthermore, the interviews have also learned that some judges argue not to mind too much when the CJEU reformulates questions, not answers certain questions, or motivates decisions poorly because that would legitimize the national court to follow its own course of action without worrying too much about what the CJEU may have meant to say.

5.7.4 *Trust and Leapfrogging*

Trustworthiness might also come into play when lower courts start using the preliminary reference procedure to bypass their own highest courts. According to Alter's inter-court competition theory,[81] lower courts would use the possibilities to refer preliminary questions to the CJEU as a 'second parent' (the national Supreme Court being the first parent) to basically appeal decisions by higher courts they have disagreements with. Others have criticized this theory because they believe that national courts would predominantly use the preliminary reference procedure simply because either they need assistance in reaching a correct solution or because they sit as a court of last instance that is

[81] K. Alter, 'Explaining National Court Acceptance of European court Jurisprudence: A Critical Evaluation of Theories of Legal Integration', in A. Slaughter, A. Stone Stweet, and J. Weiler (eds), *The European Court and National Courts – Doctrines and Jurisprudence: Legal Challenges in Its Social Context* (Oxford: Hart Publishing, 1998), pp. 227 and 242; K. Alter, 'The European Court's Political Power', *West European Politics*, 19, 3, 458–487 (1996).

obliged to make a reference.[82] The truth is, however, that we still have fairly little empirical knowledge about when and why lower courts refer questions to the CJEU. What we do know is that highest courts in general have over the years caught up with lower courts in terms of the frequency of making references.[83] Research by the Mak sisters has, nevertheless, shown that in eleven EU Member States still more than 70 per cent of the references are made by lower courts.[84] Moreover, there is research indicating that the mortgage crisis that took place after the credit crunch has incentivized lower courts there to use the preliminary reference procedure to sometimes bypass national legislation and/or decisions of higher courts.[85] Interviews with administrative courts judges in the Netherlands by Krommendijk have learned that this "leapfrogging" also takes place in this country and that the motives are sometimes a deliberate attempt to circumvent and correct the decisions by the highest administrative court.[86] He quotes, for example, one lower court judge arguing:

> already for a long time, I have this bad taste in my mouth regarding what the appellate court does in relation to EU law, which is why I want to refer (translation RvG/JdP).[87]

[82] M. Broberg and N. Fenger, *Preliminary references to the European Court of Justice* (Oxford: Oxford University Press, 2014), p. 57.

[83] A. Dyevre, A. Atanasove, M. Glavina, 'Who asks most? Institutional Incentives and Referral Activity in the European Legal Order' (August 25, 2017). Available at SSRN: http://dx.doi.org/10.2139/ssrn.3051659.

[84] C. Mak, E. Mak and V. Mak, 'De verwijzende rechter: Rechtspolitieke verandering via prejudiciële vragen van lagere rechters aan het Europese Hof van Justitie' *NJB*, 1329 (2017). S. Prechal c.s. in 2005 came to 40 per cent for the entire period 1952–2003, which would indicate an increase at least in a significant number of countries. S. Prechal e.a., Europeanisation of the Law: Consequences for the Dutch Judiciary, Den Haag: Raad voor de rechtspraak 2005, p. 25.

[85] Regarding the former. See: F. Gómez Pomar and K. Lyczkowska, 'Spanish Courts, the Court of Justice of the European Union, and Consumer Law A Theoretical Model of their Interaction' *InDret*, 4, 1–34 (2014). (www.indret.com/pdf/1093.pdf) and Case C-415/11, Mohamed Aziz v. Catalunyacaixa ECLI:EU:C:2013:164. Regarding the latter but not inspired by the mortgage crisis but by consumer credit problems: Case C-473/00, Cofidis [2002] ECR I-10875, ECLI:EU:C:2002:705, read in conjunction with: E. Carrère, D'autres vies que la mienne, Parijs: P.O.L. éditeur 2009.

[86] Other motives noted from interviews conducted by Krommendijk (see next footnote) are felt incentives from the side of the CJEU to refer cases, a desire to contribute to the development of EU law, personal career motives, such as an attempt to show off by directly addressing the CJEU, etc.

[87] J. Krommendijk, 'De lagere rechter aan banden. Is er nog ruimte voor de lagere rechter om te verwijzen naar het HvJ?' *SEW, Tijdschrift voor Europees en economisch recht*, 3, 183–196 (2018), at 186.

That this is more than just a coincidence follows from the fact that in four out of five references by lower courts in Dutch immigration law cases between 2013 and 2016, lower courts explicitly questioned decisions by the Council of State as highest administrative court.[88]

A study by Van Alphen shows that from all preliminary questions by 28 Member States to the CJEU in this same period 2013–2016, 139 references concern cases where a higher court had already provided an answer to the referred question. This does not imply that in all these cases, the lower court is deliberately trying to bypass the highest court, although some highest courts (namely: the Corte di cassazione, Tribunal Supremo and Bundesgerichtshof) are more often leapfrogged than others. In 73 cases, the preliminary questions concern a matter of compatibility of national legislation (previously upheld by a higher national court) with EU law. Although in most (108) cases, the referring court does not provide other motives than doubts about the interpretation of EU law, Van Alphen concludes that offering legal protection to citizens is probably an important driver.[89] Sometimes, however, the referring court also explicitly questions the opinion of the highest court. See for instance:

> The referring court states that the acquisition, by Romanian nationals, of the status of EU citizens after the accession, on 1 January 2007, and the lifting, on 1 January 2014, of the remaining restrictions on the free movement of workers have rendered the grounds – on which the persons who organised the

[88] Ibid., p. 186.

[89] T. van Alphen, 'Legal protection by the European Court of Justice: an empirical study on the use of the preliminary reference procedure as a citizen's infringement procedure', Master Thesis Tilburg University (2018), p. 77. 'First, many of these preliminary references (69 of the 139 preliminary references) were made in the legal fields in which there is a clear 'weaker' party – a consumer, an employee, a suspect, or a migrant – who seeks legal protection against a clear 'stronger' party – a company or State authorities. Second, these preliminary references were in most occasions in the interest of the 'weaker' party because the existing national case law was not this party's favor. Third, the referred preliminary questions are formulated in a rather concrete manner, in particular the preliminary questions in the 73 preliminary references that concerned the compatibility of national legislation with EU law. It suggests that these referring courts were just interested to know whether they could disregard or even annul the particular national legislation (and the existing national case law). Finally, in 60 preliminary references the referring courts have provided provisional answers and in 33 other preliminary references the referring courts have only provided arguments against the existing national case law, which suggests that the referring courts were to a large extent motivated to change national law. This finding is supported by the 13 preliminary references in which the particular referring courts have been open about their strategical motives to refer preliminary questions.'

immigration of those nationals were subject to criminal law sanctions in an earlier period – inoperative. That court adds that, in a judgment of 10 January 2008, the Corte suprema di cassazione (Supreme Court of Cassation, Italy), ruling as combined chambers, did not accept that the accession of Romania to the European Union meant that the act of facilitating illegal immigration committed before that accession no longer constituted a criminal offence, and that that case-law was confirmed during the period 2011–2015. Nevertheless, in the order of 8 May 2007, by which it referred that case to the combined chambers, the first chamber of the Corte suprema di Cassazione (Supreme Court of Cassation) had supported the opposite view.[90]

Under Article 267 of the TFEU the lower national courts are considerably empowered vis-à-vis the highest national courts, not only because the latter courts must bring the matter before the CJEU, if the issue is not acte clair, while the lower courts are free to do so. The CJEU has also delegated additional power to lower courts by holding in *Cartesio* that lower courts are fully independent in referring cases to the CJEU, even where a case is pending for the second time before a first instance court after a judgment has been quashed by a supreme court.[91] This implies that lower courts could use the preliminary ruling as an opportunity to overturn or bypass case-law and interpretations of their highest courts, although research by Pavone reveals there are quite high practical constraints for lower courts (e.g. workload, time, reputational damages, etc.).[92] As long as certain highest courts are reluctant to refer cases, there might be reason for the CJEU to use lower courts as watchdogs with regard to the compliance of highest court decisions with EU law.

However, this may come at a cost, because in the long run, prohibiting supreme courts to filter out, collect and synthesize preliminary references from lower courts, for example via a national preliminary reference procedure,[93] could easily affect the spirit of trust between the CJEU

[90] Case C218/15, Gianpaolo Paoletti and Others v. Procura della Repubblica [2016], ECLI:EU:C:2016:748. See also Case C-310/16 *Dzivev and Others* [2019], ECLI:EU:C:2019:30. The reference in this last case clearly indicates that the referring court submitted questions to the CJEU because it expected that the court in second instance and in cassation would not follow its interpretation of EU law.

[91] Case C-210/06 *Cartesio* [2008] ECR 8 I-09641, ECLI:EU:C:2008:723, para 94.

[92] T. Pavone, 'Revisiting Judicial Empowerment in the European Union: Limits of Empowerment, Logics of Resistance', (December 28, 2017). Forthcoming, *Journal of Law & Courts*, 6(2) 303–331 (2018). Available at SSRN: https://ssrn.com/abstract=3093895.

[93] The Dutch Supreme Court has such a national preliminary reference procedure (Article 392 Rv) where lower courts can raise question regarding interpretation of the law to the highest courts. The Supreme Court does use this procedure sometimes to forward lower court's questions about the correct interpretation of EU law as

and national courts.[94] As Bobek has rightfully argued, the *Cartesio* case-law of the CJEU leads to what might be called 'atomisation' of national judicial hierarchies and the question arises if this is a wise policy in the long run.[95] After all, supreme courts have a duty to protect the unity of national law, which is difficult for them to fulfil if the CJEU allows lower courts to bypass them in order to go directly to Luxembourg to seek individual legal protection for citizens or because they simply want to change the course of the national legislature or revise higher court precedents.

5.7.5 *Trust-Building and Another Type of Partnership*

Trust is hard to gain but easy to lose. This also holds true for the relationship between courts. If supreme courts somehow get the impression that lower courts are (sometimes) used by the CJEU to act as watchdogs responsible for supervising whether 'their' highest courts are loyal in sending preliminary questions to the CJEU and for actively enforcing EU law where supreme courts are reluctant to do so, this will affect the mutual relationships. It will not only have an impact on trust that supreme courts have in lower courts, it can also damage the believe supreme courts have in the CJEU. Komárek has therefore advocated an alternative conception of the EU judicial system:

> a conception which sees national courts as true parts of the EU judicial system. Too often national judges are only reminded of their Union mission when obligations in the name of effective application of EU law are imposed upon them. But this mission must also entail more trust in them, as well as a consideration of problems which these obligations may cause to national judicial processes. National and Union judicial processes are connected vessels and problems at one level inevitably cause problems at another. [. . .] The current preliminary ruling procedure undermines national judicial hierarchies when it allows any court to enter into a dialogue with the Court of Justice. While this openness

preliminary references to the CJEU. See for instance: ECLI:NL:HR:2014:2901, ECLI:NL:HR:2016:2834, ECLI:NL:HR:2017:342, ECLI:NL:HR:2017:346 and ECLI:NL:HR:2017:2681.

[94] In this sense Groussot is right as he argues that judicial dialogue is not only a means of communication but also a medium of power as Pierre Bordieu has argued in P. Bourdieu, *Language and Symbolic Power* (Cambridge: Cambridge Polity Press, 1991). See: X. Groussot, Matej Avbelj and Jan Komárek (ed.), *Constitutional Dialogues, Pluralism and Conflicting Identities. Constitutional Pluralism in the European Union and Beyond* (London: Hart Publishing, 2012), pp. 319–342 at 319.

[95] M. Bobek, 'Landtová, Holubec, and the Problem of an Uncooperative Court: Implications for the Preliminary Rulings Procedure' *European Constitutional Law Review*, 10, 54–89, at 74–75 (2014).

certainly played an important role in the formative years of the EU legal order, maintaining it today seems less justified. The alternative conception of the preliminary ruling procedure would thus suggest limiting the possibility to refer preliminary rulings to last instance courts only.[96]

Komárek argues that the CJEU is not merely a supranational court but also a civil, criminal and administrative law court. Because of the self-declared doctrines of supremacy, direct effect, and state liability, the CJEU is no longer an international court acting *outside* national judicial systems, but de facto an *insider* supreme court, whose task is to guide 'lower' courts in their application of EU law. Simultaneously, the Luxemburg court acts as the EU Constitutional Court by deciding disputes concerning the division of powers between EU institutions and in relation to national authorities, systemic principles of EU law or fundamental rights.[97]

With Komárek, we believe that the current preliminary reference procedure is incapable of fulfilling all these different roles at the same time. Other than normal constitutional courts, for example, the CJEU has no filtering mechanism ensuring that only important questions will arise before it. Every court in the EU may turn to the CJEU regardless of the importance of the question referred. This is ridiculous if the CJEU wants to be the most authoritative interpreter of EU law that watches over the unity, coherence and effectiveness of the law. With an increasing caseload, at some point the CJEU will have to limit the possibility of lower courts to send preliminary references in order to be able to provide national courts with proper guidance and by developing general rules and precedents that surpass the individual case.

In order to do this, the CJEU should not only speak convincingly, but also needs to stay away from pulverizing its authority by answering to each and every preliminary question – how detailed and insignificant they may sometimes be – into hundreds of preliminary rulings that cannot be coherent.[98] The CJEU simply does not have the time and the

[96] J. Komárek, supra note 8, at 468. [97] Ibid., p. 484.

[98] Although highest courts have caught up with lower courts in term of the number of preliminary questions submitted to the EU see: A. Dyevre, A. Atanasova and M. Glavina, 'Who Asks Most? Institutional Incentives and Referral Activity in the European Union Legal Order' (August 25, 2017). Available at SSRN: https://ssrn.com/abstract=3051659 or http://dx.doi.org/10.2139/ssrn.3051659.), in 11 out of the current 28 Member States, more than 70 per cent of the preliminary questions are still raised by lower courts. See: C. Mak, E. Mak and V. Mak, 'De verwijzende rechter. Rechtspolitieke verandering via prejudiciële vragen van lagere rechters aan het Europese Hof van Justitie' *NJB*, 1329

resources to check what each and every preliminary ruling means for all previous precedents, especially if the court does not discern between major legal issues and side issues. Moreover, the CJEU does not have sufficient knowledge to consider the consequences for all the preliminary rulings for the law in the each and every Member State if it is concerned with details. Furthermore, the CJEU needs to understand that highest national courts not only have a responsibility for the enforcement of EU law, but are also supposed to protect the unity and integrity of national law. This may become a daunting task when lower courts would increasingly use the preliminary reference procedure to push their luck with the CJEU to get the case law of their supreme court overruled.[99]

The other way around, national highest courts also need to take their counterpart seriously and, for example, not complain about competence creep, while at the same time asking the CJEU to decide citizen's infringement cases, where there is an incompatibility between national law and EU law. As the Witte has rightfully argued, the CJEU usually does not use 'compatibility language' but frequently hides the fact that it is basically dealing with a question of national legislation being (in) compatible with EU law by using phrases as: Article X TFEU must be interpreted as precluding legislation of a Member State pursuant to which… instead of claiming that Article A or B from Member State C is incompatible with a specific provision in the Treaties or a Regulation or Directive.[100] In our case law analysis we have also met examples of highest administrative courts using the CJEU as a scapegoat. Leijon

(2017); Prechal c.s came in 2005 to 40 per cent of the total amount of references from for the period 1952–2003. Prechal e.a., 'Europeanisation of the Law: Consequences for the Dutch Judiciary', Den Haag: Raad voor de rechtspraak (2005), p. 25.

99 We are not claiming that the most important reason for lower court's bypassing or leapfrogging of supreme courts' decisions is disagreement with the highest national court. Empirical studies in Italy and the Netherlands indicate that practical reasons constrain lower courts to refer questions to the CJEU and hence the "empowerment theory" should not be exaggerated. See: T. Pavone, 'Revisiting Judicial Empowerment in the European Union: Limits of Empowerment, Logics of Resistance' *Journal of Law and Courts* 6, 2, 303–331 (2018). J. Krommendijk, De lagere rechter aan banden. Is er nog ruimte voor lagere rechters om te verwijzen naar het HvJ?, SEW 2018, issue 5, p. 183–196. Especially this last publication, however, reveals there certainly are 'activistic' lower court judges who use the preliminary reference procedure to try to 'correct' the jurisprudence of their supreme court.

100 B. de Witte, J. Mayoral, U. Jaremba, M. Wind, K. Podstawa (eds.), *National Courts and EU Law. New Issues Theories and Methods* (Cheltenham: Edward Elgar, 2016), p. 18.

found some telling examples from her interviews with Swedish judges of how this works in practice, such as this judge arguing:

The amount of money we're talking about – then one have to, so to speak, really know what one is talking about when deciding the case (...) yes, for example if we would have said that it is obvious that this is covered by EU law (...) then it would of course have led to a lot of turmoil in the system, then all X would have requested refunds retroactively and then the government would have had to yield and pay – I can't even imagine how much money it would be, but it would be around 100 billion. (...) We did not want to put ourselves in that position – and then the question is, should we out of convenience, because we are so afraid of the consequences of such an outcome, more or less let ourselves be steered into the opposite direction (i.e. as the tax authorities did and tax them) when we did not feel we were 100 percent sure it was the right decisions and it was where we landed, and then we said that we would like to request a preliminary ruling'[101]

Dishonesty or unfairness from the side of national courts may also lie in trying to withhold questions from the CJEU in case the national court is afraid of the expected answer. We have found no evidence that this is happening on a frequent basis. A bigger risk might be that referring courts sometimes simply ignore a part of the preliminary ruling in the final decision without being transparent about it. The fact that some courts are not willing to send their final decision after the Court has ruled to Luxembourg is a reason for concern in this respect.

As we have already mentioned above, it is to some extent unavoidable, that CJEU judges and supreme court judges develop different views on matters of EU law. They have different responsibilities and are embedded in different legal orders, however interwoven these orders may be. Nonetheless, an effective judicial dialogue presupposes there is a certain reflexivity on both sides that takes into account the differences in the history, legal culture and tradition that underlie the pluralistic EU multilevel legal order. As in normal life, however, perceived strategic behaviour can easily backfire. In case the CJEU gets the impression that certain national courts are withholding cases, are unwilling to interpret national law in light of EU law, or do not faithfully implement

[101] K. Leijon, National judges as gatekeepers in European integration: Supporting further integration, protecting national sovereignty or following professional norms?, Paper prepared for the ECPR General Conference, University of Oslo, September 2017, p. 12 (https://ecpr.eu/Filestore/PaperProposal/97cb6f59–8a69–4343-8bd7-ee31d2900e0c.pdf). See also: K. Alter, *Establishing the Supremacy of European Law: The Making of an International Rule of Law in Europe* (Oxford: Oxford University Press, 2001), p. 50.

preliminary rulings, trust will be out of the window. The other way around, national judges will only (continue to) trust the CJEU in case the EU legal framework stays compatible with the fundamental principles and values on which the national legal order is based.

Of course there will be other relevant factors that can affect the mutual trust between CJEU judges and judges from national supreme courts, such as knowledge of and experience with each other's legal orders, the general climate in a certain jurisdiction towards the EU legal order or the attitude of other (non-judicial) EU institutions towards certain national legal orders (e.g. a feeling that the Polish judicial system cannot be trusted because there is too much political influence on the judiciary). Last but not least, Moreover, lack of trust is not the only explanation why the dialogue between the CJEU and supreme administrative courts may be flawed. Above we mentioned all sorts of practical stumble blocks that complicate the dialogue (e.g. language barriers, time constraints, costs etc.) and we are sure there are also complicated economic, historic, and cultural differences between national and supranational courts that have an impact on judicial communication, but this does not prevent CJEU judges and national judges to commit to trust-building in order to improve their communication. The best possible reason for this is that judges on both sides can do it themselves! For most of the other problems regarding the lack of dialogue they are at least partly depending on other actors. In the next chapter we will sketch some scenarios how this could be done depending on how far judges on both sides want to go with their ambitions to dialogue. We will distinguish between three models that move from a low ambition to a high ambition, which we label as: cooperation, coordination and collaboration.

5.8 Conclusion

In this chapter we have shown that even though the preliminary reference procedure serves different purposes (uniform interpretation of EU law, judicial EU law making and protection of rights), which may require different kinds of interaction with national (highest) courts, this interaction does not deserve the label of a judicial dialogue. Even the bare minimum of a judicial dialogue between courts would require that courts respond to each other's arguments and share responsibilities (which is more than divide responsibilities).

Procedural mechanisms that could enhance cooperation and communication, such as requests for clarification and the chance to offer provisional answers to preliminary questions are scarcely used to facilitate co-actorship and make the CJEU and national highest courts respond to each other's ideas and arguments. Our case law analysis and interviews reveal there are not only practical reasons for this but also a lack of faith in each other's competence, reliability, and intentions. More promising, at first sight, are the informal networks in which CJEU judges and national supreme court judges operate. Especially highest national courts have certainly tried to organize more horizontal communication about preliminary questions with other foreign courts and have even set-up organisations, such as ACA, to facilitate this. However, the informal communication with these other courts is freight with practical problems, such as language barriers, lack of up to date digital information on national case law, and insufficient time, resources and commitment at some courts to inform each other. As far as the informal communication with the CJEU is concerned, judges from national highest administrative courts quite often seem to be rather sceptical about official institutionalized meetings. They appear to believe more in hands-on meetings in a workshop type setting where actual dilemmas can be discussed.

Apart from this, judges from supreme administrative courts have different expectations regarding the vertical dialogue with the CJEU. Some judges clearly believe that the CJEU is better equipped than them to answer questions regarding the interpretation and validity of EU law, feel they are too busy deciding cases within a reasonable time and do not seek more responsibility. Other judges, sometimes even from the same highest court, prefer a much more active role of national courts in the preliminary reference procedure. They ask themselves what they receive in return from the CJEU when they share their views about the potential answers to preliminary questions or about the possible consequences of different preliminary rulings for the national legal orders. A number of these judges also believe that national courts should be given a more active role during the proceedings in Luxembourg, not as one of the parties, but perhaps as an amicus curiae or other type of informant to the CJEU. Especially in case of disputes about the facts of a case or about the correct interpretation of national law, these judges find it frustrating they cannot inform the CJEU, where they have a responsibility to later on apply preliminary rulings to the case at hand, which then may be built on false assumptions.

Most CJEU judges seem to see little in engaging more actively with national highest courts via requests for clarification regarding preliminary questions or responding to provisional answers. The same goes for a more prominent role for national courts during the proceedings in Luxembourg. The majority of the CJEU judges and advocates general we interviewed seem not to believe in giving more leeway to national courts with regard to what questions need to be raised (e.g. a more flexible interpretation of CILFIT), informing the CJEU during the hearing in Luxembourg or being able to raise immediate follow-up questions in case certain parts of a preliminary question are unclear to the referring court. What is perhaps more striking is that the CJEU shows such little interest in what happens with its decisions after a preliminary ruling has been issued. The fact that national courts often regularly refuse to send their final decision in the referred case to the CJEU does not seem to worry most CJEU judges even though nobody at the Court seems to know what the compliance rate with preliminary rulings actually is, while most CJEU judges seem to be well-aware of the fact that their court does not always answer all questions that were referred and also understands that some rulings might be found ambiguous by national courts because sometimes that was the only way the CJEU could come to an agreement.

We do not believe that the lack of dialogue between the CJEU and national highest administrative courts, is purely a matter of strategy, power games and inter-court competition. However, we do see clear evidence for a lack of mutual trust between CJEU judges and judges from national supreme courts. CJEU judges frequently lack faith in the competence and reliability of national highest courts to be actual co-actors in the preliminary reference procedure and are apparently reluctant to share responsibility. One good example is the fact that the idea of provisional answers was brought up by ACA members, partly, to relieve the CJEU's case load and enable the Court to introduce a 'green light procedure' in case it agreed with the proposed decision by the referring court, has never gained ground. Our interviews have proven that most CJEU judges do not believe in the idea that national highest courts could actually provide an authoritative opinion about the correct interpretation or validity of EU law provisions, which the CJEU could then rubber stamp. Instead CJEU talked about the danger of embarrassing national courts in case their provisional answers would be overruled.

Another clear example of the lack of trust between national courts and the CJEU is the way in which some national highest courts actively try to streamline preliminary questions from lower courts via informal networking, while the CJEU time and again stresses in it case law that the direct access of lower courts to bring preliminary questions directly to the Court without have to move through the national judicial hierarchy first. Here, even advocates general at the CJEU have previously argued that there are other means to discipline highest national courts who would be systematically unwilling to refer questions to the CJEU. The Luxembourg courts would not need lower courts to function as watch-dogs regarding the compliance of highest courts with the CILFIT case law in order to bring controversial questions directly to the CJEU. The down-side to this double reference system is, moreover, that the CJEU will ultimately shoot itself in the foot because it cannot handle the amount of referral anymore. Instead of hanging on to the references by lower courts, the CJEU could also try to use the highest courts to align and filter preliminary questions so that the CJEU would have more time to decide the really important cases. So far, however, the CJEU has been unwilling to move but an inch in this direction.

6 Conclusion and Future Scenarios

6.1 The Answer to Our Research Question

At the end of this book, it is time to return to our research question. We wondered whether the observation by some scholars that the self-proclaimed "dialogue" between the CJEU and the supreme administrative courts in the realm of the preliminary reference procedure does not exist is correct. If so, we wanted to learn why supreme administrative courts would go along with the fact that the CJEU still presents their relationship as a dialogue. We also asked ourselves whether the CJEU is actually prepared to (a) share power and responsibility with supreme administrative courts with regard to decisions concerning the validity and correct interpretation of EU law; (b) to enable national courts to talk back at the Court to inform it about the consequences of possible preliminary ruling for the national legal order and (c) to show accountability towards national courts regarding the way in which it has taken into account their views of how EU law should be interpreted, applied and enforced?

On the basis of our research, we believe it is safe to conclude that the relationship between the CJEU and supreme administrative courts within the preliminary reference procedure cannot be seen as a judicial dialogue, at least not one that is significantly moving beyond a question and answer (Q&A) routine. Such a Q&A procedure would not be much of a dialogue according to any standard or definition we discussed in Chapter 2. The CJEU hardly seem to use the facilities enshrined in the preliminary reference procedure, such as issuing requests for clarification before reformulating questions and making visible use of provisional answers. In its style of argumentation, the CJEU also rarely seems to respond to any information provided by supreme courts concerning the consequences of different possible preliminary rulings. Nor does the CJEU show accountability towards national courts by revealing how their views and opinions have been taken into account. Contrary to the language the CJEU is often using in which 'partnership', 'cooperation' and 'dialogue' are keywords, the Court does not appear to be willing to share actual power and responsibility with national highest courts concerning decisions about the validity and interpretation of EU law. Most CJEU judges we spoke seem to believe that sharing power and responsibility regarding the interpretation of EU law could all too easily run against the idea of supremacy of EU law. However, this argument was rarely explained in more detail. CJEU judges appeared to see it as something self-evident, although there have also been suggestions in the literature, arguing that the Court could perhaps leave more responsibility to national highest courts via, for example: a green light procedure, by limiting the rights to refer to courts of last instance, or by setting up specialized national courts functioning as decentralized EU courts in certain matters.

Does this mean that the CJEU is behaving totally inward looking? No, that suggestion would go much too far as the CJEU does seem to value informal communication channels since it organizes exchanges with national courts, CJEU judges attend conferences together with judges from national courts and participate in networks such as ACA in order to receive and provide feedback. However, these communications usually take place outside the scope of the preliminary reference procedure. What is more, the interviews taught us that quite a few judges from supreme administrative courts believe those meetings could be organized more hands-on and systematically so that national judges actually have the possibility to share their views, concerns, complaints etc. with regard to the actual legal problems they are faced with. There are certainly signs that CJEU judges and Advocates General are prepared to do this since they do participate in certain specific administrative law networks, but this is usually on a voluntary, ad hoc basis, which makes the information exchange quite opaque, even for national courts.

As we have mentioned before, national courts can also be blamed for not trying to make more out of the ideas of partnership and dialogue with the CJEU. Starting with the informal contacts between supreme administrative courts and the CJEU, for example, we are surprised how unprofessional some national highest courts still operate in this respect. To give a few examples: judges from different courts informed us there is no policy regarding who goes to (informal) network meetings with the

CJEU. Moreover, judges who are sent to represent their court are often not systematically briefed by their court regarding questions and concerns that would require debate or exchange of information and also not debriefed after the exchange with CJEU judges. Accordingly, it often depends on the ambitions of national judges that "happen" to be selected to represent their court, whether the communication with the CJEU goes beyond issues that are found relevant and interesting for the particular judge.

More in general, we highlighted in Chapter 5 that national courts also appear to be rather selective regarding the trust they put in the CJEU. On the one hand, national courts frequently seem to raise questions regarding the compatibility of national legislation with EU law in order to provide legal protection for citizen's, while those questions are basically for the national courts to decide. They are primarily responsible for the enforcement of EU law. On the other hand, national courts are not always transparent about the reasons for *not* referring certain questions concerning the interpretation of EU law, as brought-up by the litigating parties, to the CJEU. In addition, they are sometimes reluctant to leave the CJEU much leeway as to the sort of answers that may be given by narrowing down the questions to the extent that only a yes or no answer from the side of the CJEU is possible. This is unproblematic as such in case this is driven by a genuine desire to make the Court focus on a particular issue. It could also signal distrust, though, because it often minimizes the discretion for the CJEU's decisions. This could even be a trigger for the latter court to sometimes reformulate questions in case these are considered too narrow. As far as contributing to a meaningful exchange of arguments is concerned, we noticed that certainly not all Supreme Administrative Courts are willing or capable to think with the CJEU about the proper interpretation of EU law by providing provisional answers to the questions they are raising or otherwise informing the Court about the consequences that different possible preliminary rulings could have for the national legal orders.

Last but not least, Supreme Administrative Courts are also not systematically sending their final decisions that implement preliminary rulings to the Luxembourg court in order to show how they have dealt with the outcomes of these rulings. To a certain extent, this is probably just plain sloppiness or lack of time and other priorities. However, one may not rule out that, for some national courts, remaining silent towards the CJEU regarding how preliminary rulings are transposed in the national legal order also has to do with hiding that not every part of every preliminary ruling is taken for granted. Remarks during the interviews with national judges, like: if our questions are reformulated in an unrecognizable way or the ruling from the CJEU is unclear, we will feel freer to follow our own instincts, point in the direction of less than full compliance. We are not trying to blame supreme administrative courts for being primarily focused on deciding the case at hand as quickly and smoothly as possible without worrying too much about questions the CJEU has left unanswered. At the same time, one cannot have it both ways by complaining about the lack of responsiveness from the CJEU with regard to signals that national courts try to send via their preliminary references and simultaneously remain silent at the rear end of the procedure when it comes to applying preliminary rulings.

6.2 Why Keeping Up Appearances?

Why does the CJEU keeps on portraying its relationship with the national courts in the preliminary reference procedure as a judicial dialogue in which national courts share an important responsibility for a uniform interpretation of EU law.[1] The other way around, why would national courts continue to accept this? As we already mentioned in Chapter 5, an obvious reason for the CJEU to continue the rhetoric of dialogue and cooperation is that it depends on national courts for bringing up cases and for effectively implementing and enforcing preliminary rulings. A sincere cooperation by the national courts is not self-evident.

We have seen cases where supreme courts have refused to refer a question because a decision of the CJEU might have been detrimental

[1] Case C-2/06, Willy Kempter KG v. Hauptzollamt Hamburg-Jonas [2008] ECR I-411, par. 42, Case C-210/06 Cartesio Oktató és Szolgáltató bt v. Hungary [2008] ECR I-9641, par. 91 and Case C-104/10 Patrick Kelly v. National University of Ireland [2011] ECR I 0000, par. 63. That the initiation of a dialogue with the CJEU depends entirely on the national court's assessment as to whether a reference is appropriate and necessary is not telling the whole truth of course. Not only do highest national courts, which omit to refer preliminary questions to the CJEU, face the risk of a liability claim due to the Köbler case law of the Court (Case C-224/01 of 30 September 2003 ECR I-10239), but a refusal to send questions to Luxembourg can also be bypassed by lower courts addressing the CJEU. Also see Opinion 1/09 Of The Court (Full Court) of 8 March 2011 on the basis of Article 218(11) TFEU on the Draft agreement – Creation of a unified patent litigation system – European and Community Patents Court – Compatibility of the draft agreement with the Treaties), ECR I-01137.

to basic principles of national constitutional law (HS2). We have seen cases in which the national courts raising the same question twice, trying to ask the CJEU 'are you sure' you want to go in this direction, as was the case in Taricco.[2] We have seen 'difficult reception cases', like Sturgeon, where the implementation of preliminary rulings meets with serious resistance from national judges and industry.[3] Finally, we have even seen a few cases of openly rebelling, such as: the Czech Constitutional Court in the Landtóva case,[4] the German Constitutional Court in the Gauweiler case,[5] and the Danish Supreme Court in the Ajos case.[6] These, admittedly hard cases, show that the CJEU's authority is still not self-evident and the Court needs to keep in touch with the underlying values and principles of the national legal orders and cannot afford to drift too far off. Or as Paunio has put it:

> (. . .) in a legal order in which questions of broad political significance are increasingly decided by courts, the process in which general rules are justified by way of individual judgments should include discursive elements founded on a shared value-basis.[7]

This implies a dialogue between the CJEU and the national courts in order to maintain this shared value-base.[8] Determining what 'shared' values are, by definition, cannot be a one-sided exercise, but needs to include the perspective of national supreme administrative courts. As we have shown in the previous chapters, though, there is not so much to be shared by supreme administrative courts, the CJEU appears to be willing to listen to, or at least actively engage with in a way that is visible to the outside world.

The latter begs the question: what is in it for the national courts to keep the dialogue myth alive? What interest do they have in accepting

[2] CJEU 8 September 2015, C-105/14, ECLI:EU:C:2015:555 (*Taricco*).

[3] CJEU 19 November 2009, C-402/07 and C-432/07, ECLI:EU:C:2009:716 (*Sturgeon e.a.*).

[4] CJEU 22 June 2011, C-399/09, ECLI:EU:C:2011:415 (*Landtová*) and CJEU 16 June 2015, C-62/14, ECLI:EU:C:2015:400 (*Gauweiler*).

[5] CJEU 16 June 2015, C-62/14, ECLI:EU:C:2015:400 (Gauweiler).

[6] CJEU 19 April 2016, C-441/14, ECL:EU:C:2016:278 (Dansk Industri/Nalatenschap van Karsten Eigil Rasmussen).

[7] E. Paunio, 'Conflict, Power and Understanding – Judicial Dialogue Between the ECJ and the National Courts' *NoFo* 7 (April 2010).

[8] See: K. Lenaerts, 'Discovering the Law of the EU: The European Court of Justice and the Comparative Law Method', in T. Perišin and S. Rodin (eds.), *The Critical Legal Studies Perspective on the Role of the Courts in the European Union* (Oxford: Hart Publishing, 2018), p. 74.

the framing of the preliminary reference procedure as a judicial dialogue and a true partnership between the CJEU and national courts? This question is more difficult to answer. To a certain extent, it probably has to do with the fact that the presence of the CJEU is a fact of life for national highest courts and so are the doctrines of supremacy, direct effect and state liability. This does not make it very attractive to behave like a "legal irritant" for national courts. There is probably also a far more pragmatic reason, though. Many judges working for Supreme Administrative Courts do not seem to care much about whether the preliminary reference procedure is more or less 'dialogical'. They just want to have, preferably concrete, answers to specific questions having to do with the interpretation of EU law, which need to be solved in order to be able to decide the case at hand. These judges probably do not care how the preliminary reference procedure is labelled and also do not seek more power or responsibility and are happy to leave the interpretation of EU law to the CJEU. Judges in this group seem to view the dialogue rhetoric from the CJEU more as a sign of politeness and do not worry whether it is an accurate representation of the communication in practice.

On the other hand, there are also judges from supreme administrative courts, who view the idea of a judicial dialogue via the preliminary reference procedure as a fruitful concept to capture the relationship with the CJEU. The reason for this mirrors the reasons why the judicial dialogue for the CJEU represents a privileged perspective, namely: judicial law-making in the field of EU law needs to be a shared responsibility because it is about looking for 'common' principles, 'shared values' and 'legitimate expectations'. These judges believe that a dialogue provides them with the opportunity to provide input that is taken seriously by the CJEU in the making of preliminary rulings. The more the preliminary reference procedure moves further away from providing individual legal protection and moves closer towards judicial law making, the more these judges will feel their input is crucial in order to guarantee support for the outcomes of the preliminary reference procedure.

Assuming that at least a certain amount of judges from supreme administrative courts (and perhaps other national courts) would be keen to see the preliminary reference procedure transforming into a judicial dialogue that goes beyond the current Q&A routine, this calls into question whether the preliminary reference procedure as we know it does not need to be reformed.

Based on literature on interorganizational relationships,[9] we will describe three possible scenarios to improve the relationship between supreme administrative courts and the CJEU in the context of the preliminary reference procedure on the 'three Cs' of ways of working together: cooperation, coordination and collaboration.[10]

6.3 Three Possible Future Scenarios: Cooperation, Coordination and Collaboration

The term collaboration is commonly interchanged with cooperation and coordination. However, in organization theory, each concept carries a different level of structure, responsibility and communication.

The first scenario, one that could be qualified as cooperation, refers to a relationship in which the CJEU and the supreme administrative courts function separately, have both their own responsibilities and goals and convey information as needed. It seems fair to say that it represents the current low-trust inter-court relationship. Cooperation is an informal inter-organisational relationship lacking a common mission, structure or joint planning. Of course, one could argue that the joint mission of courts in the preliminary reference procedure is to establish the validity and/or correct interpretation of EU law, but our previous chapters have revealed that for many judges of supreme administrative courts this is not their primary goal. They just want to decide the dispute between litigating parties as quickly as possible without running the risk of being overruled later on. For them, raising preliminary questions is just a necessary step to offer citizens solid judicial protection. They are more than happy to leave the decision about the validity and correct interpretation of EU law to the CJEU. This is also, why we argued that the use of the term judicial dialogue is misleading. National courts do little more than bring cases to Luxembourg. CJEU judges most feel that providing an authoritative interpretation of EU law is their prerogative. They do not seem to be prepared to share much decision-making power in this respect. Nevertheless, this does not imply that the inter-court communication cannot be improved, even in this situation, which could lead to improve trust. Our first scenario sketches some

[9] P. Mattessich, M. Murray-Close and B. Monsey, *What Makes It Work: A Review of Research Literature on Factors Influencing Successful Collaboration* (Saint Paul, MN: Amherst M. Wilder Foundation, 2001).

[10] Ibid., p. 61.

opportunities how to do this without fundamentally changing the nature of the communication.

In the second scenario, the CJEU and the supreme administrative courts do engage in a judicial dialogue. Supreme administrative courts and the CJEU determine coordinate their individual missions in order to advance separate, but compatible goals.[11] Partners work together in order to build work-based trust and formal linkages are mobilized because some assistance from others is needed to achieve organizational goals.[12] Existing procedural facilities, such as the use of provisional answers and requests for clarification, could be mobilized to work together in a more productive way than currently. In this second scenario, the CJEU and the supreme administrative courts work together more actively and in a slightly more formal way. They retain their own responsibility, but they communicate and work together through the establishment of interdependent communication channels. The CJEU first and foremost striving for a uniform interpretation of EU law and the national courts primarily interested in solving the case at hand and applying EU law correctly. The interdependency here is that national courts need an answer from the CJEU to decide a particular case without disturbing the national legal order any more than necessary, while the CJEU needs questions from the national courts in order to be able to protect the uniformity and effectiveness of EU law.

Finally, collaboration is the most high-trust relationship based on the principle of sharing authority and responsibility.[13] Wood and Gray define collaboration as a process that 'occurs when a group of autonomous stakeholders of a problem domain engage in an interactive process, using shared rules, norms, and structures, to act or decide on issues related to that domain'.[14] In this third scenario the CJEU actually shares

[11] P. Mattessich, M. Murray-Close and B. Monsey, *What Makes It Work: A Review of Research Literature on Factors Influencing Successful Collaboration* (Saint Paul: Amherst M. Wilder Foundation, 2001).

[12] M. McNamara, 'Starting to Untangle the Web of Cooperation, Coordination, and Collaboration: A Framework for Public Managers', *International Journal of Public Administration*, 35, 6, 389–401 (2012), at 391.

[13] S. Hord, 'A Synthesis of Research on Organizational Collaboration' *Educational Leadership*, 43, 5, 22–26 1986. See also P. Mattessich, M. Murray-Close and B. Monsey, *What Makes It Work: A Review of Research Literature on Factors Influencing Successful Collaboration* (Saint Paul, MN: Amherst M. Wilder Foundation, 2001), p. 39.

[14] D. Wood and B. Gray, 'Toward a Comprehensive Theory of Collaboration' *The Journal of Applied Bahavioral Sciences*, 27, 2, 146 (June 1991).

power and responsibility with national supreme administrative courts. Judicial dialogue in this scenario means there is co-actorship in the process of judicial law making. The CJEU is no longer establishing the validity and correct interpretation of EU-law in a one-sided manner but needs to show how it has taken the view of the national supreme administrative court into account. The latter courts, not only have to show responsibility towards the CJEU by providing relevant input with regard to how EU law should be interpreted avoiding as much as possible disturbing the unity of the national legal orders, but also need to operate as loyal partners to the CJEU in the enforcement of EU law even when decisions are unpopular and disliked by national governments and state legislatures. As we will argue in § 6.6, this also affect the architecture of the preliminary reference procedure because the emphasis in the procedure is shifted from offering judicial protection in individual cases towards judicial law making and offering guidance beyond the dispute at hand.

6.4 Scenario I: Strengthening Cooperation by Improving the Information Exchange

One way of strengthening cooperation between the supreme administrative courts and the CJEU is by improving the information exchange. Bobek has argued that mutual trust (building) means information flows in both directions.[15] Based on our research and seen through the eyes of both the CJEU and the supreme administrative courts it is safe to conclude that improving the information flow from both sides could serve the goals that courts on both sides have.

6.4.1 *Full Text Publication of Preliminary References*

After the referring court has submitted its request for a preliminary ruling, the CJEU falls silent and the outside world has no knowledge of the case until the opinion of the advocate general is published. This provides other courts with too little information about possibly similar cases pending before the CJEU, which could lead to multiple references dealing with basically the same issues and increase the workload for courts on both sides.

[15] M. Bobek, 'Of Feasibility and Silent Elephants: The Legitimacy of the Court of Justice through the Eyes of National Courts', in M. Adams et al. (eds.) in *Judging Europe's Judges: The Legitimacy of the Case Law of the European Court of Justice Examined* (Oxford: Hart Publishing, 2013), p. 219.

Publishing the full text of all cases leading to preliminary references could improve the quality of references via horizontal communication and help other courts to decide about staying proceedings. It could benefit the CJEU by showing multiple dimensions of the legal issue at hand. We realize that translating the full reference will take time and money but if resources are the biggest stumbling-block one might do what some of our interviewees suggested, namely: not to translate the documents in all the official languages, but only in English and French or German. National courts or governments can then decide about further translation when deemed useful or necessary. The other way around, this puts more responsibility on referring courts. In order to make foreign courts understand the problem that has led to the reference they need to provide the facts and the legal context in a clear and accurate way for outsiders.

The alternative is to leave all this to national courts but this will inevitably lead to an inaccurate and not up to date information exchange that many judges will feel afraid to rely on, as is the current situation of the ACA platform.

6.4.2 *Publication of Documents Concerning the CJEU Proceedings*

The second aspect of the information exchange between the CJEU and the national courts concerns information on the proceedings itself. Quite a few judges we interviewed feel the need to take notice of what has been brought up by the parties and the intervening governments during the proceeding before the CJEU. In order to understand what the CJEU may have made to decide in a certain way, it is important for national courts, to have access to documents filed during the proceedings and transcripts of the hearings in Luxembourg.

Why not publish these documents and open up the transcripts of the hearings? Of course, we realize that some may argue that privacy is a stumble block and, in some circumstances, this might even be the case. However, this is not a convincing argument for systematically not providing this kind of information. Other federal highest courts, such as the US Supreme Court, do it and the cost do not have to be decisive here since the documents sent in by the parties and the intervening governments and the Commission already need to be translated. Regarding the transcripts, it is again better to have some language version than none whatsoever. Moreover, opening-up the black box of the CJEU proceedings serves a goal in itself. It enhances transparency, enables learning for national courts, for governments and law firms, and provides opportunities for court watchers, such as legal academics, to study which procedural strategies are likely to have an impact on preliminary rulings.

Finally, yet importantly, a proper track and trace system enabling to follow the progress that individual cases make before being decided by the CJEU, could tell us a lot more about the management of the CJEU's workflow. This could possibly lead to efficiency improvements because it enables criticism and feedback.

6.4.3 *An ACA Service to Improve the Horizontal Information Exchange?*

A third strategy to improve the information exchange between the CJEU and supreme administrative courts concerns the role of intermediary organisations, such as ACA Europe. This exchange could, for instance, provide more clarity on how to deal with the CILFIT criteria.

When judges abroad are of the opinion that a particular question is an acte clair or acte éclairé this is important information to take into account for other courts that consider referring a question to the CJEU. The CJEU, on its turn, might have an interest in a better horizontal information exchange between the supreme administrative courts as well. Not only would this enable courts to motivate better why they sometimes decide not to refer.[16] It would also provide the CJEU with cross border information on the legal and societal context of the preliminary question, which could help the Court to see the bigger picture behind a certain legal problem that may have led to preliminary questions in jurisdiction X, but also plays a role in jurisdictions Y and Z with slightly different circumstances.

ACA Europe has been giving attention to this horizontal aspect of information exchange by creating two databases called Dec.Nat and Jurifast.[17] The ACA-forum also provides a platform for judges from

[16] In the cases Dhahbi v. Italy (case 17120/09), the ECHR stated that a refusal by a national court of last instance to make a reference to the Court of Justice, providing no reasoning at all when justifying its decision, entails a breach of Article 6 ECHR. Hence, if a supreme court refuses to make use of Article 267 TFEU for no apparent reason, despite the fact that the appellant has raised it in the appeal, such refusal will breach Article 6 ECHR. Schipani v. Italy (case 38369/09) follows the same track. In this case the Corte de Cassazione had omitted all references to whether the issue was an acte clair or an acte éclairé. According to the ECHR: "it is therefore not clear from the reasoning of the impugned judgment whether that question was considered not to be relevant or to relate to a provision which was clear or had already been interpreted by the CJEU, or whether it was simply ignored". Again, the ECHR concluded there had been a breach of Article 6 ECHR.

[17] See for example M. de Visser and M. Claes, 'Courts United? On European Judicial Networks', in A. Vauchez and B. de Witte (ed.), *Lawyering Europe: European Law as a Transnational Social Field* (Oxford: Hart Publishing, 2013).

highest administrative courts to ask each other questions related to the interpretation and application of EU law. Dec.Nat database comprises judgments on EU law that the national court decided not to refer to the CJEU and Jurifast contains preliminary questions, preliminary rulings from the CJEU on these questions and subsequent national decisions. Although promising in theory, we discovered that a fair amount of judges are sceptical about how these instruments work. Some complain they do not always receive an answer (in due course) to their questions, or only receive answers from particular courts while others usually remain silent. Others raised concerns about who answers their questions (experienced judges or clerks from the research and documentation units?) and about the quality of some of the answers. Moreover, quite a number of judges confessed that language barriers still pose problems

Overall, a major concern appears to be the representativeness of what can be found in these databases. It turns out that some supreme administrative courts do not systematically forward their judgements regarding EU law and as far as they do, they often provide the decision in the native language and only make a summary available in English or French. This obstructs an optimal use of this highly relevant information. As Claes, De Visser and De Werd have rightfully argued, the impact of the contribution that judicial networks can make to alleviate the judicial knowledge deficit depends on the extent to which participating judges inform their colleagues an make them interested in the work done by the networks.[18]

A problem with the ACA network appears to be that no one in particular feels responsible for the accurateness and representativeness of the databases and the proper functioning of the information exchange platform. This should not come as a surprise because ACA as an organisation has hardly any full time staff members, which means that most of the actual work concerned with keeping-up the databases and the platform has to be done by judges and law clerks of the supreme administrative courts on top of their regular work. One way of improving the current situation could be to establish and independent ACA Research and Documentation Service that is capable of, and responsible for, facilitating a

[18] M. Claes, M. de Visser and M. de Werd, 'Operationalizing the European Mandate of National Courts: Insights from the Netherlands', in B. de Witte, J. Mayoral, U. Jaremba, M. Wind and K. Podstawa, *National Courts and EU Law, New Issues, Theories and Methods* (Oxford: Hart Publishing, 2016), pp. 114–115.

timely and accurate information exchange between the national courts that increases mutual trust.[19]

In case of a lack of funding, the idea could be to station one law clerk from every member state supreme administrative court working under the guidance of a 'mentor judge' at the secretariat in Brussels for a minimum period of one year. These clerks could be supervised by a senior judge form one of the national highest courts (taking turns) in order to lead ACA's daily operations for a couple of years.

Individual law clerks could then be assigned, among other things, with the task to signal all relevant judgements from their national court dealing with EU law in order to keep the database up to date and answer questions on the ACA platform regarding to the law of that jurisdiction. Having a more substantial staff could also enable ACA to develop manuals regarding the formulation of preliminary references, how to deal with CILFIT interpretation problems, concurrence with regard to CJEU and ECHR cases, and so on. In this situation ACA could also develop much closer working relations with the research and documentation center from the CJEU and fuel the CJEU with information required from the side of the Luxembourg Court(s). This way ACA could actually start to work like a rapid task force that is able to provide quick responses to questions concerning the preliminary reference procedure.

Of course, we understand that this will remain utopian as long as there is no money available for it. However, one cannot have it both ways. Either the CJEU and national highest courts accept that the horizontal information exchange remains what it is, or these partners make a serious attempt to improve the horizontal dialogue. In the latter case, one should be willing to invest in it, at the very least, by providing sufficient work force. The only other alternative we see is that the CJEU is going to take over some of the ACA tasks regarding documentation and information exchange, but this has the disadvantage that it will

[19] Currently we do not believe that ACA is capable of adequately fulfilling its mission statement: 'The objectives of ACA-Europe are to obtain a better understanding of EU law by the judges of the supreme administrative courts across Europe and a better knowledge of the functioning of the other supreme administrative courts in the implementation of EU law; to improve the mutual trust between judges of the Supreme Administrative Courts; to foster an effectively and efficiently functioning of administrative justice in the EU; to provide exchange of ideas on the rule of law in the administrative judicial systems and, finally, to ensure access to the decisions of the Supreme Administrative Courts implementing EU law.' See: www.aca-europe.eu/index.php/en/.

probably remain impossible to organize the same amount of expertise on national law. Moreover, it would make supreme administrative courts even more dependent on information from the side of the CJEU. In the current climate, it is unlikely that this will improve mutual trust.

6.5 Scenario II: Coordination via More Formalized Communication Channels

In the coordination scenario, the supreme administrative courts and the CJEU work together more actively to advance their separate, yet compatible missions to advance the working of the preliminary reference procedure via more formalized judicial dialogues. Hereafter, we will discuss four communication channels: the use of provisional answers; reformulation of questions and requests for clarification; a position for national courts in the proceedings before the CJEU as amici curiae, and the introduction of a more responsive style of decision making for the CJEU.

6.5.1 Interacting through Provisional Answers

6.5.1.1 Origins of the Idea of Provisional Answers

Article 107(2) of the current Rules of Procedure of the Court of Justice under the heading of the urgent preliminary reference procedure prescribes that 'the national court or tribunal indicates in so far as possible the answer it proposes to the question referred'. The scope of this rule is limited in the sense that it is an option and not a legal obligation for national courts and it is now located under the heading of the urgent preliminary reference procedure.[20]

However, outside of the urgent reference procedure, referring national courts also have the possibility to provide provisional as follows from the CJEU's: 'Information Note on References': 'the referring court may, if it considers itself able, briefly state its view on the answer to be given to the questions referred for a preliminary ruling.'[21] This possibility to offer provisional answers goes back to the 'Report on the future of the European Communities Courts System' form a working group led by former president of the Court of Justice Ole Due. This group proposed to the European Commission to change the Court's rules of procedure in order

[20] Previously this rule was found in Article 104b, par. 1, of the Rules of Procedure.
[21] Information note on references from national courts for a preliminary ruling, article 23.

to: 'include in the preliminary questions reasoned grounds for the answers that the national court considers most appropriate.'[22] This idea gained support from former advocate-general Jacobs and was also embraced by a working group of ACA-Europe in collaboration with the Network of Supreme Courts of the European Union.[23] In 2008 the idea was even picked-up in a resolution of the European Parliament.[24]

6.5.1.2 Providing Provisional Answers

An attractive feature of providing provisional answers is that it opens up a channel of communication between the referring court and the CJEU, which enables national courts to contribute directly to the development of EU-law. It encourages to do more than just pass on relevant questions to the CJEU and think out loud about possible answers.[25] The CJEU could benefit from this but in the majority of the cases we studied; supreme administrative courts do not share their view via provisional answers. As far as they do, the CJEU does usually not directly respond to the given answers. From the interviews, we took that referring courts have several reasons for not coming up with provisional answers ranging from practical hurdles, issues relating to legal culture, to the fact that the CJEU maintains a profound silence. CJEU judges usually do not respond and give different reasons for this, such as, that they do not want to embarrass national courts that might got it wrong.

We feel that the supreme administrative courts should be encouraged to deliver provisional answers, without making it a legal obligation. Not only would this require treaty reform, but whether provisional answers are useful also depends on the circumstances of the case. Some courts are

[22] Report by the Working party on the future of the European Communities Court system, January 2000, p. 18. See: http://ec.europa.eu/dgs/legal_service/pdf/due_en.pdf, accessed on November 14, 2018.

[23] Francis Jacobs, 'Possibilities for further reforming the preliminary reference procedure. Papers for the Colloquium on the Judicial Architecture of the European Union', (Papers from the Colloquium on the Judicial Architecture of the European Union, May 2004) 62. See: www.ccbe.eu/document/events/colloquium.pdf, accessed on November 14, 2018. Association of the Councils of State and Supreme Administrative Jurisdictions of the European union and Network of the Presidents of the Supreme Judicial Courts of the European Union, 'Report of the working group on the preliminary rulings procedure', (2007) The Hague. See: www.aca-europe.eu/seminars/2007_DenHaag/Final_report.pdf, accessed on November 14, 2018.

[24] European Parliament Resolution of 9 July 2008 on the role of the national judge in the European judicial system (2007/2027(INI)), sec. 31.

[25] F. Jacobs (2004), 'Possibilities for further reforming the preliminary rulings procedure', Papers from the Colloquium on the Judicial Architecture of the European Union.

probably more equipped to play the game of sending signals and indicating possible answers than others do. If the CJEU is afraid of embarrassing the referring court in case of disagreement, it could perhaps limit the dialogue to supreme courts. These should feel less insecure due to opposition from other highest courts. Provisional answers are not necessary in all cases. Only if the referring court has reason to believe that it can contribute to the decision by the CJEU by, for example, explaining the consequences of different potential answers, does it make sense. Provisional answers may also take different forms, such as (a) offering one 'right answer'; (b) offering a number of alternative answers and (c) offering several answers with an additional assessment of their potential consequences for the national legal order. Opting for one of these options may also send a signal to the CJEU regarding the expectations referring courts have. As an alternative to provisional answer, referring courts may consider giving the CJEU 'clarifications' or 'indications'.[26]

We think the CJEU and supreme administrative courts might want to consult each other in order to formulate a common policy on providing provisional answers. Why not trying a more meaningful dialogue by discussing the needs on either side? Instead of guessing what the other side finds embarrassing or not, one could also talk to each other. What is so difficult about that? We also believe that not responding to provisional answers by the CJEU will in the long run diminish the preparedness from national courts to think with the Court and will certainly not help building greater mutual trust.

6.5.1.3 Responding to Provisional Answers

The fact that the CJEU currently does not refer to provisional answers provided by the national courts, should not be taken as evidence of their irrelevance. Of course, they might be helpful to the internal secret deliberations within the chambers of the CJEU. Coordination of tasks between the CJEU and supreme administrative courts, however, will never occur as long as there is no exchange of arguments and hence a dialogue.

Responding to provisional answers, would not only signal that the CJEU takes the highest national courts seriously, it could also encourage

[26] Association of the Councils of State and Supreme Administrative Jurisdictions of the European union and Network of the Presidents of the Supreme Judicial Courts of the European Union, 'Report of the working group on the preliminary rulings procedure', (2007) The Hague. See www.aca-europe.eu/seminars/2007_DenHaag/Final_report.pdf, accessed on November 14, 2018.

the latter not to shy away from sharing their views about the interpretation of EU law with the CJEU. It might even stimulate compliance with preliminary rulings once the Luxembourg court has decided because referring courts, which feel they have been taken seriously may be expected to apply preliminary rulings faithfully.

The lack of responsiveness from the CJEU towards provisional answers touches upon more general problems regarding the style of reasoning of the Court. As we have reported earlier quite a few judges we interviewed and a more than a few academics, argue that the CJEU's reasoning is too minimalistic, apodictic, and sometimes outright concealing. Judges we interviewed, claim the CJEU often makes it look as if its decision follow almost naturally from earlier case law, whereas this is in fact not the case. Weiler has put it as follows:

> The Court should abandon the cryptic, Cartesian style which still characterizes many of its decisions and move to the more discursive, analytic and conversational style associated more with the common law world – though practiced by others as well, notably the German Constitutional court. As noted above, especially in its Constitutional jurisprudence, it is crucial that the Court display in its judgments that national sensibilities were fully considered and taken into account. And it must amply explain and reason its decisions if they are to be not only authoritarian but also authoritative. The Cartesian style with its pretense of logical legal reasoning and inevitability of results is not conducive to a good conversation with national courts.[27]

We are certainly aware of the fact that it is far from easy to change traditions and legal cultures ingrained in the Court's style of decision making. Moreover, we also understand that with the current caseload of the CJEU (see hereafter), a fundamentally different style of motivating decisions is probably unrealistic because it would take much more time and resources. However, this does not preclude the CJEU from taking little steps in the right direction. A first step could very well be the CJEU responding more actively and explicitly to the opinion of the advocate-general, the input of the parties to the proceedings, and more in particular to supreme administrative courts offering provisional answers that are meant to assist or warn the Court. The CJEU could even try to raise the level of the discourse by paying more attention to provisional answers that are well thought-through. Once national supreme courts start to see how they can have an influence on the interpretation of EU

[27] J. Weiler, 'Epilogue: The Judicial Après Nice,' in de Búrca G., Weiler J.H.H. (eds.) *The European Court of Justice* (Oxford: Oxford University Press, 2001) at p. 225.

law and/or prevent the CJEU from disrupting the national legal order in an unnecessary way, they will be more likely to start offering meaningful provisional answers if there is something to gain.

6.5.2 Launching Requests for Clarification

There is another category of cases where better coordination is possible, namely when the CJEU feels it needs to reformulate preliminary questions in order to 'save the question' or deliver a judgment that suits the legal orders or all Member States, but is thereby missing to address the problem as the referring court sees it.

An obvious course of action for the CJEU in such situations would be to invoke Article 101 of the Rules of Procedure more often to issue a request for clarification. From the interviews we took that, the CJEU seldom uses this instrument. The reasons Article 101 rarely is invoked are not very convincing though. The fact that the CJEU tried the instrument unsuccessfully in a few cases, where mostly lower courts did not provide useful additional information after a request for clarification, does not imply the instrument cannot work in relation to complex legal problems that supreme administrative courts have brought forward. This especially holds true in case there are additional signals that the case being referred is controversial or otherwise problematic. Just think of the Landtová case where two highest courts had a dispute about the interpretation of national law in light of EU law and both courts were trying to send messages to the CJEU or think about leapfrogging situations where the referring court is signalling that it disagrees with a higher national court. In such situations, it might be very good when the CJEU tries to first clarify what exactly is being referred before giving its own interpretation of the preliminary question, which could easily make things worse instead of better.

Some CJEU judges pointed at the possible procedural implications of issuing requests for clarification. They are worried in particular, that such requests will according to national procedural law lead to a reopening of the national case in order to hear the parties, which could then further delay the proceedings before the CJEU. However, we wonder how serious these concerns are. First, does the CJEU have an overview over national procedural laws that would require reopening of the referred case? Is it not likely that in many jurisdictions such a request will be seen as a practical matter that the referring court can decide for itself? After all, the referring court is also formally responsible for formulating the reference (question) and not the litigating parties.

National courts may decide to ask the litigants about the opinion concerning the questions that will be referred, but according to EU law they do not have to. Apart from that, it is not immediately clear whether it would be a problem if under some circumstances the case needs to be reopened because if the referred question is unclear and the CJEU therefore needs more time to figure out what is mean by it, the proceedings in Luxembourg will probably be delayed, which just as much affects the litigating parties. Moreover, the CJEU can attach an explicit deadline to a request for clarification, according to Article 101.

With Langer we would like to argue in favour of a broader use of this provision by the CJEU on the basis of an agreement with the supreme (administrative) courts that sets the conditions concerning when and how requests for clarification should be ordered and the sort of response that may be expected. This would not only benefit the dialogue between the CJEU and the national courts, but there is also an interest of fact finding behind it. Litigating parties, member state governments and the Commission all have an interest in a certain outcome of the preliminary reference procedure. That is why national highest courts are probably the most objective informants for the CJEU on matters of fact or national law.[28] In case national highest courts are the most objective players in the dispute that led to a reference, why not use them more actively to inform the Court in case there are doubts about the correct interpretation of the facts or the national legal provisions in a case?

6.5.3 *Supreme Courts Acting as Amici Curiae in Proceedings before the CJEU*

Some scholars have argued in favour of a more active role of the national courts during the proceedings before the CJEU. Wattel, for example, has argued that the referring court's judges should be allowed to speak at the hearing to correct misunderstandings concerning the facts or national law, or to supply additional information about the questions.[29]

This solution runs the risk of changing the nature of the hearing, but this is not a convincing argument per se. Otherwise, one would almost never be able to change anything. Nevertheless, we learned from the

[28] J. Langer, 'The preliminary ruling procedure: old problems or new challenges?', Inaugural lecture held on March 31, 2015 on acceptance of the Professorship of European law and the national legal order, p. 11. Available at SSRN: https://ssrn.com/abstract=2885256 or http://dx.doi.org/10.2139/ssrn.2885256.

[29] See http://njb.nl/blog/prejudiciele-samenwerking-en-dialoog.18560.lynkx (in Dutch).

interviews that not a single judge of the supreme administrative courts we spoke claim they should be considered to become a party to the proceedings. However, this does not exclude a more active role during the proceedings before the CJEU. A possibility would be to give the national courts a position as amici curiae.[30]

Positioning national courts as amici curiae could be done via a request for clarification or by offering the referring court an opportunity to provide a written amicus brief on the merits of the case in the run-up to the hearing especially in complex cases. The latter option would require that the CJEU provides the referring court with the documents sent in by the parties, by the national government, and by intervening Member States. Only then, could a national supreme court clarify questions of fact or of national law. In case a reference is made by a lower court, amicus briefs could also serve to inform the CJEU about matters of possible disagreement between different national courts. In particular when a lower court submits a reference because it obviously disagrees with the interpretation of EU law by a higher national court and also signals this, the CJEU could invite the supreme court to submit observations and tell its side of the story?[31]

Finally, the CJEU could decide to ask one or more national supreme courts to intervene in a preliminary reference procedure originated by a foreign court in order to inform the CJEU about the consequences different rulings could have for other jurisdictions. This idea was launched by a judge from one of the biggest Member States, who claimed that supreme courts are better equipped to provide information on the consequences a preliminary ruling could have for the legal order than government representatives. Not only do judges often have better knowledge about the national legal system than government representatives do, but for the CJEU, judges also have the advantage of being independent and impartial. The state-centred and holistic view on the representation of the member state before the CJEU easily overlooks that there might be internal, national dissenting interests and opinions. If, as Bobek has claimed, in such cases the individual actors will not be heard,

[30] See also M. Bobek, 'Landtová, Holubec, and the Problem of an Uncooperative Court: Implications for the Preliminary Rulings Procedure' *European Constitutional Law Review*, 10: 54–89, at 83 (2014).

[31] See M. Bobek, 'Of Feasibility and Silent Elephants: The Legitimacy of the Court of Justice through the Eyes of National Courts', in M. Adams et al. (eds.), *Judging Europe's Judges: The Legitimacy of the Case Law of the European Court of Justice Examined* (Oxford: Hart Publishing, 2013), p. 227

this may quickly generate the feeling of 'about us without us' or of 'law-making without representation'.[32]

6.6 Scenario III: Collaboration Between the CJEU and Supreme Courts

For the third scenario, we must look at the EU judicial system as a whole – not as a mere conglomerate of the central court in Luxembourg and the national courts in the Member States, each having their own responsibilities. In this scenario, the EU judicial system comprises national courts as true European courts that not only have obligations resulting from EU law but also take part in the making of EU law.[33] True collaboration implies that the CJEU actually shares power and responsibility with supreme (administrative) courts regarding decisions with respect to the validity and correct interpretation of EU law. In this scenario, we distinguish between two different modes of dialogue. First, supreme courts could play a much more important role in filtering, synthesizing and distributing preliminary questions from lower courts in the Member States to the CJEU. Second, the supreme administrative courts could be given more power and responsibility to answer certain preliminary questions as decentralized agents of the CJEU.

6.6.1 *Supreme Courts as Relay Stations*

The current CJEU's case law shows that lower courts can refer preliminary questions to the CJEU even when their own supreme court has already provided an interpretation over the same legal issue.[34] Interlocutory procedures before the national constitutional court or another national supreme court to filter references before these can be send to the CJEU may even interfere with the right of the lower courts to have full and immediate access to the preliminary reference.[35] The current state of the law is that lower courts should be able to (a) refer questions

[32] M. Bobek, 'Landtová, Holubec, and the Problem of an Uncooperative Court: Implications for the Preliminary Rulings Procedure' *European Constitutional Law Review*, 10, 54–89, at 74–75 (2014).

[33] J. Komarek, 'In the Court(s) We Trust? On the Need for Hierarchy and Differentiation in the Preliminary Ruling Procedure' *European Law Review*, 32, 4, 467–491, at 475 (2007).

[34] Case C-166/73 Rheinmühlen-Düsseldorf v. Einfuhr- und Vorratsstelle für Getreide und Futtermittel (1974), ECLI:EU:C:1974:3.

[35] Case C-188-10 and C-189-10, Melki and Abdeli.

to the Court, at whatever stage of the proceedings they deem appropriate, even at the end of the interlocutory procedure, any question which they consider necessary; (b) to adopt any measure necessary to ensure provisional judicial protection of the rights conferred under the EU law and (c) to leave aside the national legislative provision at issue if it is considered contrary to EU law.

Although the CJEU seems to provide some room for coordination of preliminary references at the national level, it emphasizes that this should not distract a lower court from referring whatever question it considers necessary. In the collaborative scenario, there are good reasons for the CJEU to reconsider its position in this respect and give highest courts more leeway to conduct a preselection of the questions form lower courts. In order to guarantee that preliminary questions are precise and relevant, it is important that the problem which led to concerns about the alignment with EU law has been thought-through in the national judicial hierarchy. More instances assessing the legal problem, usually also means more accuracy about the nature of the problem that is related to the interpretation of EU law.[36] Apart from that, supreme courts are capable of pooling and coordinating cases from lower courts in such a way that the legal issue is presented in the best possible way to be referred. We add to this, that national highest courts are also better positioned to filter-out questions that are acte clair or acte éclairé than lower courts that usually have less experience, knowledge, and resources to draft preliminary references.

In case the CJEU is serious about a judicial dialogue it should view supreme courts more as co-actors with a shared responsibility for the proper functioning of the preliminary reference procedure, especially since the number of references cannot be controlled without this in the long run. Obviously, such a position as relay station requires institutionalized communication channels and in some Member States, such as Spain and the Netherlands, there is already a possibility for lower court judges to ask advice from the supreme courts before submitting references. However, the question is if one should not take this one step further. We do not see, for example, why the CJEU would not allow some sort of front office to gain access to preliminary reference procedure. This could be done in various ways. Just think of a commission consisting of members of the supreme courts and representatives from

[36] Komarek supra note 31, at p. 488.

lower courts that decides when and how preliminary questions are fit to be send to the CJEU.[37]

We realize that some highest courts, and in particular constitutional courts, have been reluctant in the past to submit preliminary questions, but not only do these days seem to be as good as over,[38] there are other possibilities for the CJEU to address that problem. Moreover, involving national supreme courts more actively in this respect would also show the CJEU considers them as trustworthy partners, which is more likely to have a positive effect on the inter-court cooperation than that this will lead to further obstruction of the preliminary reference procedure.[39] Komárek has argued there is little reason to believe the uniformity and the development of EU law would be endangered by limiting preliminary references to highest courts.

Far more important than the practical reasons for allowing supreme courts a greater role in the filtering of preliminary questions, such as the caseload control of the CJEU, is the fact that the only way the CJEU can gradually develop into a genuine constitutional court for the European Union is to give national highest courts a more prominent role as well and involve them in the development of EU law more actively, let alone because as Feteris has argued supreme courts nowadays generally recognize that law making is not exclusively a task for the legislator, but must involve in particular the highest courts in the state(s). In the long term, highest courts, including constitutional courts, will probably not accept an exclusionary role for the CJEU as the sole interpreter of EU law

[37] In Dutch civil law for example, the lower courts can already refer a question to the Dutch Supreme Court if this question is of special interest for the development of the law. We know of at least five cases in which the lower courts referred a question containing an EU law dimension to the Dutch Supreme Court that in turn referred these questions to CJEU. See: J. Krommendijk, 'Samenloop van nationale en Unierechtelijke prejudiciële procedure: straight to the top of een hink-stap-sprong?' *Rechtsgeleerd Magazijn Themis* 179, 4, 149–158 (2018).

[38] A. Dyevre, A. Atanasova, M. Glavina, Who asks most? Institutional incentives and referral activity in the European Union legal order (August 25, 2017). Available at SSRN: https://ssrn.com/abstract=3051659 or http://dx.doi.org/10.2139/ssrn.3051659.

[39] See also M. Bobek, 'Landtová, Holubec, and the Problem of an Uncooperative Court: Implications for the Preliminary Rulings Procedure' *European Constitutional Law Review*, 10, 54–89, at 75 (2014), who rightfully argues that the CJEU´s attitude rests on a widely spread legend, which would need to be empirically confirmed first, namely that (a) for the construction of the EU legal order, the direct engagement of the Court with any first instance court in the middle of nowhere is essential, because it is these courts which send the most important, progressive questions; and (b) national superior courts are opposed to this fact and are trying to block the access of lower courts to the Court or prevent the effects of the judgments of the Court in the national legal order.

in case the Court does not also allow other highest courts to look over its shoulders and provide some kind of checks and balances.

6.6.2 *Towards a Decentralized Decision-Making Model*

As already mentioned, one of the main future challenges for the preliminary reference procedure is to deal with the enormous workload while at the same time upholding its primary function in the development of the EU law. There have been warnings in the literature that the attachment to the preliminary rulings procedure in its current form is in the end detrimental to the authority and authoritativeness of the CJEU. Broberg and Fenger, for instance, stated:

> if no measures are taken it is not unlikely that both the unity and the impact of the Court's decisions will diminish as their number increases and as they deal more frequently with questions of secondary importance or of interest only in the context of the case concerned.[40]

The question that needs to be address and that also follows from § 6.6.1 is whether the CJEU should not evolve from its present role of being a 'jack of all trades' into the EU's true constitutional court. In case one answers this question in the affirmative, this cannot be done without focusing more on the bigger issues of general importance for all Member States in the development of EU law.[41] One of the instruments to relieve the Court would be a certiorari system similar to the one applied by the US Supreme Court whereby cases of lesser importance for the uniformity and development of EU law are weed out.[42] Such a docket control system would enable the CJEU to concentrate on the most notable issues of EU law. However, a docket control system involves the risk of having a distorting effect on the judicial cooperation between the national courts and the CJEU instead of facilitating the judicial dialogue.[43]

An alternative model to control the Court's docket could be to build on the idea of provisional answers we discussed under the second scenario

[40] For example, M. Broberg and N. Fenger, *Preliminary References to the European Court of Justice* (second edition), (Oxford: Oxford University Press, 2014), p. 24.

[41] See also: J.H.W. Weiler, 'Epilogue: Judging the Judges – Apology and Critique', in M. Adams, H. de Waele, J. Meeusen and G. Straetmans, *Judging Europe's Judges The Legitimacy of the Case Law of the European Court of Justice* (Oxford: Hart publishing, 2013), p. 253.

[42] Discussed, for example, by H. Rasmussen, Remedying the Crumbling EC Judicial System, *Common Market Law Review*, 37, 1071–1112 (2000).

[43] A. Arnull, 'Judicial Architecture or Judicial Folly? The Challenge Facing the EU', in A. Dashwood and A.C. Johnston (eds.), *The Future of the Judicial System of the European Union*, (Oxford: Hart Publishing, 2001), pp. 41 and 45.

above. In case supreme courts are prepared to take the idea of provisional answers more seriously, this would allow the CJEU to introduce a 'green light procedure'.[44] One option might be that the CJEU could dispose more cases by an order in which it simply refers to one of the answers already provided by the referring court. In such a case, it should be clear, though, whether the CJEU agrees only with the outcome of the provisional answer or also with the underlying legal reasoning. This problem could be solved via a combination of giving 'green light' in combination with an abbreviated motivation in case the Court only partly agrees with the underlying reasoning of the referring court.[45] A combination of relying more on (solid) provisional answers with the possibility of an abbreviated motivation and possible referral to the ordinary reference procedure would not only speed up the process, but also offers the CJEU the opportunity to differentiate between cases of general importance and dime a dozen cases. From the perspective of trust building it would have the advantage that it involves national supreme courts more directly in the process of judicial law making via preliminary rulings and gives them responsibility instead of treating them as a judicial post-box.[46] We believe this is likely to (further) improve the relationship with the CJEU.

A final option could be for the CJEU to establish decentralized "auxiliary courts" with judges from supreme courts and perhaps constitutional courts that would decide more practical oriented preliminary questions that currently flood the docket of the Luxembourg court. This remedy might work both ways. On the one hand, it could relieve the caseload of the CJEU and enable it to focus on the legal problems that really matter and provide leeway for the CJEU to spend more time and energy on judicial law making with regard to problems that affect the unity of EU law. On the other hand, it would also involve judges from national courts much more actively in the development and maintenance of European law. The latter might also create more support for and acceptance of preliminary ruling from the side of national governments and

[44] F. Jacobs, 'Possibilities for further reforming the preliminary rulings procedure', Papers from the Colloquium on the Judicial Architecture of the European Union November 15, 2004, p. 62–69 (available at: www.ccbe.eu/document/events/colloquium.pdf).

[45] See for example the Dutch Article 81 RO (the Judicial Organization Law Act) providing the Dutch Supreme Court with the possibility of an abbreviated motivation.

[46] See Jacobs supra note 41 and Allan F. Tatham, *Central European Constitutional Courts in the Face of EU-Membership: The Influence of the German Model in Hungary and Poland* (Leiden: Martinus Nijhoff Publishers, 2013), p. 317.

would literally bring EU law closer to citizens. Last but not least, such auxiliary courts could become a breeding ground for the recruitment of judges for the CJEU and the General Court and ensure that judges can be selected solely on the basis of merit.

6.7 The Future

The CJEU is embedded in a unique system of checks and balances.[47] Different actors on the European and the national level try to balance each other's power within the individual branches of government. This means that the legitimacy of the judicial lawmaking process in the European Union depends heavily on the willingness of the CJEU and the national courts to cooperate. Kochenov and Van Wolferen go as far as to claim that 'the interaction between national courts and the Court of Justice of the EU is the only way through which the EU can be precluded from becoming a self-defining, tyrannical, constitutional order.'[48] Although, this may sound a bit too dramatic, we believe the authors do make an important point. The problem they see is that the CJEU has not so much adhered to values enshrined in the rule of law as to the basic principles of EU law that it has often self-created. The CJEU does not allow other highest courts, including the ECHR, to look over its shoulder in order to criticize the way in which the Court deals with fundamental rights and guarantees the uniformity of EU law.

The essence of the rule of law, however, is that no public power is absolute and without scrutiny. This also applies to the CJEU. Opening up to a true judicial dialogue with other highest courts could facilitate the checks and balances that are much needed to protect the values laid down in Article 2 TEU.[49] In fact, an important reason why the idea of a

[47] M. Rosenfeld, 'Comparing Constitutional Review by the European Court of Justice and the U.S. Supreme Court' *International Journal of Constitutional Law*, 4, 4, 618–651 (2006), https://doi.org/10.1093/icon/mol027.

[48] D. Kochenov and M. van Wolferen, The dialogical Rule of Law and the breakdown of dialogue in the EU, EUI Working papers, LAW 2018/01, p. 1 (abstract).

[49] We could not say it any better than Dean Spielman, Judge at the General Court of the European Union Former President of the European Court of Human Rights, who argued in a lecture organized by the Leuven Center for Global Governance studies on 27 March 2017 about the relationship of the ECHR to the CJEU that: 'External review will always be an added value for EU, as it is in the case of a sovereign state. In fact, the existence of an independent external control will contribute to an improvement in the protection of fundamental rights within the European Union. This is all the more true, if one takes into account the current architecture of fundamental rights' protection mechanism in

"judicial dialogue" has become so influential is that, in a globalizing world, different courts on different levels have gotten involved in law making. At a conference of the Network of the Presidents of the Supreme Judicial Courts of the European Union in Madrid in 2016, Feteris said it like this:

> Today, it is generally recognised in many countries that law-making is not exclusively a task for the legislator, but also for the courts. In the Hutchinson case, the European Court of Human Rights (ECtHR) recalled that in the Convention States the progressive development of the law through judicial interpretation is a well-entrenched and even a necessary part of legal tradition. Today we have moved far beyond the caricature drawn centuries ago by Montesquieu of the judge as a speaking puppet, an expressionless being who merely repeats the words of the statutes.[50]

What many are overlooking, however, is that judicial law making is also less and less reserved for highest courts. The preliminary reference procedure is itself a good example, because lower courts can use the procedure to bypass their legislature or higher courts in order to avoid or nullify national legislation or judicial precedents. Engaging in judicial law making by lower courts goes beyond the preliminary reference procedure. An eye-catching case in point from our own country is the Urgenda climate case, decided by the district court of The Hague in 2015.[51] To the surprise of many, this court ruled in a blistering decision

Europe. The European edifice of fundamental rights' protection is not a pyramidal construction with a unique supreme court on top of it. It is a sophisticated "multi-level" protection model which involves three main actors: the national courts, the ECtHR and the CJUE. All three of them interact simultaneously over an overlapping legal space. As it has rightly been observed by Andreas Voßkuhle, the president of the Federal Constitutional Court of Germany, Europe's judicial structures should be thought in terms not of "pyramid" but of a "mobile", a kinetic sculpture which consists of an ensemble of balanced parts which are not revolving around their own axes, but are instead constantly engaged in a dialogue triggered by the movements of the other parts.' The lecture, entitled The Judicial Dialogue between the European Court of Justice and the European Court of Human Rights Or how to remain good neighbours after the Opinion 2/13 is available at: www.fp7-frame.eu/wp-content/uploads/2017/03/ECHRCJUEdialog.BRUSSELS.final_.pdf. See also L. Glas and J. Krommendijk, 'From Opinion 2/13 to Avotiņš: Recent Developments in the Relationship between the Luxembourg and Strasbourg Courts' *Human Rights Law Review*, 17, 567–587 (2017).

[50] M. Feteris, Development of the Law by Supreme Courts in Europe. *Utrecht Law Review* 13, 1, 155–169 (2017), at 156. DOI: 10.18352/ulr.401. See also: H.M. Kritzer and M.J. Richards. 'Taking and Testing Jurisprudential Regimes Seriously: A Response to Lax and Rader' *Journal of Politics* 72, 2, 285–288 (2010), who have argued that mechanical theories of jurisprudence are largely dead, at least in the U.S.

[51] District Court of The Hague, 24 June 2015, ECLI:NL:RBDHA:2015:7196.

that the Dutch State must ensure that greenhouse gas emissions in the year 2020 would be at least 25 per cent lower than those in 1990 in order to avert the imminent danger caused by climate change in view of its duty of care to protect and improve the living environment. The Court of Appeal upheld the decision by the district court in 2018.[52] Although the moment we write this, the Dutch Supreme Court can still reverse the decision of the Court of Appeal, this initially prospectless looking case is important when thinking about the future relationship between supreme courts and the CJEU for at least three reasons.

First, the case shows that existing judicial hierarchies are increasingly blurred in our globalizing legal world. As Stein and Castermans have argued, the Urgenda decision marks a sea change in jurisprudence and lays the basis for a broader recognition of the application of human rights norms, tort law claims, and public interest litigation, to counter the global climate change crisis.[53] This is not so much due to the impact the case has had on the Dutch government's environmental policy, but because NGOs in other countries have followed suit in holding their governments liable for the consequences of climate change and foreign courts referring to this case.[54] The Dutch Supreme Court nor the CJEU can prevent this from happening.

The oil slick effect of decisions, such as the Urgenda ruling of the district court in The Hague, is strengthened by the fact that it is becoming more and more easy to access the case law from foreign courts, which is why some authors claim that a global community of courts with growing interdependencies is developing.[55] There is no single

52 The Hague Court of Appeal, October 9, 2018, ECLI:NL:GHDHA:2018:2610.

53 E. Stein and A.G. Castermans, 'Case Comment – Urgenda v. the State of the Netherlands: The "Reflex Effect" – Climate Change, Human Rights, and the Expanding Definitions of the Duty of Care' *McGill Journal of Sustainable Development Law* 13, 2, 305–324 (2017), at 318–319. See: www.mcgill.ca/mjsdl/files/mjsdl/6_stein_web.pdf.

54 See, for instance: Leghari v. Federation of Pakistan, [2015] W.P. No. 25501 (Lahore High Court Green Bench Pakistan), online: blogs2.law.columbia.edu/climate-change-litigation/wp-content/uploads/sites/16/non-us-casedocuments/2015/20150414_2015-W.P.-No.-25501201_decision-1.pdf and Rabab Ali v. Federation of Pakistan & Another, [2016] Constitutional Petition No. / I of 2016, filed 6 April 2016 (Supreme Court of Pakistan), online: www.elaw.org/system/files/Pakistan%20Climate%20Case-FINAL.pdf and also Juliana v. United States, 217 F Supp (3d) 1224, (D Or 2016) [Juliana]. See also: See: www.theguardian.com/environment/2018/mar/20/can-climate-litigation-save-the-world.

55 K. Knop, 'Here and There: International Law in Domestic Courts' *New York University Journal of International Law and Politics*, 32, 501 (2000); A.M. Slaughter, 'A Global Community of Courts' *Harvard International Law Journal*, 44 191, 192 (2003); see also A. Alkoby, 'Theories of Compliance with International Law and the Challenge of Cultural

'super court' able to supervise and control this global community of courts. Perhaps the clearest, is the situation with regard to human rights law where it is impossible to say what is the highest human rights court in Europe. Perhaps the best way to describe the situation is to argue that the CJEU, ECHR, and national constitutional courts have competing competences.

Second, the Urgenda case reveals a new method of judicial law making that shows how legal sources from national, foreign and supranational legal orders become intertwined.[56] The district court of The Hague used the open (tort law) norm in the Dutch civil code to define the State's duty of care toward its citizens but interpreted this duty by interpreting it in light of the constitutional duty to protect the environment (Article 21) and Constitution,[57] general environmental principles of law (e.g. the precautionary principle), international soft law (e.g. UNFCCC and the Kyoto Protocol) and personal rights under articles 2 and 8 of the European Convention on Human Rights. What is more interesting is that the court held that the duty of care in the civil code should be interpreted in such a way that the State can be presumed to be in compliance with these international legal obligations, which it called the 'reflex effect' on national law.[58] Moreover, it used policy statements from the State,

Difference' *Journal of International Law and International Relations* 4, 151 (2008); E. Benvenisti, 'Reclaiming Democracy: The Strategic Uses of Foreign and International Law by National Courts' *The American Journal of International Law*, 102, 241 (2008); M.R. Ferrarese, 'When National Actors Become Transnational: Transjudicial dialoque, between Democracy and Constitutionalism' *Global Jurist Frontiers*, 2009, 1–31. A bit more skeptical are: A. Wiener and P. Liste, 'Lost Without Translation? Cross-Referencing and a New Global Community of Courts' *Indiana Journal of Global Legal Studies* 21, 1, 263–296 (2014).

[56] M.A. Loth, 'Climate Change Liability After All: A Dutch Landmark Case' *Tilburg Law Review*, 21, 1, 5–30 (2016). https://doi.org/10.1163/22112596-02101001.

[57] Article 21 reads: 'It shall be the concern of the authorities to keep the country habitable and to protect and improve the environment.' See: www.government.nl/binaries/government/documents/regulations/2012/10/18/the-constitution-of-the-kingdom-of-the-netherlands-2008/the-constitution-of-the-kingdom-of-the-netherlands-2008.pdf.

[58] District Court of The Hague, June 24, 2015, ECLI:NL:RBDHA:2015:7196, at par. 4.43: 'From this it follows that an international-law standard – a statutory provision or an unwritten legal standard – may not be explained or applied in a manner which would mean that the state in question has violated an international-law obligation, unless no other interpretation or application is possible. This is a generally acknowledged rule in the legal system. This means that when applying and interpreting national-law open standards and concepts, including social proprietary, reasonableness and propriety, the general interest or certain legal principles, the court takes account of such international-law obligations. This way, these obligations have a "reflex effect" in national law.'

negotiated agreements signed by the Dutch state and scientific evidence recognized by the government to interpret the state's duty of care enshrined in the Civil code. One of us has previously labelled this as judicial law making 3.0 in order to set it apart from more traditional methods of interpreting open norms via extensive (teleological) interpretation of legislation (1.0) or filling-in lacunas in written law by using legal principles and comparative law (2.0).[59]

Third and finally, the Urgenda decision shows that law making in general, and judicial law making in particular, increasingly takes place in networks,[60] which are not necessarily institutionally, legally, or hierarchically entrenched in a (single) system of constitutional checks and balances, but are often formed ad hoc and with regard to particular subjects (e.g. climate change, minority rights, data protection).[61] From a normative perspective,[62] judicial dialogues are about the only way to create correction mechanisms in a system where there is no final word in the process of law making and judicial decisions are the result of a continuous process of deliberation, persuasion and contention. Within the realm of the preliminary reference procedure, a dialogue between the CJEU and supreme administrative courts that actively involves the latter in the decision making process and shares responsibility, is

59 R. van Gestel and M. Loth, 'Urgenda: roekeloze rechtspraak of rechtsvinding 3.0?' *Nederlands Juristenblad* 37, 2598–2605 (2015).

60 The literature discerns, for example, between citation networks, prestige networks and amicus curiae networks. See: J.M. Box-Steffensmeier, D.P. Christenson and C. Leavitt, 'Judicial networks', in J. Nicoll Victor, A. Montgomery and M. Lubell (eds.), *The Oxford Handbook of Political Networks* (Oxford: Oxford University Press, 2016). Available at: https://polisci.osu.edu/sites/polisci.osu.edu/files/Judicial_Networks_Steffensmeier.pdf.

61 See former Advocate General to the Dutch Supreme Court: J.B.M. Vranken, 'Taken van de Hoge Raad en zijn Parket in 2025', in A.M. Mol, I. Giesen and F. G. H. Kristen (eds.), *De Hoge Raad in 2025: Contouren van de toekomst van de cassatierechtspraak* (Den Haag: Boom Juridische Uitgevers, 2010), pp. 29–46.

62 See Lize R. Glas, *The Theory, Potential and Practice of Procedural Dialogue in the European Convention on Human Rights System* (Antwerpen: Intersentia, 2016), pp. 71–75, who discerns between a descriptive and normative concept of a judicial dialogue. Loth explains that as a normative tool: 'the concept of judicial dialogue is used to express a preference for reciprocal lawmaking over the established alternatives, like the sovereignty of parliament (which gives the parliament the last word), a strong form of judicial review (which gives the judiciary the last word), or a judicial hierarchy (which gives one court authority over another).' See: M.A. Loth, 'Who Has the Last Word? On Judicial Law Making in European Private Law' *European Review of Private Law*, 25, 1, 45–70, at 47 (2017).

probably the best way to ensure the CJEU preliminary rulings are conceived as legitimate in the sense of being: fair and unbiased, politically acceptable, open and transparent.[63]

[63] M. Pollack, 'The Legitimacy of the European Court of Justice: Normative Debates and Empirical Evidence', in N. Grossman, H. Grant Cohen, A. Føllesdal and G. Ulfstein (eds.), *Legitimacy and International Courts* (Cambridge: Cambridge University Press, 2018), pp. 143–173.

Index

Introductory Note

References such as '178–79' indicate (not necessarily continuous) discussion of a topic across a range of pages. Wherever possible in the case of topics with many references, these have either been divided into sub-topics or only the most significant discussions of the topic are listed. Because the entire work is about 'dialogue', the use of this term (and certain others which occur constantly throughout the book) as an entry point has been minimised. Information will be found under the corresponding detailed topics.